Fancy Dresses Described

Fancy Dresses Described

A Glossary of Victorian Costumes

Ardern Holt

Illustrations in
Colour and Black and White
by Miss Lilian Young

Dover Publications, Inc.
Mineola, New York

Bibliographical Note

This Dover edition, first published in 2017, is an unabridged republication of the work originally published by Debenham & Freebody and Edward Arnold, London, in 1896 under the title *Fancy Dresses Described, or What to Wear at Fancy Balls*. The twenty color plates scattered throughout the original edition have been gathered together in a color insert found at the beginning of this volume.

International Standard Book Number
ISBN-13: 978-0-486-81425-4
ISBN-10: 0-486-81425-4

Manufactured in the United States by LSC Communications
81425401 2017
www.doverpublications.com

The Plates

Fig. 1.—ARMENIAN.

[See page 14.]

Fig. 2.—BOULOGNE FISHER GIRL.

[See page 27.]

Fig. 5.—DRESS OF CHARLES II. PERIOD.

[See page 46.]

Fig. 8.—Di Vernon.

[See page 68.]

Fig. 9.—DRESDEN SHEPHERDESS.

[See page 71.]

Fig. 11.—DUTCH COSTUME.

[See page 72.]

Fig. 12.—DRESS OF EDWARD IV. PERIOD.

[See page 89.]

Fig. 13.—DRESS OF PERIOD 1837.

[See page 270.]

Fig. 14.—DRESS OF PERIOD 1830.

[See pages 215 and 270.]

Fig. 21.—DRESS OF GEORGE II. PERIOD.

[See page 108.]

Fig. 23.—DRESS OF GEORGE III. PERIOD.

[See page 113.]

Fig. 24.—MODERN GREEK.

[See page 119.]

Fig. 26.—SPRINGTIME IN JAPAN.

[See page 140.]

Fig. 27.—DRESS OF LOUIS XVI. PERIOD.

[See page 152.]

Fig. 30.—NORWEGIAN BRIDE.

[See page 185.]

Fig. 34.—Rose Garden.

[See page 222.]

Fig. 37.—SCOTCH FISHWIFE.

[See page 96.]

Fig. 39—SPANISH COSTUME.

[See page 242.]

Fig. 42.—BUNCH OF SWEET PEAS.

[See page 253.]

Fig. 50.—ZINGARI.

[See page 293.]

PREFACE.

THE FIFTH Edition of *Ardern Holt's* "FANCY DRESSES DESCRIBED" being exhausted, we have arranged for the publication of the SIXTH Edition in a greatly improved form.

The work has been practically rewritten, and many new characters added.

An important feature in the new edition are sixty illustrations by *Miss Lilian Young*. The sketches were made in each case after consultation between Artist and Author, and with special reference to the descriptions given in the letterpress. In many cases these sketches are printed in colors, and in all they are executed with such attention to detail as will enable ladies, should they wish to do so, to have the costumes made at home.

DEBENHAM & FREEBODY.

WIGMORE STREET (CAVENDISH SQUARE),
LONDON, W.

Fancy Dresses Described

LIST OF ILLUSTRATIONS.

COLORED. (See color insert.)

UNCOLORED.

INTRODUCTION.

BUT, WHAT ARE WE TO WEAR?

This is the first exclamation on receipt of an invitation to a Fancy Ball, and it is to assist in answering such questions that this volume has been compiled.

It does not purport to be an authority in the matter of costume, for, as a rule, the historical dresses worn on such occasions are lamentably incorrect. Marie Stuart has been known to appear in powder; Louis XIV. wearing a beard; and Berengaria in distended drapery. No one would probably view the national costumes with more curiosity than the peasantry they are intended to portray, although certain broad characteristics of the several countries are maintained by Fancy Ball-goers.

Several hundred costumes, which a long and varied experience has proved to be the favorite and most effective, are here described, with every incidental novelty introduced of late years. A glance through these pages will enable readers to choose the one which will best suit them, and learn how to carry it out.

Among the Characters adapted to BRUNES are Africa, Arab Lady, Arrah-na-Pogue, Asia, Autumn, Bee, Gipsies of various kinds, the Bride of Abydos, Brigand's Wife, Britannia, Buy-a-Broom, Carmen, Cleopatra, Colleen Bawn, Connaught Peasant, Diana, Druidess, Earth, Egyptian, Erin, Esmeralda, Fenella, Fire, Greek, Harvest, Maid of

Saragossa, Maritana, and Rose of Castille, together with Italian, Spanish, and Oriental dresses.

For FAIR WOMEN, among others, the following are suitable:—Arctic Maiden, Air, Bride of Lammermoor, Aurora, White Lady of Avenel, Canada, Canadian Snow Wreath, Danish Peasant, Day, Dew, Elaine, Fair Maid of Perth, Fairy, Flora, Gabrielle d'Estrées, La Belle Dame sans Merci, Marguerite in Faust, Moonlight, Norwegian costumes, Ophelia, Peace, Polish Peasant, Rainbow, Rowena, Sabrina, Swiss, Schneewittchen, Titania, Twilight, and Water-Nymphs.

The most notable HISTORICAL DRESSES described are Queen Anne, Anne Boleyn, Catherine of Arragon, Catherine Howard, Catherine Parr, Catherine de Medici, Charles I. and his Family, Madame Elizabeth; Elizabeth, Queen of England; Elizabeth of York, the Georgian Period, the James II. Period, Princess de Lamballe, the Reigns of Louis XIII., XIV., XV., XVI., Marguerite de Valois, Marie Antoinette, Marie Stuart, the Queen's Maries, Tudor, Philippa of Hainault, and the costumes of successive centuries.

For ELDERLY LADIES the following costumes are to be recommended:—Mrs. Balchristie, Griselda Oldbuck, the Dowager of Brionne, My Grandmother, a Lady of the Olden Time, Night, Puritan, some Vandyke dresses, Quakeress, Mrs. Primrose, wife of the Vicar of Wakefield, Peacock, the Duchess of Orleans, a Maltese Faldette, Mother Hubbard, Mother Shipton, a Sorceress, a Gallician Matron, and some Gainsborough and Sir Joshua Reynolds's dresses.

GENTLEMEN'S FANCY COSTUMES are not included in this volume.*

A Husband and Wife might select Jack and Gill, Cock and Hen, any Kings and Queens, a Wizard and Witch, Night and Morning, or Night and Day.

Fancy Dresses are never more piquante and charming than when worn by children; the several characters in the Nursery Rhymes are admirably adapted for them, and I have given a special selection of dresses for boys in the Appendix, children's fancy balls being on the increase.

For Calico Balls, which of late are somewhat out of favour, among

---

* They are published in a separate work, entitled "Gentlemen's Fancy Dress: How to Choose It."

other characters I suggest the following:—Fille de Madame Angot, Bo-peep, Mothers Hubbard, Bunch, Shipton, &c., all the several Fish-girls, the dress carried out in striped and plain cottons instead of woollen stuffs; Cabaretière, Five-o'clock-tea, Flower-girls, Flowers, Normandy, and most of the other Peasant Dresses; Polly-put-the-Kettle-on, My pretty Maid, Shepherdesses, Poudré and Watteau costumes, Alphabet, Miss Angel, Scott's and Shakespeare's heroines, Bertrade, Bonbonnière, Queen of the Butterflies, Buy-a-Broom, Charity Girl, Chess, La Chocolatière Cinderella, Columbine, Coming-through-the-Rye, Dresden China, Dominoes, Friquette, Germaine, Harvest, Incroyable, Lady-Help, Magpie, Olivia and Sophia Primrose, Rainbow, and One of the Rising Generation. But it must be borne in mind that the word "calico" is of elastic meaning on such occasions, including cotton-backed satin and cotton velvet. Tinsel trimmings replace gold; ribbon is allowed; net takes the place of tulle; and very few people dream of adopting cotton gloves or mittens.

To be properly *chaussé* and *ganté* are difficulties at fancy balls. With short dresses the prettiest and most fashionable shoes are worn, either black with colored heels and bows, or colored and embroidered shoes to match the dress, the stockings also worked or of plain colors or striped. With the Vivandière dress Wellington boots are best.

To avoid glaring inconsistencies, it is well to remember that powder was introduced into England in James I.'s reign, though not very generally worn. It attained the height of its glory in the Georgian period, and in 1795 fell a victim to the tax raised by Pitt on hair-powder; those that wore it subsequently were called guinea-pigs, on account of the guinea tax. Periwigs were first mentioned in 1529. High-heeled shoes were not heard of till Elizabeth's reign.

It is uncomfortable to dance without gloves, so consistency yields to convenience. For most Peasant dresses mittens are best; but when gloves are worn they should be as little conspicuous as possible. For the Poudré costumes, long mittens and long embroidered gloves are ruffled on the arm. Gloves were never heard of till the 10th and 11th centuries, and not much worn till the 14th; still, what can pretty Berengaria do if she wishes to dance and does not care to appear ungloved?

With regard to **Hair-dressing.** For Classic costumes the hair is generally gathered together in a knot at the nape of the neck, and bound with a fillet, a few curls sometimes escaping in the rear when the knot is carried higher up at the back of the head. For Modern Greek costumes, loose curls fall over the shoulders, or the hair hangs in two long plaits. For Italian, the two plaits are tied with colored ribbon, and often entwined with coins or beads, or the plaits are twisted up into a coil, thrust through with pins. For an Egyptian costume, the hair is flat in front, with ringlets at the back. The Turkish women plait their hair in innumerable tresses, entwining them with coins and jewels; and round flat curls appear on the side of the forehead. At fancy balls often only two long plaits are worn, but it would be more correct to add to the number. For Scotch dresses the hair is worn flat in front, and curled at the back; for an Irish girl there is a coil at the nape of the neck. With regard to the German Peasantry; about Augsburg they wear the hair flat to the face, and a loose chignon at the back. At Coblentz and Baden, it is plaited and tied with ribbons; and near Dresden and elsewhere, where the peasantry sell their hair, a close-fitting cap hides all deficiencies. In Norway, the women wear it plaited and pinned close to the head, or allow the plaits to hang down. The Swedes turn it over a cushion, and let it fall in curls. The Poles dress it in two long plaits, the Russians braid it round the head. Marguerite, in Faust, wears two pendent plaits tied with ribbon. A Vivandière has hers rolled in a coil, or in plaits; Britannia, floating on the shoulders, like Undine, Winter, Snow, Fairies, &c., but in their case it should be powdered with frosting, applied by shaking the powder well over, after damping with thin white starch. A Normandy Peasant should have the hair flat on the forehead, and in broad looped-up plaits at the back. A Puritan has a close coiffure and a coil is best beneath the cap. For Ophelia, it should float on the shoulders entwined with flowers. The hair is worn hanging down the back for Berengaria, Gipsy, Druidess, Elaine, Fairy, Fenella, Peace, République Française, &c.

With regard to **Historical Characters,** up to Queen Elizabeth's time the hair was parted in the middle, and either allowed to float on the shoulders or was bound up under a coif; Elizabeth introduced frizzing and padding. For Marie Stuart it should be turned over side-rolls, so as to fill the vacuum beneath the velvet head-dress. During the time of the Stuarts a crop of curls was worn over the forehead, and long ringlets at the back. As people desire to look their best at fancy balls, it is advisable to adapt the style required as much as possible to the usual method of dressing the front hair, leaving the more marked change for the back.

For **Poudre Costumes,** it is wisest, if possible, not to have recourse to wigs, they are heavy and unbecoming. It is far better to powder the hair, using violet powder, and a little brillantine before applying it; this entails, however, a great deal of trouble in subsequently removing the powder. Some hairdressers cover the head with a thick soap lather as a preliminary. The powder is applied thus: A puff well filled is held above the head, jerking the elbow with the other hand. The process should be repeated again and again, and it is incredible the amount that ought to be used to produce a satisfactory result. An easy mode of dressing is to part it across the head from ear to ear, turning the front over a high cushion, making the back into a long loose chignon, with a few marteaux or rolled curls behind the cushion. Sometimes the roll in front is replaced by a series of marteaux placed diagonally. Sometimes the centre-piece only is rolled over the cushion, with marteaux at the sides, and the back has four marteaux on either side, put diagonally, with others behind the ear, or a bunch of loose curls fall at the back. All this may be made easier by having false marteaux and curls, which have a far better effect than a wig. It is, however, much the fashion to powder the hair as it is worn now, viz., with curls in front and a coil or twist at the back, a style which accords well with the dress worn when powder was in fashion.

The giving of Fancy Balls requires more pre-arrangement than an ordinary entertainment. The men-servants are often put into the costumes of family retainers of old days, the women dressed as Waiting-maids of the 18th century; the Band also dons fancy attire.

The Decorations should be arranged with some regard to the many vivid colours worn by the company. Chinese lanterns hung in passages and balconies have a good effect, and the flowers should not be of too brilliant a hue; green foliage is the best background.

Occasionally the hostess elects that her guests shall appear in costumes of a particular period, and Poudré Balls find many patrons. At these sometimes the lady guests only wear powder with ordinary evening dress, the gentlemen making no change in their usual attire, save perhaps that white waistcoats and button-holes are enjoined.

A marked feature at most Fancy Balls is a specially arranged Quadrille. (*See* Quadrille.)

Country dances are being resuscitated for costume balls; the Maltese country dance, the May Pole dance, the Swedish dance, Sir Roger de Coverley, the Tempête, Morris dance, ribbon dance, and others. The most effective pre-arranged dance, is a well-performed Minuet or the stately Pavane. The See-saw Waltz, the Staffordshire Jig, Le Carillon de Dunkerque, Ribbon Dance, Mazurka, a Highland Schottische, a Norwegian dance, a Polonaise in Watteau Costume, or the Cachuca in Spanish dresses are attractive. But nothing is so popular or so fashionable as the Cotillon*. At juvenile fancy balls dancing is not, as a rule, the sole amusement. Conjurors, Ventriloquists, Christy Minstrels, a Punch and Judy Show, and a magic-lantern, please the little ones, but possibly no thing so much as a Horn of Plenty, out of which a liberal number of presents are distributed, or the old familiar Christmas Tree, a Gipsy Cave, or a Fairy Pool, where the children fish for presents; and the Brandy-ball Man (one of the guests with a tray of sweets), who distributes goodies to the children.

Fancy Balls were brought over to this country by a German lady, Mrs. Teresa Cornelys, at the end of the last century, when they were held at Carlisle House, Soho. Lady Waldegrave, Lady Pembroke, and the Duchess of Hamilton were among the beauties. But then, as now, the fashions of the day asserted their sway in the costumes of old times. Fashionable materials are always used, however inappropriate. When crinoline was the mode, even the peasants' dresses were slightly distended; during the reign of the jersey, elastic silk served for the bodices of Gipsies, Folly, and many others; and materials tinted with aniline dyes are used for historical raiment of very early periods. A march round which sometimes takes the form of a Polonaise shows off the dresses to advantage.

There is much in a name,—A Coquette, a Lady of the Past Century, Petite Sole à la Normandie, the Bounding Ball of Babylon, His Picture in Chalk, a Duchess of the Next Century, &c., have attracted attention to very mediocre costumes ere this.

Any popular play or opera will be pretty sure to originate the most fashionable costumes of each season, or possibly some pretty pictures

* Full particulars of the several figures are given in a small volume, the "Cotillon by Ardern Holt," published at Windsor House, Breams Buildings, Chancery Lane, E.C.

Mr. Walter Crane's and Miss Greenaway's charming sketches suggest many of the quaintest dresses at children's fancy balls; and costumes of the early part of this century and the latter part of the last, as also the styles of the sixteenth century,—flowing skirts, low square bodices, and puffed sleeves richly embroidered.

It behoves those who really desire to look well to study what is individually becoming to themselves, and then to bring to bear some little care in the carrying out of the dresses they select, if they wish their costumes to be really a success. There are few occasions when a woman has a better opportunity of showing her charms to advantage than at a Fancy Ball.

ARDERN HOLT.

ERRATA.

Page 2, line 14, "on a lace" should read "or a lace."
„ 20, line 15, "Marchvnd" should read "Marchand."
„ 22, last paragraph, after "Beckett" add "by."
„ 25, last line, "with lace and full" should read "with lace and frill."
„ 27, last line, "billed frill" should read "kilted frill."
„ 37, line 13, "black gauge" should read "black gauze."
„ 46, line 18, "ruffle, gloves" should read "ruffled gloves."
„ 69, line 19, "Doll Paper" should read "Paper Doll."
„ 78, line 17, "and" should read "with."
„ 115, line 6, "order or Gipsies" should read "order of Gipsies."
„ 115, line 31, "stand" should read "standing."
„ 144, line 13, "jewelled hand" should read "jewelled band."
„ 153, line 33, "WALTER" should read "WATER."
„ 197, line 36, "filled" should read "fitted."
„ 205, line 17, "up one" should read "upon one."
„ 222, line 25, "A Rose Tree" should read "A Rose Garden."
„ 239, line 31, after "1640" add "Dress of Period."

FANCY DRESSES DESCRIBED.

ABBESS, LADY, together with Novice and Nun, are costumes sometimes adopted at fancy balls but not altogether suitable. They wear flowing dresses of dark material, a knotted cord about the waist, a rosary at the side and either a white or black head-dress; following the garb of some particular order, though by no means necessarily consistent. The sleeves are often lined with black silk, the head-dress made of crepe lisse with a flowing black gauze veil, the robe black cashmere. Or sometimes grey lined with a color. The white coif is frequently made of lawn. The Dominican and Augustine Nuns wear black and white with a black head-dress; for the former order square over the face turned up with white and extending below the shoulder over the important linen cape. A long black cloak envelopes the figure. The Benedictines and Ursalines have sometimes white linen hoods and capes, according to their degree, the forehead bound with white linen. A Novice on such gala occasions as fancy balls is robed in a long white muslin gown and veil attached beneath a wreath of white roses, a chatelaine of white beads at the waist. This is hardly consistent with the costumes of any order. The **Royal Abbess of Whitby** was represented at a fancy ball in a plain white woollen robe, fastened with a fibulæ, set in a small square-cut band at the throat, and a girdle at the waist worked like the neck-band with crosses in gold thread, as also the hem of skirt and long hanging sleeves; over-mantle also embroidered; abbess' staff, a book in hand; long veil of black muslin.

ABIGAIL. A favourite French dress, could be rendered with a short white silk skirt, and green-velvet trellis-work interspersed with flowers of all colors. Tunic turned up *en laveuse* lined with jonquil silk; the bodice trimmed with jonquil and dahlia color, also the muslin cap; jonquil silk stockings; dahlia shoes, with buckles.

ABRUZZI PEASANT. (*See* ITALIAN.)

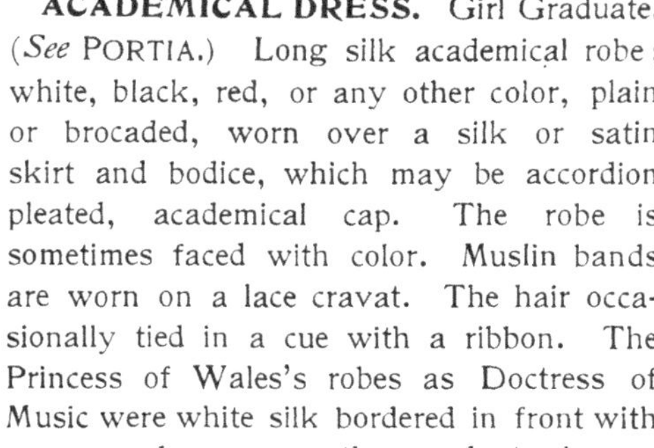

ACADEMICAL DRESS. Girl Graduate. (*See* PORTIA.) Long silk academical robe; white, black, red, or any other color, plain or brocaded, worn over a silk or satin skirt and bodice, which may be accordion pleated, academical cap. The robe is sometimes faced with color. Muslin bands are worn on a lace cravat. The hair occasionally tied in a cue with a ribbon. The Princess of Wales's robes as Doctress of Music were white silk bordered in front with red as were the pendant sleeves. The hood red; the college cap edged with gold having a gold tassel.

AIDA. Dress of barbaric splendor formed of multi-colored striped Algerian stuff forming a double skirt, edged with Angola fringe, a heavy jewelled girdle round the waist, one end falling in front. The bodice covered with chains of beads and jewels. No sleeves, massive gold bracelets above and below the elbow united by chains. The head is encircled by fringes of sequins, the hair unbound, floating on the shoulders.

ADRIENNNE LECOUVREUR. *Madame Bernhardt* in this character wore two Louis XV. costumes, one with paniers and draperies of ivory satin over pale blue satin bordered with roses; the other after a portrait of Madame de Pompadour, a rose colored and blue satin dress, the train brocade, the ground silver-grey, strewn with garlands of eglantine.

AFRICA. Short skirt and bodice made *à la vierge* of white Algerienne material, trimmed with cross-cut bands of yellow satin and goat fringe; gold belt; crimson cashmere scarf across the bodice, fastened on left shoulder with a lizard, ends floating on dress. Tiger skin attached to the back, gold diadem with stiff red feathers peeping above it. Necklace and large earrings of beads of all colours. Africa is sometimes dressed in more realistic fashion; the skin blackened; short skirt of cotton, bright colored scarf draped around the head and body; bead ornaments, large bracelets, ring in nose, hand and arm tattooed; or, as a **Negress** in a gay cotton gown, a bright yellow handkerchief tied about the shoulders, and a red one round the head; large gold earrings.

AGNES SOREL. (*Mistress of Charles VII., who reigned in France,* 1422-1461.) Soft brocaded white dress, made long, caught up over gold and white brocade both bordered with ermine. Jacket bodice of white brocade, with wide revers edged with gold; tight sleeves, puffed and slashed at elbow. Hair in two plaits; high pointed head-dress of period, with gauze veil. Pearl ornaments. (*See* also style of dress in Illustration, Fig. 12. Period Edward IV.)

AGRICULTURE. A wreath of wheat ears and poppies, marguerites and cornflowers encircling the head. Garlands of similar flowers on the classic gown of soft wool, draped over a cuirass bodice of silver cloth.

AIR. A white tulle or gauze dress with several skirts, one over the other, or blue over white, light and gossamer, made long for an adult, short for a child. The lower skirt is covered with silver swallows and other birds, the upper edged with silver fringe or lace, bestrewn with silver insects such as bees, etc. The low bodice similarly trimmed, a silver-spangled scarf loosely thrown across; a veil attached to the head with silver butterflies and aigrette feathers. Silver ornaments, birds and insects, satin shoes, with silver butterflies on the bows. Or a short blue satin skirt, painted red towards the waist; a windmill on one side, a balloon on the other. The low blue bodice draped with grey tulle, forming the tunic, but starting from a gold brooch in the form of a face; crimson embroidered waist-band, bellows and horn hanging from it; birds nestling in the tulle. Head-dress, a gold weather-vane.

ALBANIAN. The actual dress varies in different districts. In some parts the women wear red cotton garments, some white wool, with a skull cap formed of coins, or a shawl is folded like a helmet, with clasps under the ears. The costume consists of a sleeveless tunic over another woollen tunic embroidered at the edges, the sleeves of a lighter material than the over-dress. Scarlet sash, silk tassels. Brides have handsome silver gilt girdles. The bodice may be replaced by a paletot to the knee over a white chemisette, a scarf of many colors round waist. Or a dark blue velvet bodice laced with gold cord over light blue; an amber velvet jacket trimmed with ruby to match the skirt, bordered with gold; a silk scarf twisted about the head. Or a green velvet jacket and gold waistcoat, white satin skirt with gold border, red satin tunic; red, white and green cap.

ALBERT DURER (*Period of* 1471-1528.) His wife is depicted wearing a head-rail of white linen cloth covering the hair completely, and passed round neck and shoulders. Low, square bodice of soft woollen stuff with velvet stomacher; long sleeves, with puffs at elbow and shoulder; mittens; long plain skirt, with girdle round the hips, drawing up the dress on one side, a book attached. (*See* FIFTEENTH CENTURY.)

ALCESTES (Euripides). (*See* ANCIENT GREEK.)

ALDGATE SCHOOL (Costume of). Dark grey serge prescribed by Sir John Cass in 1710; the bodice opening and laced over a white vest. Deep collar and broad pink revers, pink buckled belt, full, deep basque. Red quill in the hair, recalling the fact that Sir John signed his will endowing the foundation, having broken a blood vessel.

ALCESTIS. (*See* CHAUCER.)

ALGERIAN COSTUME. Skirt, just touching the ground, of blue and gold brocade; red and gold embroidered scarf round the waist; full muslin under-bodice sewn to a broad black velvet band at the neck; short jacket of blue velvet elaborately embroidered in gold, with long hanging sleeves, tight-fitting gold under ones coming to wrist. Hair almost hidden by a red handkerchief with the ends tied in front.

ALICE BRIDGENORTH (*Peveril of the Peak*). Puritan dress in grey, brown or fawn, high to the throat, with small ruff; muslin cap and kerchief; fair curls; keys hanging at the side. (*See* PURITAN.)

ALICE IN WONDERLAND. The characters in this tale are favourites with children. **Alice** is dressed in a white muslin short frock with low bodice and sash, hair in curls; the **Lion** and **Unicorn's** heads are faithful copies of their pictures, the dress modern. The **March**

Hare, a brown coat, waistcoat, and trousers with hare's head and feet. **White Rabbit,** a check suit, with rabbit's head and feet. **Cheshire Cat,** wears a coat of chinchilla. The **Duchess,** a pale rose-colored over-dress with lilac front trimmed with ermine; horned head-dress of ermine; pendent veil. The **Rose,** satin rose leaves mounted as a large cap; the bodice and skirt like rose leaves; pink sleeves and bodice, intermixed with green satin. **Lily,** the flower forms head-dress; bodice and skirt of yellow silk, brown border to hem, and tall lily in the hand. The **Caterpillar** is cleverly adapted from Tenniel's sketches, with green cap and body coverings like a caterpillar. The **Chess Men** represent the pieces in chess. **Cards,** after those in the pack. (*See* CARDS for Queens of the Pack.) Kings, wear golden crowns, velvet robes, and the insignias of the suits.

ALICE LEE. A dark blue hat, or a fillet of blue beads and pearls. Plain stone colored train; light blue front, trimmed with gimp. Basqued heart-shaped bodice of dark blue velvet, piped with light blue, opening over a white stomacher. The sleeves wide at top, tight fitting at wrist, puffed at elbow; or the bodice may be low, with muslin kerchief, showing the neck.

ALINE. (*See* SORCERER.)

ALL IS NOT GOLD THAT GLITTERS. Dress of gold colored satin, with gold stars and gold lace. Crescents and stars cover the front of the costume, and a cap of cloth of gold is adorned with diamonds. Shoes and stockings worked with gold sequins.

ALMANACK. Fashionably made spangled white satin gown with the almanack printed on it or sewn as a card on the front. Smaller cards on each shoulder. Or a white and blue costume made short with the signs of the Zodiac carried round it and introduced on the white silk stockings and shoes. A white satin tabard in front displays an almanack; and the date of the year in diamonds is worn as a coronet.

ALMEH. Sleeveless pointed bodice and skirt of tulle spotted with mother of pearl, a sash of striped gauze about the waist, velvet senorita jacket. Small velvet skull cap trimmed with gold braid and edged with coins. Veil of tulle. Many gold bracelets and sequin jewellery.

ALPHABET. White kilted cashmere short gown, a horn book slung as a chatelaine at the side. The bodice black satin, with a white satin label in front displaying the letters. Quills and ink bottles introduced on the shoulders. Short black underskirt bordered with gold Roman letters; second skirt white, with old English letters in ruby velvet; third skirt blue, covered with black velvet letters; black velvet low bodice; muslin fichu and apron; blue cap with word "Alphabet" on band, or a battlemented crown, a letter on each; aigrette of goose-quills; birch rod and primer as chatelaine. Any evening dress may be utilised by wearing a belt across the bodice, a band of black velvet round the throat, and high cap all adorned with letters, or a white satin front with black letters upon it. Or a black tulle evening dress, may display silver letters stuck on spirally; huge A, B, C on train. Large black fan with A, B, C upon it; the same on shoes; the vowels on velvet round the neck; black capitals on the handkerchief.

ALSATIAN. The distinctive feature is a large flat bats-wing bow on the top of the head, composed of black silk, with two loops and two ends, attached to close-fitting gold or silver-embroidered velvet cap; short, bright-colored cloth skirt, trimmed with gold and black velvet; long, straight black silk apron, edged with black lace; low black velvet bodice, embroidered with gold or silver in front. The peasants wear this sewn to the skirt; black bows on shoulder-straps; full muslin under-bodice to neck and wrists; black lace or many-colored kerchief at throat; black shoes, red heels; stockings to match; hair in pendent plaits; tiny bodice bouquet of white heather; tricolor on cap. **Alsatian Gleaner.** Same, with the handkerchief about the head in lieu of cap. Alsace and Lorraine are sometimes represented together, and wear a shield with arms at the side.

ALTREVAL, COUNTESS D'. (In *Ladies' Battle*. *See* L.)

AMAZONS, and QUEEN OF THE. Short scarlet satin petticoat, covered with an appliqué of symbolical animals, in black velvet and gold cloth, bordered with gold cord. The bodice of tiger skin; a helmet and shield. Bracelets above and below elbow, high boots and leggings.

AMBULANCE NURSE, GENEVA SISTER, RED CROSS NURSE, OR SISTER OF CHARITY. Black stuff dress, hardly touching the ground, plain high bodice, sleeves to wrist, linen collar and cuffs; muslin cap. (At fancy balls the gown is sometimes made of green or blue merino.) Bibbed apron of cambric, the lower edge turned up, forming pockets, with rolls of lint for bandages, and small cases of plaster. The badge, viz., a red cross on white, fastened on right arm below the shoulder, either cloth or muslin.

AMERICA. Short white satin skirt, with red and blue stripes; blue satin tunic, edged with silver fringe, covered with silver stars, or draped with the American flag; white satin waistcoat; blue satin jacket, revers at neck, coat-tails at back trimmed with red and silver: mousquetaire sleeves; all-round collar, muslin tie; blue satin high boots; blue felt cocked hat, with white and red rosette, and bound with blue; or skirt half stars, half stripes, leather bodice high to throat; feather coronet; gun in hand.

AMERICAN INDIAN QUEEN, NORTH. A brown satin cuirass bodice and skirt, or black cloth embroidered with red, yellow, and white, bordered with cut leather fringe; sandals: a diadem of colored eagles, and vultures' feathers; birds' wings in front, and bead jewellery. It is best to obtain the real fringed leather dress with its colored grass and bead embroidery and the feather head-dress, from the country.

AMPHITRITE. Sea-green gauze dress powdered with silver; silver tunic with shells, coral, and seaweed; a bandelet of sea shells round the head, the flowing hair studded with precious stones and crystal drops: green shoes and stockings. (*See* WATER NYMPH.)

AMSTERDAM ORPHANAGE, DRESS OF. Short, plain, full gathered skirt, one side black, the other red, the plain tight bodice similarly divided; white tucked apron; large kerchief worn over the dress, crossing in front; thick white muslin cap, the front close-fitting and flat, the back full.

AMY ROBSART. An Elizabethan dress of the richest materials, velvet, satin, or brocade, in any colors such as cherry colored velvet and white satin; the skirt or train worn over a hoop is full, touching the ground and bordered with a jewelled band; the front breadth of contrasting tint or fabric may be quilted or embroidered, and sewn with gems. Low plain bodice bordered at waist with frill of material; large upstanding wired lace ruff from shoulders; sleeves, one puff at top, tight to wrist, close ruffles; head-dress a slightly pointed cap of velvet, pearls, and feathers. Any rare lace and jewels may be worn; pearls encircle the neck.

ANDALUSIAN. (*See* SPANISH.)

ANGEL. (As worn by the Marquise de Gallifet at a ball in Paris, time of Napoleon III.) Short petticoat of white cashmere, embroidered in gold; the bodice glistening metal scale armour, white feather wings attached to each side, descending below the knee; golden hair floating over the shoulder; a diamond star on the forehead; a small steel sword carried in the ungloved hand.

ANGEL, MISS, identical with **ANGELICA KAUFFMANN.** Thus described in Miss Thackeray's novel: "Sacque and petticoat of white silk, a grey brocade upon it resembling network, embroidered with rosebuds; deep-pointed stomacher, pinked and gimped; the sleeves fitted the arm closely to a little below the elbow, from which hung three point-lace ruffles; her neckerchief was of point, confined by a bunch of rosebuds; three rows of pearls were tied with a narrow white satin ribbon; her small lace cap floated over curls and powdered hair; shoes with heels three inches high to match the dress." Mittens may be worn. The sacque is brocaded sometimes with silver.

ANGLO-SAXON PERIOD, WOMEN OF, had loose dresses touching the ground, consisting of tunic, gunna or gown, kirtle, and mantle with large over-sleeves. The tunic was worn over the under garment, then made of linen, with tight sleeves at wrist; the word kirtle has many meanings, it was here applied to the loose under-skirt. The head out of doors was enveloped in a veil of stuff, silk, or wool. The skirt bordered with embroidery, a girdle round waist, bodice high to the throat meeting a gold necklet. Regal velvet robe from shoulder of distinct tone. Gold circlet on head. Red, green, and blue are the colors of the period. Cloth, silk, or linen the materials.

ANGLING GIRL. (*See* FISHER GIRL.) Wears a blue and white striped gown with fishing rod and landing net, and fish basket at back.

ANGOT, FILLE DE MADAME (*Clairette*). Short skirt, striped or plain blue; low velvet or pink satin bodice trimmed with black, muslin kerchief inside, the ends tucked under a bib of the black or pink silk apron, bordered with lace, half-hidden by a muslin apron, scalloped at edge, the left corner tucked into waistband on right side; large full muslin cap, red cockade at side, or a straw hat poised at back of head, with velvet trimmings and pink roses; sleeves to elbow; large gold cross and ornaments. In the early scenes she wears a bridal dress. (*See* LANGE, MDLLE.)

ANGOT, MÈRE. White crepe lisse cap, trimmed with Valenciennes, large red butterfly bow fastened at the top, another at the side; yellow satin short skirt, red satin overskirt, the front breadth barred *en tablier* with black satin, and over it an apron of white crepe lisse, one corner turned up. Crepe fichu, leaving throat and neck uncovered, crossed under a cerise satin corslet bodice.

ANNA DANICHEFF. Russian costume, (*See* RUSSIAN PEASANT.)

ANNE, QUEEN OF ENGLAND. (1702—1714.) Long plain skirt of satin or brocade over small hoop, low pointed bodice with stomacher; sleeves in one long puff to elbow; gold girdle; velvet furred train from shoulder, fastened with jewels; hair turned off from face and hanging in curls, entwined with pearls; small round crown; long embroidered gloves. Sometimes the bodice was continued as a sort of polonaise, and looped back on the hips; pillow-lace ruffles and tucker.

ANNE: DRESS OF QUEEN ANNE'S PERIOD. 1702-14. Much the same as the latter part of Louis. XIV., who ruled in France from 1643 to 1715. The fashions vary considerably during this reign, and are often mistaken for those of George I. Satin is the stuff most worn, also flowered brocades and damask trimmed with gold and silver. A sacque is a necessary part of the dress, and patches, a square bodice, and elbow sleeves, lace lappets, the commode head-dress of plaited gummed lace, made on a frame of wire with ribbons and lace in tiers, standing up crest wise; it assumed in time very large proportions. It may be replaced by the hood worn then—a strip of soft silk placed flat on the head, and loosely knotted under the chin, sometimes lined with a contrasting colour. At the end of Queen Anne's reign, powder was worn, and high cushions and lace caps with lappets. Fans are indispensable. Flounced silks, long gloves, trains caught through the pocket hole, are among its distinguishing features. Hoops came in, in the middle of the reign. Kneller's portraits are good guides. The following is a correct costume. Petticoat, pale yellow silk with flounce of old lace. Sacque of old running-patterned brocade, green and yellow, caught back on skirt; French lawn apron trimmed with old point; stomacher and commode head-dress to match; high heeled yellow shoes, very pointed, with buckles; Watteau fan, and Mousquetaire gloves.

ANNE OF AUSTRIA (*Wife of Louis XIII.* 1610). An historical costume which admits of rich materials and splendid jewels. High close-fitting bodice, with ruff at throat, long sleeves puffed longitudinally, ruffles at wrists, bodice pointed and coming on to hips, bordered with jewels and embroidered; plain skirt over hoop, trimming of gold and jewels carried down the front and round the hem. Velvet, brocade or satin and gold tissue are suitable. Small velvet cap, with jewelled heron's plume, fastened with emeralds; hair curling on the forehead.

ANNE OF BRETAGNE (*Wife of Charles VIII. of France and second wife of Louis XII.* 1498-1515.) As worn at the fancy ball at Buckingham Palace, 1842. Full plain trained skirt of red velvet, bordered with gold and jewels, opening on one side over a panel of gold and silver richly embroidered, and turned back with ermine. Low square bodice outlined with gold, gold pendant girdle, gold jewelled galon down the centre of bodice; long hanging sleeves bordered with gold. Crimson velvet coif; gold crown, tulle veil.

ANNE BOLEYN. Velvet surcoat, full, touching the ground, bordered with jewels and ermine: distinct front breadth of satin or gold cloth, embroidered and jewelled; girdle of gems with pendent end in front; long-waisted bodice square-cut, displaying beneath a partlet, viz., chemisette of satin embroidered in gold; deep hanging ermine-lined sleeves, over close-fitting ones matching the front: velvet diamond-shaped hood, often embroidered with jewels, forming bag at back, with triple-pointed coronet close to face showing but little hair; splendid jewels. The costume may be of black, purple, or ruby velvet, with white satin or cloth-of-gold; blue velvet and amber satin, &c. Pointed shoes with diamond stars. (*See* Illustration of TUDOR PERIOD, Fig. 43.)

ANNE OF CLEVES (*Fourth wife of Henry VIII.* 1557). Similar costume to that worn by Anne Boleyn. She is generally represented in a stiff bodice of ruby or green velvet, or gold brocade, cut as a low square, showing the bare neck, with a jewelled velvet band encircling the throat; long sleeves slashed, girdle round waist; a velvet cap called French hood, with white gauze visible beneath. A bag hangs at the side of the velvet or brocaded skirt, which is jewelled down the front. A round ostrich feather fan carried in hand.

ANNE OF DENMARK, 1548 (*Daughter of Christian III. of Denmark, and first wife of Augustus, son of Duke of Saxony*). Dress worn at the fancy ball at Buckingham Palace, by Viscountess Canning. Skirt of violet velvet touching the ground, opening up the side to show a petticoat of cloth of gold. Low bodice set over a white chemisette; gold stomacher; jewelled belt; sleeve puffed and slashed, of velvet and muslin with gold embroidery, the embroidered cuff falling over the hand. Large picturesque hat with feathers.

ANNE OF GEIERSTEIN (*Sir Walter Scott*). An old-fashioned Swiss dress made with a short red skirt, bordered with gold and blue bands, the low bodice laced in front over a stomacher; the white chemisette gathered into a band at the throat; short overdress of blue opening in front, sleeves to wrist with cuffs and epaulettes; round Swiss hat trimmed with crimson. Or, in full dress she wears a long brocaded skirt, low bodice formed of alternate perpendicular puffings of satin and velvet, sleeves tight to wrist, a puff at the top; band of same color as the dress round the head.

ANNE PAGE (*Merry Wives of Windsor*). Velvet skirt touching the ground, opening over a sky blue, pink, or maize satin petticoat, the sides bordered with lace and pearls; ruby, blue, or black low bodice, the basque in tabs, satin stomacher, high vandyked lace, ruff from shoulders, puffed satin sleeves to wrist, with turn-back cuffs of lace; conical velvet peaked hat bordered with pearls lined with satin to match petticoat; pearls round neck; velvet pointed shoes; a veil is sometimes worn. Sir W. Calcot painted her in a white satin dress, a pink bodice, and long jacket basque, open in front and edged with swansdown. The sleeves puffed at the shoulders come below the elbow not quite to the wrist, finished off with a ruff. The bodice is half-high, bordered with vandyked lace; a muslin kerchief within this. Hair dressed in curls, not powdered, a blue rosette on one side.

ANNIE LAURIE. This heroine of Scotch song wears a simple white satin or muslin dress; a satin plaid, fastened on the shoulders with a brooch; Scotch bonnet of black velvet, or merely a blue ribbon snood.

ANNE OF WARWICK, WIFE OF RICHARD THE THIRD, 1483—1485. Her coronation robes were of crimson velvet furred with minever, the shoes crimson tissue. She is described by Planché as wearing a kirtle and mantle of white cloth of gold, trimmed with Venetian gold, furnished with ermine "garnished with seventy annulets of silver gilt and gylt." At fancy balls she appears in a pale satin skirt, green or blue, bordered with a trellis-work of gold edged with fur; a close fitting jacket edged with ermine; turnover collar and cuffs of fur; her hair in ringlets, surmounted by a crown or a gold caul, with a kerchief at the back of fine lawn distended by wire. The trained velvet mantle from the shoulders bordered with fur.

ANNOT LYLE (*Legend of Montrose*). Short tartan skirt, overskirt of blue satin, both trimmed with silver gimp, and the blue velvet jacket bodice with slashed sleeves and lace ruffles. Blue and silver snood, blue shoes, silver chain, key, and ornaments. The hair may be left loose.

ANT. Short skirt and bodice of greyish blue stuff, embroidered with brown ants; sleeves to elbow of deep red, and the girdle, a large ant forms the ornament on the soft red cap.

ANTIGONE. (*See* Greek, Ancient, and Illustration Classic, Fig. 7.)

ANTWERP, DRESS WORN AT. The Flemish peasant costumes seen here consist of a stuff gown, large apron, colored handkerchief crossing in front of bodice, and the long black silk or stuff cloak with hood, wired round the edge. The cap has a high full crown with pendant sides of lace like a hound's ears.

APPENZELL, PEASANT. (*See* SWISS.)

APPLE BLOSSOM. Fashionable evening dress of soft pink and white tulle, silk or satin trimmed with the blooms. A basket of the flowers carried in the hand. A wreath for head-dress, with long tulle veil. Apple and Pear Blossoms are good dresses for two sisters. (*See* GALEUSE DE POMME.)

APRIL. Short skirt of pale blue satin, a black velvet sun on one side, the other veiled with crystal tulle. The black bodice with puffed sleeves showing silver moons; grey tulle wound round head and shoulders like a filmy cloud descending from a head-dress formed of silver horns, the points turning down in the centre.

AQUARIUM. The idea of this dress is taken from the anemone tanks of an aquarium. The dress, pale shot coralline and green satin; the trimmings, fringes and groups of natural seaweeds, all of the most delicately-tinted kinds, small pearly shells, coral, and large pink anemones, imitations of the real actiniae, with their spreading tentacles placed here and there all over the dress—on the shoulders, front of bodice, and in the hair (interspersed with seaweed), and looping up the satin skirt. Shells, coral, and silver fish ornaments. Character also called **Gem of Ocean.** On the shoulders are small silver fish with fins erect. The hem bordered with vandykes of brown plush to simulate rock. For a realistic rendering. Head-dress, a miniature aquarium with water and fish. A gown of green, silk covered with cork and seaweed.

ARABIAN WOMAN. Loose gauze or muslin trousers to the ankles over silk; cerise silk short skirt, covered with white striped gauze; a silk sash knotted at side, open gold-embroidered velvet-faced under-bodice of folded muslin; long hanging gauze sleeves; red silk turban with sequins, studded with gold and jewels; hair hanging interplaited with flowers; red embroidered slippers, bangles round ankles; gold bracelets, rows of coral and beads. Chains about the neck; Burnous cloak.

ARBLAY, MADAME D'. The famous Fanny Burney, lady in waiting to Queen Charlotte. Pale blue satin petticoat embroidered with pearls and silver braid. Flowered satin over skirt, with a white ground, made short in front to show blue hose, and high heeled shoes with diamond or silver buckles; powdered hair; a high cap of white lace tied under the chin. Bodice square cut, with elbow sleeves showing a muslin kerchief crossed in front.

ARCADIAN SHEPHERDESS. Short blue satin skirt; a narrow white satin apron, bordered with pink, and ornamented with pink bows. A white underskirt comes to a point about three or four inches below the waist, and is covered by a low blue bodice with revers, leaving a diamond-shaped piece of the white visible; the sleeves are blue, made full and trimmed with pink and white; the hat is straw garlanded with roses and tied beneath the chin over powdered hair. A short crook with blue, pink and white ribbons. (*See* DRESDEN SHEPHERDESS. Fig. 9.)

ARC-EN-CIEL. (*See* RAINBOW.)

ARCHANGEL. (*See* ANGEL.)

ARCTIC MAIDEN AND ARCTIC QUEEN. (*See* WINTER.)

ARGYLE, COUNTESS OF. Time of the regency of Mary, Queen of Scots, from David Wilkie's picture of John Knox preaching to the Lords of the Congregation, in our National Gallery. The dress satin brocade or velvet. The bodice and skirt united at the back, the front shows a distinct petticoat. The long pendant sleeves are lined with ermine, and are part and parcel of the slashed shoulder puffs. The bodice is half high, with wired muslin shoulder ruff matching the turn-back cuffs of the tight under sleeves. The velvet hood is lined with cream and bordered with pearls, forming a point turning upwards in front; a plain gauze or tulle veil falls at the back; a jewelled cross hangs from girdle. This is a good illustration of the costumes of the middle of the sixteenth century, 1547 to 1579; Henry II., Francis II., Charles IX., reigning in France; Edward VI., Mary, and Elizabeth in England.

ARIEL. *(Tempest.)* Short white diaphonous tulle dress, low bodice and pendant, sleeve with silver wand and silver gauze wings. Hair floating on shoulders, confined by a silver band round the head, with star in centre.

ARLINE. (*Bohemian Girl.*) Black or rose-colored tulle or satin dress covered with coins and gold braid; scarf of many colors round the waist; gold armlets below and above the elbow, connected by gold chains; gold net on the head with coins, a multi-colored striped satin skirt, with blue tunic; gold embroidery is effective.

ARMENIAN in Fig. 1 wears a soft silk Princess robe opening down the front over a white chemisette, a silk scarf of many colors round the waist, short open jacket bordered with ball trimming, sleeves pendent from elbow, matching the skirt. Striped head-dress, rows of beads and jewelled necklace. In the country they wear shoes with toes turning upwards, full silk trousers, a white muslin under-dress, open at the neck; a silk scarf round the waist; velvet embroidered coat, opening wide in front, occasionally showing a gold embroidered waistcoat; the round cap of velvet, which may be supplemented by a beaded fringe over the forehead; hair in plaits, and a yachmush out of doors. Handsome silver clasps are sometimes added to the belt. Long gauze veil and plenty of ornaments admissible.

ARMIDA (*Tasso's Jerusalemme Liberata*). Niece of Idraot, Prince of Damascus. The golden hair should fall about the shoulders, the head encircled by a band of gold; long flowing loose robe of cashmere or any soft woollen stuff of greyish tint, low at the neck, the sleeves loose and hanging, a girdle at the waist; edge of skirt and bodice bordered with gold.

ARRAH-NA-POGUE. (*See* IRISH PEASANT.)

ART. (*See* CLASSIC.) It is generally rendered by a gown in this style made of soft cream wool or in pale blue and brown satin, a palette and brushes on one side, modelling tools on the other, the hair bound with bay leaves, or displays a palette and brush aigrette. Antique gold ornaments.

ARUM. Long white satin dress, the low white velvet bodice folded as the flower, yellow folds rising above. Sleeves like Arum and the head-dress, and a bunch of blooms on shoulder.

ASHTON, LUCY. (*Bride of Lammermoor.*) Antique bridal dress of white satin. Long pointed low bodice, a deep frill of lace falling downwards from the top in front, ruff at back; sleeves in one puff to elbow, and ruffles; pendent sleeves from shoulder; train, front breadth and stomacher worked in pearls and silver, and trimmed with lace; silver girdle; lace veil and wreath, pearl ornaments; a blue ribbon attaching broken coin around neck.

ASHTON, MRS. (*Bride of Lammermoor.*) Black velvet train trimmed with ermine, opening over grey satin, long pointed, square cut bodice with embroidered stomacher, elbow sleeves; lace commode head-dress.

ASIA. Magnificent Oriental dress, a blaze of jewels and gold. Eastern robe of purple silk, embroidered in gold, underdress of gold brocade; rounded at the throat, embroidered in front; mantle of gold brocade from shoulders; a scarf of many colors about waist; tiara of emeralds, rubies and diamonds.

ASLANGA (*Fouque's Aslanga's Knight.*) Robe of white cashmere; a gold belt round the waist of low full bodice, gold embroidery on the skirt, neck, and sleeves; long circular mantle embroidered to match the skirt, fastened with gold brooch; shoes of white undressed doeskin, embroidered in gold; fair hair, loose and flowing.

ASSYRIA, QUEEN OF. Ample robes of white cashmere, embroidered in gold, with wreaths of lotus leaves edged with a gold fringe; jewelled girdle; regal cloak fastened on the shoulder with lotus flowers and precious stones; crowns of lotus leaves; necklet of the same in gold.

ASTROLOGY. Skirt made short, of amber, red, and black striped satin, cabalistic signs on a band of amber, displaying cats' heads.

Bodice and paniers of red satin with the same insignia, all studded with gold and silver stars; short shoulder cape of black satin, black pointed cap with similar signs; powdered hair. Book and telescope carried in the hand.

ASTRONOMY. Blue satin skirt and bodice; the former bordered with the signs of the Zodiac, and stars, sun and moon; the latter descending to hips, where there is a black velvet band with stars and at neck; the hat resembling the half of the celestial globe; a telescope slung at side; ornaments stars.

AS YOU LIKE IT. Shakespeare. (*See* AUDREY, CELIA, PHOEBE, and ROSALIND.)

ATHENS, MAID OF. Greek dress, short white full skirt edged with gold; blue sash; coin head-dress, or red cap, spangled veil. Short Greek embroidered jacket; white under-bodice; full white sleeves to elbow; girdle round waist; silk trousers to ankle.

AUDREY (*As You Like It*). Loose yellow woollen dress, high to throat, with long open sleeves, rope round the waist; large felt hat; hair loose on shoulders. Sometimes she wears a rough figured woollen tunic and handkerchief of the same over low bodice; or a bodice and tunic made with short sleeves, the white under-dress showing in the full sleeves to wrist and the stomacher; a sort of sun-bonnet on the head.

AUGUST. Short red skirt trimmed with amber, a gauze tunic of red over yellow, low bodice trimmed with the same; the tunic draped with grapes and leaves, poppies and wheat. An aigrette of birds and wreath of roses in the hair and on the shoulder. A staff in the hand entwined with grapes; the soft white gauze fichu and sleeves caught up with the flowers. (*See* HARVEST).

AURORA. Lower skirt white, the second grey blue, the third pink, spangled with gold stars, the whole over-draped with light yellow spangled tulle; veil of the same. A blue velvet tiara with star in centre; ornaments, gold suns and stars. The bodice of shaded rose, colored velvet, gold zone. It may also be rendered in grey and pink.

AUSTRALIA. Short violet skirt and bodice embroidered with wheat and trimmed with grapes caught up with yellow velvet, below which a kangaroo is painted above the hem. A gold coronet, a yellow silk scarf attached to the back.

AUSTRIAN PEASANT. A short dress of red or green woollen material; the bodice a low, square, laced in front, a red and yellow kerchief beneath; with long white sleeves to wrist; a large pleated collar is attached to underbodice. The hat is high and pointed, with flowers at the side. In Upper Austria, on fete days, the girls wear a helmet-shaped head-dress of gold gauze, a black velvet low, square, sleeveless bodice, and a bright colored cotton short skirt, boots, and embroidered apron. (*See* GERMAN PEASANT.)

AUTUMN. Dress of brown, ruby, maize, or pale green silk, satin, gauze or tulle, trimmed with chatelaines of purple and white grapes on a velvet trellis work round short skirt, vine or red-leafed Virginia creeper, and other shaded autumn leaves; or bouquets of poppies, corn-flowers, convolvulus, wheat-ears, barley, oats, grasses, blackberries, apples, and other autumn fruits. Beehives, bees, birds, and a sickle are further insignia; head-dress, wreath and tulle veil, or straw hat wreathed with flowers; ornaments of dead gold, or flowers; silk stockings to match the dress, and shoes with flowers; a basket of fruit and flowers may be carried in hand. Sometimes a panther skin is fastened on one shoulder and draped to the hip; a wand carried in the hand. Sometimes Autumn is dressed in classic drapery (*see* CLASSIC), with the flowers and other insignias of the season, or a gown of crimson velvet trimmed with autumn leaves and a sickle. (*See* SEASONS.)

AUVERGNAT. Striped black and white skirt; red, low, square bodice outlined with black, a bunch of flowers on one side a boullonné at waist. Satin cap, with small round crown descending in points to the ears; red apron; silver heart peasant jewellery, or cross, black shoes, red stockings, a straw hat with flat crown. A muslin fichu may be worn on shoulders.

AVELINE (*La Marjolaine*) (*See* NORMANDY PEASANT.)

AVENEL, WHITE LADY OF. (*See* WHITE LADY.)

AZALEA (*See* FLOWERS.)

AZORES. The distinctive feature of dress here is a long full silk cloak with a gigantic hood which extends a quarter of a yard beyond the face. A cap is worn beneath it.

AZUCENA. (*Il Trovatore*). Tawny yellow loose woollen robe, confined at waist by leather belt with pendent tassels; scarf of red and other colored silk fastened into girdle and on shoulders; head bound with a many-colored striped handkerchief tied at the back; rows of beads round neck.

BABES IN THE WOOD. The girl wears an evening dress of green and white tulle, with over-skirt of silver-spangled tulle, covered with autumn leaves, garlands of foliage, and robins; the hair hanging down, head encircled by a wreath of leaves. The boy has long red stockings and puffed trunks striped with blue; a close-fitting red jerkin, cut in tabs at the waist; the tight sleeves with epaulettes also cut in tabs; round cap; materials velvet and satin.

BABET *(Blaise and Babet).* Plain brown or blue skirt and tunic; large bows at the side; red corselet bodice over a low white one; sleeves made in two puffs; hair in curls, surmounted by a straw hat with ribbons and flowers.

BABOLIN. Short blue skirt bordered with white kilting headed by two rows of black velvet, one plain and one embroidered. A blue broché bodice with black velvet paniers. A muslin fichu drapes the square bodice and is held in place on the bust by a strip of black embroidered velvet. A band of the same edges the short sleeves. The pink Bourbonnais cap is fashioned like a close fitting bonnet with a plaiting of muslin round, forming a slight curtain at the back. A wreath of flowers at the junction with the soft crown. Black shoes and blue stockings.

BABY. Grown-up people often appear in a long lace trimmed infant's robe and cap, a rattle hung at neck, a toy lamb under the arm. (*See* WATER BABY.)

BABY BUNTING. Suitable for a very small child, who wears a cape combined with a cap having upstanding ears; like the dress, all made of white fur.

BACCARAT. Short skirt of white velvet with red satin bodice, all covered with cards, and hearts, clubs, diamonds, and spades, which appear also on the tricorn hat.

BACCHANTE. White tulle dress, green satin, gold belt, tunic and bodice, leopard's skin attached to the back. Or classical dress of apple green soft silk, the draperies caught up with white and purple grapes; large wreath of grapes on the head; flesh colored stockings; the sandals tied with purple ribbon. Or fawn cloth dress, loose tunic and bodice in one. Skin of fawn on shoulders, loose sleeves to elbow; hair in classic knot, entwined with ivy and vine leaves. Drinking cup in one hand, spear in the other. A half-mask may be worn and wine-colored raiment.

BACKGAMMON. Low bodice formed of squares of black and maize satin, shoulder knots of white, crimson, and black ribbon; the short maize skirt bordered with backgammon pieces simulated by circles of red and white satin with jet and gold braid; the upper skirt cut in deep points alternately cerise and black satin, edged with gold braid; velvet necklet, backgammon men as pendants. Enamel dice for ear-rings and bracelets. Cup for dice suspended by gold cord from waist to hold handkerchief. Cap simulating dice, with scarlet aigrette at the side: red fan and shoes and stockings, black gloves.

BACON, LADY. Reign Queen Elizabeth. Skirt of dark blue and red brocade on a cream ground, distended by huge hoops; front of skirt of light blue silk, covered with long muslin apron, hem-stitched in squares bordered with pointed lace. The bodice of the brocade, with stomacher of lighter tone having dark blue bands at the top and waist, matching those on sides of skirt. A plaited muslin partlet to the throat with huge unplaited ruff in three points from the shoulders, bordered with vandyked lace, and edged with wire, so that each point turns down; a short sleeve over tight dark blue striped ones; turned back cuffs of vandyked lace at the wrist; head-dress of the Marie Stuart shape, edged with lace.

BADMINTON. (*See* LAWN TENNIS, with which the dress is identical, but shuttlecocks replace balls.)

BADRABADOUR, PRINCESS (*Arabian Nights.*) Amber satin skirt, opening over under-dress and bodice of pale blue satin, embroidered with gold and made with tight amber sleeves, and hanging blue satin ones outside; red scarf draped about hips; hair in two long plaits, blended with pearls; gold and pearl ornaments; red scarf turban round the head; blue shoes, embroidered with silver.

BAHAMA FRUIT SELLER. Dress of lilac print, cut low in the neck; white linen apron with scarlet braid; white muslin turban; beads round the neck; tray on head with fruit. The face should be colored.

BAIGNEUSE. Soft white serge knickerbockers; full loose bodice and short skirt trimmed with red braid, red scarf round the waist; espardelles on the feet, with flesh-colored stockings; red cap.

BALCHRISTIE, MRS. (*Heart of Mid-Lothian*). The portly housekeeper wears a dark dress. Plain, woollen, satin, silk, or velvet skirt, low square bodice, kerchief tucked inside; sleeves to elbow and muslin ruffles; square muslin lace-edged apron covering front breadth; muslin cap with bows and ends of ribbon. Stick in hand; bunch of keys at side.

BALEARIC ISLES, PEASANTS OF. Dress of black silk or merino; bodice made half-high, with elbow sleeves, and metal buttons down the entire length; the bodice is trimmed in front with silver beads and chains; full plain skirt, large striped apron. The rebozello, viz., the head-dress is in two parts, one made of muslin or lace, like a half handkerchief, the centre point falling at the back, two ends in front, the other closer fitting is fastened at the back of the head, and brought together beneath the chin like a nun's veil. The hair floats loosely beneath it.

BALAIS, MARCHVND DE. (*See* BUY-A-BROOM.)

BARBARA ALLEN. A muslin gown, short, with frill at foot, low bodice, long tight sleeves, blue sash. Straw cottage bonnet tied with blue ribbons underneath, beneath the chin.

BARBARA YELVERTON, LADY. (*See* GAINSBOROUGH.)

BARBER, LADY. Short blue stuff gown with bibbed apron, sleeves blue and white like twisted barber's pole, comb stuck in hair, aigrette a shaving brush, razor in hand, strop fastened to side.

BARMAID. (*See* LOUIS XVI.)

BARNABÉ, MADAME (*La Timbale d'Argent.*) Short skirt of sky-blue cashmere, with five graduated rows of black velvet; blue bodice cut in tabs round the waist, trimmed with black velvet, showing a low linen chemisette above, bordered with blue ruching; muslin apron trimmed to match; black kid shoes with black straps across the instep, and buckles. The hair turned back and entwined with blue scarf.

BARRY, MADAME DU. (1715-1748.) Court dress of Louis XV.'s reign, generally pink and white. Very low pointed bodice, with stomacher, bestrewn with diamonds, silk revers at the top, lace and muslin within; a garland of roses from the right shoulder to left; brocaded train and paniers over a satin petticoat, trimmed with lace, silver flowers and pearls; sleeves to elbow and ruffles; ornaments pearls. Hair powdered and worn over high cushion, curls at the back, with pearls and pink roses intermixed.

BASKET OF VIOLETS. Skirt of violet satin, plain and short, covered with straw in trellis pattern carried to hips, with green moss peeping out between. The space below the waist is filled in with perfumed white, dark, and light artificial violets, sewn close together, intermixed with moss and leaves; bodice, violet satin, hidden by violets and green leaves; wreath of violets and leaves. A half hoop of straw passes over the head with a bow on one shoulder, this forms the handle of the basket, firmly fixed and immovable. Violet fan and ornaments, long gloves. Any other flowers may be substituted, sometimes the skirt is replaced by basket work encasing the two legs rendering it difficult to walk, the figure above the waist is framed by the basket handle, the black velvet hat trimmed with the particular bloom worn over powdered hair.

BASQUE PEASANT. Short kilted skirt of red flannel; embroidered and striped stomacher of same laced with gold cord showing beneath black jacket trimmed with gold; or light blue bodice; red stockings with blue garters. Head-dress a blue drooping bag attached to black velvet band worn over white lace cap; gold brooch, cross and ear-rings. For a bridal dress white satin in same style with high lace cap.

BAT. Short dress of grey, blue and gold with long sleeves attached to arm from shoulder to wrist, in the semblance of bats wings. A bow on the front of the bodice recalls a bat with outstretched wings. Bat in hair.

BATH, WIFE OF *(Chaucer).* Short striped scarlet petticoat, green over-dress, pinned together at back, the gathers arranged in honeycomb smocking from waist to the depth of five inches, the same on the upper part of the sleeves made of green like the tunic; bodice cut square, showing chemisette of linen. Hair in net, with kerchief knotted beneath the chin and fastened with ornamental pins; over this a rough beaver hat turning up on one side, peaked at the other, a feather round the crown; riding-whip and spurs, distaff in other hand.

BAVARIAN PEASANT. A red or blue petticoat, with black and silver bands; a black velvet corselet bodice, laced across with silver cord and ornaments; a white under-bodice; white apron; a turn-down ruffle of lace at throat, a colored handkerchief beneath, crossed in front. Hair in long plaits surmounted by round black cap, or a low-crowned black felt hat, with silver tassel; bead or massive silver necklace studded with bright-colored stones; white stockings, buckled shoes, and mittens. In Algan, in Bavaria, the women wear a curious wheel-shaped black head-dress on the back of the head; made of black gauze on a wire foundation, trimmed with black lace and satin ruches, long broad black ribbon streamers depending. The size varies according to the age of the wearer, and the shape is of ancient origin. (*See* GERMAINE.)

BAYADERE, LA PETITE. Short princess dress of white or some bright-colored cashmere bordered with rows of braid and gold embroidery; a low red-velvet sleeveless bodice over it, ending above the waist; white lace frill falling from top; long white sleeves; round black cap with aigrette.

BEADLE PARISIENNE. (*See* WATTEAU.)

BEATRICE D'ESTE. Duchess of Milan. A princess gown of bright blue and black stripes on orange, the sleeves slashed, with white undersleeves showing to wrist; collarette round the throat, from which pearls fall on to the bodice. The hair is worn smooth, with a pearl fillet or coif.

BEATRICE (*Much Ado about Nothing.*) Satin gown touching the ground; muslin apron bordered with vandykes; low bodice slightly pointed, a kerchief inside; a close plaited muslin ruff turned back, displaying the neck; sleeves to elbow, puff at shoulder, and caught up inside the arm with a button. The hair in curls; pointed satin hat worn at the back of head. At the Lyceum Theatre, Beatrice wore an over-dress of gold and terra-cotta brocade opening straight down the front over a petticoat of the two colours. The over-dress was bordered with gold, the stomacher matching the petticoat, the sleeves high at the shoulder, full to the elbow, with lace ruffles and lace rabato at throat. Knot of crimson ribbon in the hair. Second Dress: Travelling robes of stamped pale green plush, jewelled girdle, white satin puffed sleeves and under-skirt, quilted in large patterns. Third Dress: White and gold brocaded gown, over white satin under-dress, slashed sleeves.

BEAUTY, SLEEPING. Long robe of white and silver, trimmed with pearls, bodice opening slightly at neck; pearl girdle; hair flowing. **Beauty** (*Beauty and the Beast*) in the Fairy-tale Quadrille, at Marlborough House, wore a white spangled tulle dress, full bodice, silver belt, and pendent sleeves; a silver fillet round the head.

BECKETT (*Alfred, Lord Tennyson. See* ELEANOR OF AQUITAINE, and FAIR ROSAMOND.)

BEE, Hornet, Wasp. Short skirt of yellow and brown satin in horizontal stripes, or plain brown skirt with tunic painted back and front with yellow horizontal stripes; bodice edged and striped with gold, made as a deep cuirass, or as a coat, the tails having the markings of a bee; long sleeves, and gloves; wings of yellow gauze bordered with gold, distended on wire attached to back; brown velvet cap like the head and antennæ of the insect; black high-heeled shoes with yellow bows; yellow and black striped stockings. **Hornet and Wasp** are similar dresses, but the stripes are more decided. For the **Queen Bee,** skirt formed of yellow tulle boullonés to resemble a bee-hive with bees dotted about them, the train to represent the insect, made in gold and brown satin, with a panel of honey-giving flowers at each side; low bodice of golden brown velvet over white tulle, chemisette, worked in honeycomb edged with bees; long transparent gauze wings fastened to the shoulders with jewelled bees; a bee nestling in aigrette of flowers.

BEER. Fawn colored short skirt, with brown bands like barrel hoops, hops growing up one side and falling in profusion from the top of the close fitting low bodice, having bunches of barley on the shoulders. Head-dress fashioned like a pewter pot, of silvered cardboard.

BEETLE. Dress of green tulle or green and gold tissue trimmed with irridiscent beads, the design beetles, which appear on the head-dress, shoulders, and looping up the skirt; a pointed velvet cap or a couple of toy beetles in hair.

BEETLES, QUEEN OF. Short black skirt with horizontal stripes of red and yellow; the same combination carried round the top of the black bodice; a black pointed cap, the whole covered with ever-moving toy beetles. A sceptre in the hand, surmounted by a beetle.

BEGGAR. (*See* MACAIRE, GYPSY, ETC.)

BEGUM. (*See* INDIAN).

BELLA DI TIZIANO. (*See* VENETIAN.)

BELLE, LA, DAME SANS MERCI. *(Keats' Ballad).* Long mediaeval robe of blood-red satin cut in one with the bodice and moulded to the figure; low at neck, the sleeves full and long; a velvet mantle fastened to shoulders; a gold torque round throat. The garland for the head, the bracelets, and "fragrant zone," should be made of grasses and wild flowers; the hair left loose and floating; a branch of some wild-berried plant in the hand.

BELLENDEN, EDITH. *(Old Mortality. See* E.)

BELLE STRATAGEM. *(See* MISS LETITIA HARDY.)

BEPPA *(La Bonne Aventure).* Short pink skirt, made with three black lace flounces headed by a trellis-work of black velvet; pink close-fitting high bodice, pointed at the waist; black senorita jacket with gold epaulettes trimmed with gold ball fringe. Mandoline carried in hand. Hair dressed with high comb and red roses; pink stockings, black shoes with pink heels.

BERCEUSE. A white satin gown quilted in a brocaded pattern, over it a plain satin tunic with low pointed bodice and double puffed lisse sleeves to the elbow. A handkerchief tied over the head of bright coloring. Period Louis XIV.

BERENGARIA OF NAVARRE *(Wife of Richard I.* 1189-1199.) Satin skirt, bordered with ermine; the front embroidered with the arms of England; long cuirass bodice, jewelled and embroidered stomacher, top and edge of cuirass outlined with ermine; regal velvet mantle of tawny red bordered with ermine from shoulders; embroidered all over with a diapered pattern, or waving crossed lines in dull gold-colored silk. A pearl and gold collar round the throat, and a girdle of the same about the waist. The sleeves cut rather tight to half-way below the elbow, thence hanging in round long points. Fair hair, loose and flowing; gauze gold-edged veil; royal crown.

BERGÈRE. *(See* SHEPHERDESS).

BERNE, PEASANT OF. *(See* SWISS).

BERTRADE *(Heloise and Abelard).* Valois costume: short skirt of maize and blue or pink and white perpendicularly striped with velvet; tunic, and low square bodice with white muslin kerchief folded beneath deep hanging sleeves, bordered with velvet, tight-fitting, under ones of contrasting color velvet, aumoniere at side; high stiff pointed Valois head-dress matching tunic, striped with velvet; pendent tulle veil; cross round neck.

BETTINA *(La Mascotte, Piedmontese Peasant.)* Short blue skirt, brown tunic, white under bodice with elbow sleeves and turnback cuffs; low brown over-bodice laced in front; straw hat and flowers. Second costume: a princess dress of silk brocade, puffs at the top of the sleeves; bodice low, square; a pointed cap with gold trimming.

BETTY, LADY. Large hat, with upstanding brim and five red feathers; short princesse dress, with square bodice; long cloak from shoulders; large green parasol.

BILL POSTER. A short gown and low bodice made in brown paper or calico covered with bills of all sorts, some forming hanging sleeves, smaller ones bordering the top of bodice, and massed together form a couple of rosettes placed on either side of the hair.

BILLIARD TABLE. Short green cloth skirt and high bodice, with epaulettes like the pockets of a billiard table, circles of red and white cloth round the hem and carried in a double line down the bodice. Cues crossed as aigrette in hair.

BIMETALLISM. Long Directoire coat half gold half silver brocade skirt of yellow and white brocade veiled with gold and silver gauze, sprinkled with sequins: three-cornered hat looped with coins; tall walking stick, gold and silver coins attached by yellow and white ribbons; coin ornaments.

BIRDS. (*See* BULLFINCH, CANARY, COCKATOO, COCK ROBIN, CROW, DUCK, PARROT, RAVEN, SNIPE, SPARROW, STORK, SWALLOW, WHAT-A-TAIL, ETC.) They are mostly carried out with feather bodices and wings, over tulle or satin skirts; a cap like the head of the bird.

BIRMINGHAM. Battlemented mural crown in silver, the crest of the city; a short dress with sleeves to elbow and fashioned like a tabard in red, blue, and gold silk, bordered with ermine, displaying the arms of the town; a close muslin ruff at throat.

BLACK-EYED SUSAN. Short full skirt of blue serge or linen; banded bodice, with blue sailor collar and cuffs; black silk handkerchief tied in sailor's knot in front; black tarpaulin sailor's hat with a bunch of white flowers; or a short chintz dress, white muslin cap and apron, colored kerchief.

BLACK FOREST, PEASANTS OF. A red skirt, with bands of green closely plaited at waist; long white apron, white under-bodice and sleeves; low square black velvet bodice—at Kintzig and elsewhere supplemented by a yoke-piece of black velvet on the shoulders, with silver embroidery; scarlet plastron laced with silver; hair in long plaits. The head-dresses differ in different parts. Some are of black silk, round, placed at the back of the head, with pendant black ribbon, bordered with lace and full; some have a black bow, like the Alsatians.

BLANCHE REINE (LA). Dress *à la* Marie Stuart, made in white silk or satin with pearls; the Marie Stuart cap and veil.

BLANCHE OF CASTILLE (*wife of Louis VIII., France,* 1223-1226.) A white satin skirt and bodice, embroidered with crescents, lilies of the valley, and white roses, drawn in at waist with jewelled girdle; black satin mantle powdered with silver stars and pearls; pearl pouch at the side; tiara of pearls and silver stars; white tulle wimple.

BLANCHISSEUSE. (*See* WASHERWOMAN.)

BLUEBELL. Short and narrow blue silk skirt, cut in deep scallops and framed on wire; the low blue bodice scalloped at the neck and sleeves, showing under-bodice of pale yellow, laced across with blue cord; blue shoes and stockings; cap of silk in the form of the flower with green stalk; bluebells of Scotland about dress.

BLUE CHINA. (*See* CHINESE.)

BLUE COAT DRESS. (Worn by a woman.) Short blue cloth skirt with leather belt; quaint short-waisted bodice to match; fastened with gold buttons. Muslin band at throat.

BLUETTE. Cream satin short skirt gathered at the foot, the fulness kept in place by blue bands fringed with cornflowers, a trellis work of velvet over pink satin forming belt; bodice of blue satin cut like petals, gauze fichu and sleeves; tied up with the flowers, employed also as epaulettes; close-fitting cap made of bluettes.

BLUE GIRLS OF CANTERBURY. A charity dress of blue twill or serge, with jaconet mob cap and apron.

BOADICEA. Classic dress of soft blue, red, or yellow woollen stuff, bordered with gold; bodice full, cut in one with skirt, and confined at waist with gold girdle; cloak fastened by a brooch on either shoulder, no sleeves; gold torque; hair flowing, confined by gold circlet; spear or diadem in hand.

BOGIE GIRL. Short dress of flame-colored satin trimmed with silver, silver wings and ornaments; head-dress, horns in hair. A sister is often accompanied by her brother as **Bogie Boy** in flame-colored tights and habit, with silver dragons, crescents, etc., Mephistophelian quills; red wand and red shoulder cape.

BOHEMIAN GIRL. (*See* ARLINE.)

BOLEYN, ANNE. (*See* A.)

BONBON. Cocked hat made of mauve, old gold, and salmon tulle, surrounded by outstanding cosaques; low, mauve silk bodice and skirt; the latter half mauve and half salmon silk, a narrow yellow ruching at hem, pendant crackers round the waist, a ruff at the shoulders formed of them, a staff in hand surmounted by large crackers, striped stockings, mauve shoes.

BONBONNIÈRE. Short red, white, and blue skirt; low square crimson bodice, trimmed across the front with blue; muslin apron and cap, with blue and red ribbons; a basket of bonbons in the hand, and a pair of scales. Or short cream satin skirt trimmed with bands of pink, chocolate, and gold; pink and chocolate striped upper skirt, ribbons at side, pink satin bodice over muslin chemisette, pink pointed cap, powdered hair; basket of sweets in hand.

BO-PEEP. A short pale blue satin skirt, pink bunched-up tunic, black velvet low bodice, laced in front with colored ribbons over white muslin stomacher, short sleeves, straw hat with velvet ribbon streamers and flowers. Or a black velvet cocked hat or mob cap; crook, tied with a bunch of ribbons; a toy lamb under arm; black shoes, colored heels and stockings; large blue apron or small muslin one may be added; ruffles, Dolly Varden silk, plain chiné, or brocaded satin or chintz suitable. Hair powdered or not, as preferred.

BOULANGÈRE, LA BELLE. Orange silk short skirt, with deep flounce of white gauze headed by boullonnes; short, low bodice, pointed in front, cut in one with the train, of striped red, blue, and white satin bunched up; elbow sleeves; thick muslin apron with bib and pockets; white cook's cap; hook with baker's "mark-boards" hangs at side; small loaf on one shoulder.

BOULE DE NEIGE. *(Gueldre Rose.)* Dress of frosted tulle over white satin, the front a mass of white gueldre roses and leaves, spangled with dewdrops. Long white satin bodice and waistcoat of silver brocade, edged with green leaves; a cluster of white gueldre roses on the left side. Long white gloves, with three bands of small leaves, tuft of the flowers and leaves at the top of each; fan of green leaves, scattered over with gueldre roses; wreath of the flower and leaves. A few white petals about the hair.

BOULOGNE FISH GIRL. Is depicted in Illustration Fig. 2, wearing a full striped petticoat, dark blue woollen apron and sleeves, a bright-hued shawl crossing the figure, a pleated muslin cap with billed frill.

BOULOGNE FISHWIFE. Scarlet flannel skirt, high black jacket, sleeves to elbow turned up with muslin; scarlet band at neck, black and white tunic *à la laveuse*—viz., turned up in front and caught together at back; cap as in sketch with a stiff pleated frill round; scarlet half-handkerchief over it; pockets of white calico outside the dress; large gold ear-rings and cross.

BOUQUETIÈRE *(Louis XV.)* Coat of biscuit colored flowered broché silk, bound with garnet velvet; paste buttons; lace cravat falling over white satin waistcoat; short pink skirt, a white one bordered with gold appearing below. Hair powdered, a tall, pointed-crowned pink satin hat with low brim, placed at the side, having three large ostrich plumes with the tips turning downwards rising from a tuft of roses; gilt basket of flowers slung round the figure with velvet.

BOURBONNAISE, LA BELLE. Yellow short skirt, bound with black. Blue overskirt, low black velvet bodice, with long sleeves and laced in front. A quaint straw poke bonnet at the back of the head, trimmed with black velvet and red roses; silver arrow in the hair, violin carried in the hand.

BRADWARDINE, ROSE *(Waverley).* Costume of eighteenth century; watteau train, and low-pointed bodice of old brocade, satin, or velvet, over quilted petticoat; elbow sleeves and ruffles; small satin hat, with roses and feathers; powdered hair.

BRANKSOME, LADY OF *(Lay of the Last Minstrel).* Long velvet train, worn over satin petticoat slashed high bodice, white lace ruff; embroidered sleeves; jewelled coronet and veil.

BRENDA AND MINNA TROIL *(The Pirate).* Good costume for two sisters. Minna, dark, proud, and sad; Brenda, fair and glad. The scene is laid in 1724, and the dresses are of Norwegian type. Minna a short, amber petticoat trimmed with fringe: a gold bronze velvet, low, square bodice over white chemisette high to the throat; hair hanging in two long plaits, amber handkerchief knotted about it. Or pale amber silk sacque over petticoat of cream quilted satin, ruffles to sleeves, kerchief and apron of old lace, double falling ruff at neck, and snood of yellow ribbon. Brenda, same in salmon and cinnamon. Minna may also wear a riding-dress, with cavalier hat and plume, and Brenda, blue skirt bound with brown, full-sleeved chemisette bodice of cream colour, with old silver charms and clasps; sleeveless jacket of pale blue Indian silk; blue silk stockings, shoes of untanned leather; flowing hair bound with old silver beads or ribbon.

BRETON. Short colored skirt with horizontal rows of black velvet to waist, or bordered with Breton embroidery; low Breton bodice forming a point on either side of the bust edged with a band of the same. Short sleeves of contrasting color, showing high white linen chemisette and sleeves to wrist; large square embroidered apron trimmed with silver fringe, and oblong pockets; black shoes, clocked stockings; Breton lace cap with flowers and jewelled pins, large silver Breton cross and ornaments on black velvet. The peasant women of to-day wear black, the skirt short and full, a shawl daintily pinned about their figures. The distinctive feature is the cap, the ordinary shape has a close-fitting under cap shaped like a half moon, which extends from the forehead to the nape of the neck, hidden by a band of starched linen pinned over the forehead and would hang down either side like hound's ears, only the further corner from the face is turned upwards; tape like strings passing under chin, are tied on left temple. The caps are sometimes of embroidered muslin and edged with lace. Some of clear muslin with broad hems are mere wide scarves, passing over the head attached to a close fitting head-piece, the ends rolled under, stretching far back like tunnels.

BRIDAL CAKE. White gown trimmed with silver flowers, cupids hovering on shoulders. Head-dress of white sugar like a tazza, with flower aigrette.

BRIDES. (*See* ASHTON LUCY, OLIVETTE, ORANGES AND LEMONS, POLISH, NORWEGIAN, GERMAN PEASANT for Mecklenberge, and Starnberg.) Ordinary bridal dress is sometimes worn at fancy balls by children and adults.

BRIDE OF ABYDOS. Byron's heroine wears a rich Greek dress. Short skirt bordered with gold; bodice opening over white chemisette, striped with gold, red sash at waist; long Greek sleeveless casaque of velvet edged with embroidery; small satin toque at side of head, and covered with sequins; ornaments, sequins. (*See also* GREEK.)

BRIGAND'S WIFE. Short stuff skirt with yellow, blue, scarlet, and black stripes. The bodice a double-breasted brown velvet jacket, with revers and gold buttons, cut in tabs at waist; red waistcoast; striped stockings; black high-heeled shoes. Hair in two long plaits with coloured ribbons and coins entwined. High brown velvet hat surrounded by red and green ribbons, cock's feathers at side. Stiletto hanging on skirt at side.

BRIONNE, DOWAGER OF (*Rôle de Madame Dejazet*). Plain black satin dress, high to the throat, with black lace ruff, miniature attached, jewelled brooches down the front, chatelaine at waist: train of grey satin caught to the side by loops of beads; white hair, velvet coronet with dome-shaped lace crown. This costume is well suited to a matron of mature age, also to younger women; she carries a tall headed cane and fan.

BRISTOL RED-MAID (*Charity Girl*). Wears a red short full skirt to ankles, bodice made with basque, long sleeves, with linen cuffs, long linen apron and cape of jaconet: mob cap tied with blue ribbon; gray stockings, low shoes: white cotton gloves.

BRITANNIA. A gold helmet, trident, and shield, with Royal arms. The dress white satin or cashmere with a steel cuirass: blue mantle lined with crimson satin fastened to shoulders; silver belt with lion's head at waist. The robe is made in Classic style; the short sleeves fastening with three buttons outside the arm. Sometimes the Union Jack is draped on skirt.

BRUNHILDA AND KRIEMHILDA (*Niebelslungen lied*). Suitable for two sisters. They wear rich gold stuffs made in the Burgundian fashion of the thirteenth century. Brunhilda, under-dress of brocade, over-dress of gold tissue caught up at the side: low square bodice bordered with jewels, jewelled stomacher, silver girdle: sleeves puffed at elbow and shoulder: gold crown, hair in coil entwined with pearls. Kriemhilda: under-skirt of rich stuff, bordered with bands of gold: upper-dress of embroidered cloth of gold, edged with ermine: low bodice much jewelled in front, long sleeves lined with ermine, and bound with gold, tight sleeves to wrist; hair on shoulders, surmounted by a crown.

BUCKHOUNDS, MISTRESS OF. Powdered hair, bag wig: black velvet cap with peak and white plumes: green habit, skirt bordered with gold: top boots: jacket bodice with gold brodequins down front: Steinkirk tie, sleeves with ruffles and embroidered gauntlet cuffs, hunting crop.

BUCKINGHAM, DAUGHTER OF JOHN VILLIERS, FIRST DUKE OF (*after Gerard Hornthorst*). White satin dress with a point lace Medici ruff, the puffed sleeves edged with tiny lace ruffles drawn in with pink ribbons tied into bows. The waistband and front bow are formed of ribbons of the same color; the bell shaped under-skirt is, like the bodice, arranged in narrow plaits, and the over-skirt opens in front. The latter appears, in the original at Hampton Court, to be made of silver-striped gauze or muslin; strings of pearls from the necklace and the armlets, and a chain of jet beads hangs across the bust.

BULGARIAN PEASANT. Short blue petticoat, trimmed with bands of red and gold, over-skirt of paler blue stuff bordered and embroidered in three stripes with red, white, and gold. The red velvet bodice, which is close-fitting, is cut out heart-shape in front, the opening bordered with similar embroidery, showing an under-bodice of white cashmere, also embroidered in a heart-shape; tight sleeves, with bands of embroidery at the shoulders and cuffs; sash of many colors round the waist; helmet-shaped woollen cap; necklet of beads. In the country the unmarried girls wear wreaths of flowers, and rows of gold coins about the neck, a white embroidered scarf round the head. The married women wear beads; a belt with copper-gilt buttons.

BULLFINCH. Grey velvet cap with bullfinch head; corselet bodice with red feathers in front, grey velvet at back; short grey skirt with a broad band of feathers; grey shoes with red heels and grey stockings with red clocks.

BULLRUSH. Light-green satin short pleated skirt with green bullrush leaves falling from the waist of brown velvet bodice; bullrushes introduced between the pleats of the skirt; crown of bullrushes set in gold band; brown stockings and shoes.

BUNCH, MOTHER. (*See* HUBBARD).

BUNCH OF KEYS. A fashionable black dress on which gilt paper keys are sewn at intervals. A bunch of keys are suspended from the waist. The head-dress, necklace, and ear-rings are made of gilt keys.

BURMESE PEASANT. Black velvet tunic; short, narrow petticoat of rainbow tinted woollen, with embroiderey in colors, cut in one with the loose bodice; this opens at the neck to show a white low chemisette. Beads round the neck; the sleeves come half way to the elbow; a large, gracefully twisted scarf encircles the head, or a black pointed hat.

BURNEY, MISS FANNY. (*See* ARBLAY.)

BUSY BEE. (*See* BEE.)

BUTTERCUP. Yellow satin dress draped with gauze. Bodice of green satin, fringed round neck, armholes, and waist with buttercups, a garland about the throat, clusters with ribbons on side of skirt; the cap made in yellow satin with green calyx to represent the flower. Yellow satin shoes and stockings; ornaments, buttercups, screen fan made on twigs covered with buttercups. Also rendered with trimmings of buttercups on a yellow gown.

BUTTERCUPS AND DAISIES. Short white satin dress, arranged to represent petals of buttercups and daisies, and caught up with garlands and wreaths of the same flowers; wreath of same on head; basket of the same carried in hand. **Little Buttercup** (*Pinafore.*) Old fashioned straw bonnet, print gown, a black and red shawl pinned across the shoulders.

BUTTERFLY in Fig. 3 is depicted wearing a diaphonous skirt with panels showing the markings of the wings; a brown velvet bodice with handsome gold and velvet applique ornamentation; two gold cords falling like the antennae. The folded tulle above is caught up with similar ornaments on shoulders, wings at the back, antennae in the hair. A tulle evening gown with a flight of butterflies across it, gauze, wing butterflies on hair and shoulders. **Butterfly** (*For young child.*) Short skirt of blue foulard, with an over-skirt of gauze; low bodice, having a waistband fastened in front with bows; two wings are attached to the middle of back, made of gauze, edged with fine wire; silk stockings; blue satin shoes. Or, **Canadian Butterfly.** Bodice of green plush elongated into a point which falls on to the short yellow tulle skirt; short, puffed sleeves; gauze wings at back forming tunic; butterfly on head; green shoes with butterflies; butterfly fan. **Queen of Butterflies.** Dress draped with tinsel gauze, black velvet tunic shaped and pointed like wings; low bodice, with bands of gold across the front, blue gauze wings attached to back; short sleeves, with butterflies; a crown with a butterfly hovering behind it; black shoes with blue butterflies.

BUY-A-BROOM (*Marchande de Balais.*) Short blue and white skirt, poppy-colored tunic, and loose bed-gown chintz bodice with belt round waist; sleeves to elbow turned up with muslin; muslin kerchief, cap, and apron, hair in plaits, straw hat with red and blue ribbons; small

Fig. 3.—BUTTERFLY.

brooms in hand, and dispersed about the dress; high-heeled shoes, blue striped stockings, mittens. Originally this character was represented by a Dutch peasant as follows: Full short skirt of dark woollen material; square cut bodice, a stomacher shaped like a shield on front, shoulder straps over a white chemisette, long loose sleeves, covered with gold drops and spangles. Head-dress of scarlet cloth, like an inverted saucepan; girdle of scarlet embroidered cloth; white stockings, black shoes and buckles.

BICYCLING. Grey satin short skirt with wheels formed of black velvet and white satin on either side, full low bodice with folds of black velvet and white lisse, a bunch of red roses at side, epaulettes fashioned like wheels; a red bicycling lamp with electric light on head.

CABARÈTIERE. Short skirt of striped black and amber; blue tunic turned up on either side. Low black velvet pointed bodice, laced at back. White silk plastron, barred with black velvet, edged with blue and amber, short sleeves. Muslin apron, trimmed with the two colors, caught up on left side. High cap of goffered muslin and black velvet. Tankard and key at side. Gold cross and ear-rings.

CACTUS. A red tulle skirt, with low satin bodice; the stiff cactus leaves forming braces; clusters of the flowers on the top of the sleeve. At waist the leaves form a shower downwards tipped with the flowers. The long leaves arranged as an upstanding comb at the back of head.

CAKE. (*See* BRIDE.)

CALABRIAN BRIGAND WOMAN. (*See* BRIGAND'S WIFE.)

CALENDAR. (*See* ALMANACK.)

CALVADOS, FISH GIRL OF. (*See* FISH-GIRL.)

CARMARGO. The Costume owes its name to an opera dancer in the time of Louis XV. A short blue skirt, with cross bars of black velvet; tunic and bodice of brocade, half high, with folds of muslin coming across the neck and tucked into the front of stomacher; black velvet and blue silk ruches carried round the top of bodice. Short sleeves, bordered, with frills of plaited muslin and blue ruching round.

CAMILLE *(Le Beau Nicholas).* Short skirt of crimson and yellow satin, striped and bordered with frilling; yellow satin bodice with elbow sleeves; white silk bibbed apron, tied beneath the puff at the back, and bordered with black velvet; large straw granny bonnet with yellow ribbon and black velvet strings; mittens.

CAMMA *(The Cup).* Sea-green soft silk peplum, gemmed and embroidered in gold, green, and scarlet; chiton worked and fringed with gold; bodice set in regular folds, sleeves long, fastened with studs at the elbow; white coif bound with golden cord; sceptre in hand; bracelets; suede shoes; hair like Venus of Milo. As a priestess: Golden satin chiton; gemmed peplum in green, scarlet, and gold; diamond diadem; saffron veil.

CANADA. White cloth skirt and jacket bordered with silver cloth, trimmed with puffings of silver tulle and cloth of silver; a blue scarf round hips, edged with silver sleigh-bells, and caught up with Canadian blue bird and beaver. The jacket braided and frogged with silver; wreath of maple leaves and rowan berries across bodice. Blue cap after Scotch shape trimmed with swansdown, embroidered with silver; hair powdered; blue satin muff, small bird at side. Chatelaine of snow-shoes, toboggans, canoe, and skates. Or, a classic robe of white with a wreath of maple leaves round the bodice and head, hair flowing, or a helmet with maple leaves and effigy of Peace and the beaver. In left hand oval shield representing Union Jack, about two feet high, "Canada" inscribed in centre. Another rendering is the dress worn in the Canadian winter, made of blanket flannel with many colored striped border; epaulettes of the stripes; bright crimson sash; a cap of dressed beaver skin.

CANAL, SUEZ. Long flowing classic robe of cloth-of-gold, brocaded with waves of blue satin bordered with pearls; under-skirt of red satin embroidered in Egyptian designs. A gold key at the girdle; Egyptian head-dress of pearls, turquoise, and diamonds; girdle of roses and lilies.

CANARY BIRD. Dress of yellow plush or satin, short basqued jacket, from the folds at back a feather tail emerges; canaries on the shoulder, the bird's head forming the cap. Sometimes the yellow is embroidered in pearls, and canaries are scattered all over the dress.

CANDOUR, MRS. *(School for Scandal).* Light-green satin skirt with three gathered lace flounces headed by button roses; pointed bodice and watteau train of dark floral brocade embroidered with steel; elbow sleeves, powdered hair, large mauve velvet hat and feathers turning up in front. In the course of the play she dons a hooded mantle.

CANTINIÈRE. (*See* VIVANDIERE.)

CAP O' RUSHES *(Fairy Tale).* Cap formed of light green rushes tied in a knot at the top descending to the shoulders. Soft pink silk gown, narrow in the skirt, the low bodice full, the two cut in one, girdled with jewelled embroidery beneath the arm-pits. Short sleeves, two bands of ribbon crossing each other on the arm.

CAPE COLONY. Black skirt, feather ruche at foot, blue sash on hips, with Cape Colony in silver upon it; a panache of black plumes at side; leather, low bodice, upper portion draped with black and blue revers; ostrich feathers replacing sleeves. Black felt hat turned up at side, trimmed with feathers; whip in one hand, a Cape lily in the other.

CARDS, PACK OF. Black satin skirt festooned with red and black gauge caught up with red or black spades, diamonds, hearts or clubs. A scarf of two colors round hips tied in a bow at side with falling cards; coronet of cards; cards as epaulettes—enamel card ornaments. Black and red striped stockings; black shoes, red heels. For the **Queens** sometimes the dresses are copied from the playing cards, or from those quaint packs which depict famous actresses in their several rôles. Or any of the Queens might be carried out as follows:—Short white satin skirt, trimmed with bands of black and red velvet enclosing diamonds, spades, hearts, or clubs. Square bodice and elbow sleeves, draped with chiffon, caught down with the pips. On each sleeve a facsimile of the card also up the front of gown, placed slantwise and bordered with gold. The gloves white, with a miniature card painted on the back; the head-dress a turban of red and gold, with a large black satin club on the left side, fastening a small white feather, turned over the front of the turban. The fan white satin, painted to match. Sometimes the Queens of the several packs wear long velvet or silver lisse dresses of mediaeval make, with ermine and gold crowns and sceptres; or white ball-gowns with powdered hair, the insignias of the several suits appearing in velvet or jewels about the dresses; crowns on the heads. **Queen of Hearts** is occasionally represented by the Duchesse De La Vallure *(See* V). **Queen of Clubs** by the Duchess d' Estampes, period Francis I. A good rendering is a pink satin dress covered with black velvet clubs, forming the stomacher to the bodice and the crown. **Queen of Spades** is represented by Odette *(see* Charles XI.), and the **Queen of Diamonds** by Gabrielle d'Estrees *(see* G.).

CARMEN *(heroine of Bizet's Opera).* In the first act, a short dress of deep orange satin, trimmed with black chenille; black velvet Spanish jacket over a white chemisette; bright green sash and shoes; black mantilla. Second dress (a gipsy costume), short skirt of Armenian embroidery in all colors, arranged with bands of the same at the back. Muslin bodice; Spanish jacket of silver cloth, with short and pendant sleeves. Necklace of many rows of silver coins; armlets and bracelets of the same. Head-dress, silver braid, coins, and roses of three colors. Third dress (a brigand woman), short stuff petticoat, striped blue, yellow, black, and red; scarf of same draped round it. Yellow waistcoat, brown Senorita jacket, with long sleeves, trimmed with black ball fringe. Linen cuffs and collars, blue necktie, red handkerchief tied about head. Round black Spanish cap. Fourth costume, short white satin skirt, with three rows of gold blonde, headed by bands of ruby satin, bordered with gold; down the front bows of gold braid tagged; stay bodice of white satin, with gold buttons, pointed back and front. Senorita jacket of ruby satin, with long sleeves, gold blonde ruffles. Mantilla of gold blonde, diamond ornaments, roses at the side. With all but the brigand dress gold embroidered stockings and shoes. Prosper Merimée describes the wayward gipsy as wearing a short black silk, with low bodice and short sleeves, or square bodice with elbow sleeves, plain skirt, rather full' black mantilla, and a great bunch of white jasmine fastened high to the head. A large plain black fan, or one of the ordinary Spanish fans.

CARNATION. Bodice of carnation-colored velvet, low and plain, headed by a silk ruche cut like the petals. Sleeve made in the form of the flower, the upper portion covering the shoulder, of green velvet. Skirt of carnation velvet, with triple flounces, pinked and veiled with draperies of green tulle. Hat resembles the flower, with green satin and carnation-colored frills.

CARNIVAL. Short white skirt bordered with red. A double-breasted, close-fitting bodice with red buttons, two short white basques in front with a double line of red at the edge starting from the side; a full basque on the back, white satin revers at side of the bust; white turn down collar , a ruche of black coque feathers inside. Full black sleeves, deep gauntlet cuffs of white satin bordered with a row of small red diamonds. Powdered hair; black chapeau-bras, a rosette on each point at the side. Red pointed shoes, black stockings; mask and domino. For **Ice Carnival** this is produced in white, with icicles and silver fringe.

CAROLINE, QUEEN OF GEORGE II. (1727-1760.) White satin embroidered skirt, with hoop, train of purple satin bordered with ermine, coming from shoulders and looped across front with pearls and gold; low bodice of same, with ermine and jewelled stomacher; gold girdle; pendant sleeves; diamond and gold ornaments, gold crown.

CARRIER PIGEON. Grey satin skirt with tunic in the shape of wings composed of white feathers; pigeons in the hair and on shoulder. Band of red ribbon across bodice from right shoulder to under left arm, with letter attached; letters falling from feather fan; head-dress, cap like pigeon's head. Or the gown may be grey cloth, the draperies caught up by pigeons, and the edges bordered with feathers; the bodice entirely composed of feathers.

CASSANDRA. Classical Dress (*See* CLASSIC, Fig. 7) of light blue tone; head encircled with bay leaves.

CASTILIAN MAID. Pink satin petticoat, bordered with gold gimp; black velvet Senorita jacket, open in front, and laced across a white chemisette with thick gold cord; a small black lace apron; shoes of pale pink satin, with ribbon sandals; Spanish hat of black velvet, with ostrich plume, poised on one side of the head; hair in two long plaits or fastened in a coil.

CAT. Generally represented by a **White Cat.** Short white silk, cashmere, or satin skirt, edged with several rows of white fur or swans-down; low square or high jacket bodice, similarly trimmed; at the back, from the shoulders hangs a loose white fur mantle; head-dress, a cap of white fur, like a cat's head, with ears and red bead eyes; round the neck either a red collar and bells, or a red velvet collar with the words "Touch not the cat but with the glove." Hair powdered. High white satin boots bordered with fur, and long gloves edged with fur, hanging at sides; kitten perched on shoulder; fan painted with a cat. **For a black, tabby, or tortoiseshell cat,** the same in the appropriate coloring, the hair not powdered. **For a Child**: White skin paws encased in mittens. Square red handkerchief tied about the neck so that the point comes between the ears of the cat's-head cap, the other hangs down the back. A pair of scissors are attached to the sash at the waist. White fur dress.

CATERPILLAR. (*See* ALICE IN WONDERLAND.)

CATHERINE DE MEDICI. Ample skirt of velvet or rich brocade, just touching the ground, distended with hoops, satin front breadth, jewelled gold bands carried across jewelled girdle. Bodice pointed at waist, seams defined with jewels; low stiff ruff on wire foundation from shoulders. Sleeves to wrist in perpendicular puffings, full at top, cuff turning upwards; over these, gossamer sleeves from shoulders to hem of dress. Hair turned off face in roll; diamond crown or coif after Marie Stuart order, but not so pointed. Shoes broad-toed, sewn with pearls. Yellow, red, and black, favourite colors, and rich arabesque brocades worn.

CATHERINE HOWARD. Tudor garb of bright colored, rich flowered brocade; the cap round and hood-like, showing the hair, or replaced by a diamond tiara. Train of velvet trimmed with pearls. The sleeves, which at this period were movable and distinct, were attached to the shoulder, with a wide border of fur reaching almost to the knees; under sleeve slashed and puffed to the waist, ending in a ruffle. The richly-wrought petticoat embroidered in cloth-of-gold. *See* illustration of Tudor period, Fig. 43.

CATHERINE OF ARRAGON. Dark velvet robe, bordered with ermine, displaying satin or cloth of gold, front breadth trimmed with pearls or rich embroidery. A low, square, stay-like bodice to waist, with jewelled girdle; broidered stomacher with jewels. A satin habit-shirt, or partlet, worked with gold and pearls, tight under-sleeves to match; pendant velvet sleeves lined with ermine. Black velvet hood, with triple-jewelled front; gauze veil at back. Pointed velvet shoes, slashed. A sprig of lavender carried in the hand. Leslie painted the queen after her divorce wearing a dress of dark green velvet or silk, shot with gold, the bodice cut square and low, trimmed with a deep bordering of black velvet, covering a third of the bodice in front, fastened with jewels, attached to this a jewelled pendant and chain; white muslin apron; the sleeves full, sewn into a piece at the wrist, fitting the arm, opening on the outside with jewelled links; the hair dressed plain to the face, a velvet head-dress rounded at the ears and falling at the back in heavy folds. **Catherine Howard** similar Tudor Dress. Fig. 43.

CATHERINE OF RUSSIA (as worn by Baroness Brunnow at the Queen's Fancy Ball, 1842). White satin skirt, with pelisse of rose colored satin, trimmed with ermine, having gold brodequins across the front; round cap to match, with jewelled aigrette and heron's plume; long hanging sleeves, tight ones beneath. Blue ribbon Russian order.

CATHERINE OF PORTUGAL (*wife of Charles II.*, 1660—1685). A satin train bordered with ermine, pointed bodice trimmed with black lace, gold and pearls. Petticoat of maize satin trimmed to match. (*See* PERIOD OF CHARLES II.)

CATHERINE PARR. Dress of cloth-of-gold, train two yards long; kirtle or petticoat of silk brocade; pendant sleeves, lined with crimson satin; jewelled cross at neck; jewelled girdle. Hood head-dress, with crescent-shaped coronet, a blaze of jewels. (*See Illustration*, TUDOR PERIOD, Fig. 43.)

CATHERINE SEYTON (*The Abbot*). Pale blue satin petticoat, studded and embroidered with pearls, over-dress of blue velvet. Stomacher of diamonds and opals, high lace ruff. Blue velvet cap, lisse veil trimmed with pearls; a jewelled girdle round the waist.

CAUCHOISE. (*See* NORMANDY PEASANT.)

CAVALIER PERIOD. (*See* PERIOD OF CHARLES I. AND II.—*Maid Servant.*) A short maroon stuff gown with three rows of black velvet, a light blue bodice cut low, showing white chemisette set in collar band. Long sleeves and turn back linen cuffs, cut in vandykes; a large white apron reaching to the hem, with a bib and vandyked braces, a round linen cap with band of black velvet.

CECILIA, ST. Long loose overrobe of rich gold and green brocart, the neck cut round at throat and bordered with jewelled band, matching the edge of trained under-dress of pale green, having pendant sleeves, tight sleeves beneath. Hair in coil with jewel in centre of brow. She carries a small harpischord.

CECILY HOMESPUN (*Heir-at-Law*, by George Colman). Plain cotton tunic, and low bodice over short petticoat of same; muslin cap, kerchief, and apron, made in the style worn in George III. reign. (*See* GEORGE III. PERIOD.)

CELIA (*As You Like It*). A shepherdess with crook ornamented with roses. White silk short skirt; pale blue tunic and bodice festooned with silver gauze, trimmed with silver cord, blonde and roses. Small satin hat, blue slippers, pink roses on both. Or, 1st Dress: Mousse green brocade with bands of blue; flowing skirt, looped on one side, belt and bag, square bodice bordered with blue; puffed sleeves; cap. 2nd Dress: Red skirt; the grey over-dress looped up on one side, square bodice; puffed sleeves.

CERES. (*See* HARVEST). After Flaxman, classic dress of maize-colored cashmere bordered with gold, trimmed with garlands of grapes, field-flowers, poppies, corn-flowers, daisies, etc., caught up in front to hold a lapful of the same. Cornucopia filled with fruit and flowers carried in the hand. A child would represent the character in a short maize tulle with full bodice, a garland of the above flowers round the head, skirt, and waist; a sickle in the hand.

CHAMBERMAID, FRENCH. A short skirt, square cut bodice, elbow sleeves of white and pink striped silk. The silk sleeves end above the elbows in a frill turning upwards, a puff of muslin encloses elbow, lace ruffles, frilled muslin apron with bib, a bunch of roses one side, muslin cap with pink ribbons.

CHAMPAGNE BOTTLE. Cuirass bodice of old gold satin, with full sleeves; green satin skirt, white satin label on front printed with "Jules Mumm, Rheims. Very dry," or any suitable lettering; head-dress a full gathered cap of fawn cloth set in a band like top of cork; wine glass attached to one shoulder; gold nippers slung from waist.

CHAPEAU DE BRIGAND (*From Famous Picture*). Red cloth under-skirt, green velvet full-basqued jacket with long sleeves, white turn-back cuffs, brown revers showing low white under-bodice, large red lace-edged collar turning down from neck; brown felt hat with three bands bearing effigy of virgin, peacock's feather, and green velvet on broad brim; rosary in hand.

CHAPERON, ROUGE. (*See* RED RIDING HOOD.)

CHARITY GIRLS. Foundling dress. Short dark-blue or brown skirt, plain bodice with sleeves to elbow. Cambric tippet, with collar coming to waist, back and front; sleevelets from elbow to knuckles, with place for thumb, meeting elbow sleeve; muslin cap with upstanding crown, high in front, the latter-piece with crimped border, turned up at ears. Blue ribbon falling on tippet, with medal. At **St. Botolph's School** the dress is dark green, dark green ribbon on cap; amber stockings and leather shoes. At **St. Giles's-in-the-Fields** and **Lady Owen's School** the dress is light blue. **Orphan Girl, Soldier's Home, Hampstead,** red skirt and bodice, white muslin tippet, cap and

Fig. 4.—DRESS OF CHARLES I. PERIOD.

apron. **Carleon Charity Girl** wears blue and yellow. (*See* ALDGATE SCHOOL, AMSTERDAM ORPHANAGE, BRISTOL RED MAIDS, and BLUE GIRLS OF CANTERBURY, etc.).

CHARBONNIÈRE. Skirt of short green woollen, brown tunic, red scarf round waist, jacket bodice, white stomacher fastened with gold buttons, turn-back cuffs to elbow sleeves, white sleeve beneath; red cap. (*See* COAL.)

CHARITY, SISTER OF. (*See* AMBULANCE NURSE, ABBESS.)

CHARLES I., PERIOD OF. The gown in Fig. 4 is such as was worn by Queen Henrietta Marie, wife of Charles I. It is made of white satin, with pearl and diamond trimming on skirt, bodice, and sleeve. The cape collar peculiar to this period is edged with Vandyke point lace, and insertion above. Pearls encircle the neck and are frequently introduced across the head, or a band of brilliants. The hair is dressed in soft curls on the forehead; it was sometimes cut square in front and there were also ringlets at the back. A pearl girdle was often worn, and sometimes pearl embroideries on sides of skirt, a heavy velvet train in plaits from shoulders. White, pink, or yellow satin, or black, or ruby velvet suitable. Round feather fan carried in hand. The Princesses, as children, wore skirts touching the ground, sewn in plaits at the waist; the bodice square, with sleeves puffed or coming to wrist, and Vandyke cuffs. They were made in dark blue, drab, black, or gold satin or velvet (sometimes with sacque from shoulders), and were almost hidden by a large, square muslin apron, bordered with vandyked lace, having square bibs and lace epaulettes. They had close fitting net caps, with lace, like those of an infant. The ordinary costume of a middle-class woman, during this reign, was a skirt touching the ground, distended, in the earlier portion, by the farthingale, when the extra length formed a puff round the waist, falling in graceful fulness. The bodices were stiff, coming only to the waist, for the countrymen and citizen's wives, and had either vandyked or stuffed epaulettes, or a brace-like trimming on the front, the aprons reaching to the hem of the dress, and having a bib. In this rank, the ruff was of linen, close under the chin; higher class women wore them deeper, secured to the back of the shoulders; the French hood covered the hair and head; the commonalty preferred the high-crowned hats with broad brims like the soft felt hats of to-day. Before the end of the reign, the French hood and the ruff went out. The falling collar succeeded, the plain, graceful skirt and full sleeve, curls resting softly on the face. Another style of hair-dressing must have been borrowed from the Dutch; the hair combed straight back and the curls at the side only. Hollar represents a woman thus habited in his "Ornatus Muliebris Anglicanus," date 1645. She wears a long pointed bodice laced across the front, with an upper robe caught up in a species of panier at the hips, a tippet of linen, and long gauntlet gloves. It was in the reign of Charles I. that patches first began to be worn, which Bulwer, in 1650, speaks of as "a vaine custom of spotting their faces with an affectation of a mole to set off their beauty." When this absurd fashion came in, they were scattered all over the visage in a variety of shapes—stars, crescents, and even a coach and horses—and this folly lasted many years.

CHARLES II., PERIOD OF. The dress illustrated Fig. 5, may be carried out in plain satin. The skirt full, the bodice low and stiff, with handsome jewelled trimming on front at neck, and fur bands which can be replaced if desired by a fall of lace, a full sleeve to elbow with an undersleeve of muslin and satin caught up in the fore-arm with a jewel. Ruffle, gloves, pearls round the throat, and a small bouquet of flowers at the side of the head. The women's dress of this era is familiar from the bevy of beauties associated with it at Hampton Court in *néglig*é attire. The bodices expose rather than cover the bust and neck; the curled locks fall on the shoulders, and are simply confined by a row of pearls; the arms are bare from the elbow; a train and distinct front breadth form the skirt, and there is a plethora of lace. More homely women wore plain skirts, an upper one of a contrasting tone; pointed bodices, high to the throat, with a plain turn-down collar; the full sleeves to elbow are caught up with jewels at the bend of the arm; the shoes high on the instep, and very high in the heel, with roses or buckles. The following is a good example:—Long skirt of blue and gold brocade, with flounces of gold embroidery and point d'Alencon lace, train of old gold satin puffed and looped at the side with bows and pearls; bodice low with lace turning downwards from shoulders, sleeves fastened into elbow with diamond ornaments; diamond tiara.

CHARLES VI. OF FRANCE, PERIOD OF. (1380-1422.) Rich white satin skirt; bodice open in front and barred with fur carried round the braces and short basque; train of cloth of gold bordered with sable, and studded with diamonds. Veil of Indian muslin; horned head-dress of gold and white satin with jewels.

CHARLES VII. OF FRANCE, WOMAN OF RANK, PERIOD OF (1422-1461). Blue satin trimmed with ermine and black velvet, over old gold satin petticoat; belt at waist, revers on bodice, long tight sleeves; conical head-dress of black velvet, trimmed with tulle. Silk girdle. Ornaments, pearls and diamonds.

CHARLES IX., PERIOD OF. White satin, quilted front, trimmed with gold and pearls, black velvet train and bodice; shoulder ruff, puffed sleeves to wrist. (*See* MEDICIS PERIOD and FRANCIS II.)

CHARLES V. OF GERMANY. (*See* FRANCIS I.)

CHARLEMAGNE, PERIOD OF. Robe of coral pink, deep gold embroidery at the foot, pleated into bodice descending to the hips, the lower portion a white corslet with gold lattice work, a jewelled band at upper and lower edges, one end falling on to centre of skirt. Pink continued to throat and cut slightly on cross. Pendent, pink sleeves, white satin close fitting ones covered with gold lattice work. Crown and gauze wimple. Long white embroidered cloak.

CHARLOTTE CORDAY (1768-1793). Short, scanty skirt of white muslin or grey cashmere, bordered with a gathered flounce. A muslin fichu over the short-waisted bodice, crossing in front and tied at back; long, tight sleeves. Large muslin cap, which goes by her name, having a full crown, encircled by deep frill, plain in front, much gathered at back; ribbon about crown, bow on right side, tricolor cockade on left. Lamartine thus describes her attire: "A Normandy cap, the lace of which flapped on her cheeks, a large green silk ribbon pressed the cap round her brow. Her hair escaped from it on to the nape of her neck, and some curls floated down. On her early arrival in Paris she had a high conical hat. As a girl she wore dark cloth robes; a grey felt hat turned up at the edge and trimmed with ribbon."

CHARLOTTE, QUEEN (WIFE OF GEORGE III.). Skirt of white satin over hoops, trimmed with flounces and boullonnes, front embroidered in gold; train and bodice of pink flowered satin with lace; square, bodice and lisse fichu, wide ruffles to elbow; sleeves; powdered hair, surmounted by lace and ribbon head-dress; pearls, feathers, and diamonds. At the end of her reign she wore short waists, beneath the arm pits, narrow skirts, and for Court functions high upstanding feather.

CHASSERESSE. (*See* HUNTRESS.)

CHATELAINE. Gown of black velvet, large muslin mob cap, fichu and apron, silver girdle and chain with pendant keys at side. Lace mittens; ebony stick. Suitable for woman of middle age.

CHAUCER. There are many characters in Chaucer adopted to fancy balls; they include **Alcestis.** A soft green silk patterned with daisies, a long green tippet over the shoulders. The dress narrow, stiff, and angular. Chaucer's age was characterised by a profusion of colors, some stiffness in the patterns. The **Prioress** is arrayed in the violet robes of a religieuse. For **Arcite** and **Walter of Saluces,** boy's dresses, *see* Appendix. The **Wife of Bath** in a stuff gown with an overskirt drawn up on the side to show the underskirt. **Canace.** Dress of terra cotta silk, close fitting; long pointed shoes of old gold satin; hair plaited round the ears; silver coronet; gold veil; falcon on wrist. **Dorigen** wears the sideless gown, the hair in two long plaits. A gold net over the head and a short depending veil, the throat protected by the gorget. **Arcite:** A juste au corps of brown moire antique, gold belt, dark blue trunk hose. (*See* PERIOD OF EDWARD III. for styles worn by some of Chaucer's heroines.) **Hostess of the Tabard:** Brown cloth dress and hood, with a large holland apron worked with runic devices; head-dress of period.

CHERRY (*Bunch of Cherries, Cherry Ripe.*) Quilted red satin skirt, white muslin tunic, bodice, and puffed sleeves; broad red sash all trimmed with ripe cherries, and plenty of leaves. Mob cap suitable for child; or a tied down hat with wreath of fruit, and a basketful under arm. Dress of white tulle, muslin, or grey silk, trimmed all over with cherries, a coat of red satin, plastron of cherries beneath; ear-rings and necklace of pendant cherries. Basket of cherries carried in hand; wreath to match; fan bordered with cherry-leaves; cherry-colored stockings; black shoes.

CHERRY RIPE. A large mob cap, muslin dress and fichu, with ribbon sash, and mittens, after Millais's picture.

CHESS. Short black and white checked skirt bordered with a band of white on which are black velvet appliques of the several pieces. Low black velvet bodice with white satin braces, the epaulettes formed of a chess-board with the chess-men attached; the stomacher is also of black and white check. Black and white ribbons hang at the side. The ornaments are composed of chess-men. The hair is powdered, and surmounted by a black velvet academical cap fashioned like a chess-board; or a coronet is formed of the chess-pieces.

CHESS, LIVING. The several pieces are thus represented:—**Pawns,** red or blue dresses *à l'Amazon;* skirts and bodices trimmed with gold and silver fringe; gold and silver helmets, with plumes; spears and shields carried. **Knights** in complete armour, bearing swords, one side gold, the other silver. **Bishops** in archiepiscopal robes, with mitres and crosiers. **Rooks** in gorgeous mediaeval dresses. The **Castles** wear towers on their heads. **Kings** and **Queens** in royal robes of satin velvet and ermine, with diamonds, sceptres, etc. **Heralds** in tabards. Chess-board blue and white, 32 feet square. At the court of the first French Empire there was a representation of living chess where sixteen ladies were dressed as Egyptian mummies to represent Pawns. These figures were closely draped in black with either blue and silver or red and silver scarves. They wore the sphynx head-dress. The four rooks were concealed beneath a painted canvass tower. The bishops were replaced by "fous" in jesters' garb. The king and queen were in regal robes.

CHICKEN, WHITE. Gown of white China silk. Skirt arranged in accordion plaits. The edge of the skirt, the top of the bodice and the waist are bordered with feathers headed by a band of scarlet velvet matching the head-dress which represents the comb. The sleeves have bands of feathers over the shoulders, pendent wings of silk falling at the back, the points tipped with a red button. Scarlet stockings and shoes which have points at the heels to simulate the spurs. The top of wand resembles a chicken's head.

CHIEFTAIN'S DAUGHTER (*time of Prince Charlie*). White silk or muslin skirt trimmed with rows of tartan ribbon; black velvet bodice with plaid on shoulder; gold aigrette, with badge of gold birch-leaves; Cairngorm ornaments.

CHINA. A fashionable character carried out in several ways. For **Dresden China** almost any *poudre* dress may be worn, with or without a sacque. It is generally thus rendered: Quilted short skirt; high-heeled shoes and clocked stockings; chintz or brocaded Watteau tunic; muslin apron; low bodice; short sleeves with ruffles; coloured stomacher laced across; bow of ribbon or black velvet round neck; straw hat or muslin cap and apron; powdered hair. Bows of ribbons and flowers can be introduced on the shoulders, with a tiny china figure in the centre. A satin chapeau bras might have flowers springing from centre. Crook and high-heeled shoes. (*See* also DRESDEN SHEPHERDESS. Fig. 9.) **White China.** The same entirely white satin; white roses, lace and pearls; a close lace ruffle at throat; large white fan. **Blue China.** Worcester blue and white circular head-dress simulating a china plate; a low square bodice pointed at the waist of blue and white cotton or brocade, the patterns resembling those on china; puffed sleeves nearly to wrist; a blue scarf about the hips, skirt silver lattice work on white satin, lace frill beneath hem. Blue brocaded paniers meeting under front of bodice; a wand surmounted by a dove carried in the hand; blue shoes and stockings. **Etruscan China.** Egyptian red, black and gold. The hat, a mere coronet, of black velvet, embroidered in red and gold; black low square bodice, with red stomacher trimmed with gold; short sleeves; red, short skirt; black tunic, bordered with band of red, worked with gold; Etruscan tazza and vases in the hand. **Faience de Longwy** might be carried out in cretonne with a green mousse ground, black lines and white flowers. A coronet of the same white flowers for head-dress; the bodice has a rounded yoke-piece bordered with gold, a full white muslin bodice showing between it and the corselet; bodice and tunic cut in one, bordered with gold fringe; plain short skirt; a hand-screen of the same coloring carried in the hand. **Vallauris Ware.** A low square bodice and tunic in one, of dark green satin outlined in gold, over white satin skirt; a plastron of white flowers down the front, white sleeves, head-dress like a green plate edged with gold. **Wedgwood.** Cottage hat of blue and white with the Greek key bordering; a white under-bodice low and heart-shaped; a blue cuirass over this, edged with the same key pattern on white; tunic of blue and white bordered with a band of blue, blue tassels at side; blue short skirt, a blue and white caladium leaf carried in the hand. **Japanese.** Square cuirass bodice and tunic of red and gold satin in Japanese designs; plain red satin skirt; a head-dress fashioned like a Pagoda top to a vase; red gloves and stockings, black shoes. For **Sèvres** the hair is powdered; a coquettish pink satin hat worn on one side of the head, with a bouquet of roses; low square cuirass bodice and tunic, white with gold fleurs-de-lis and roses, bands of pink satin for trimming; pink satin under-skirt with two festooned lace flounces, the edge of skirt cut in battlements edged with gold, pleated lace beneath; bunches of roses on the shoulder; a fleur-de-lis wand.

Fig. 6.—CHINESE COSTUME.

CHINESE COSTUMES should be dresses brought from the country. Narrow skirt and loose over-dress with large hanging sleeves of two-colored satins, such as yellow and chocolate; long tunic embroidered in gold and colored silks; silk trousers, and ankle-bangles; hair *à la Chinoise*, with flowers and silver pins; fan in hand; Chinese shoes; a gold girdle or a sash tied at back encircles the waist. The Illustration Fig. 6 of a Chinese dress displays a gown of deep blue and cardinal satin, richly embroidered with flowers. Hair dressed in the usual Chinese style, decked with pins and flowers.

CHOCOLATIÈRE, LA (*From Léotard's Picture in the Dresden Gallery.*) Short dark-grey skirt; white apron with low bib, reaching to the hem of skirt; yellowish-brown velvet jacket with short, full, all-round basque; a striped yellow and black three-cornered fichu crossed in front; sleeves to elbow, turned back cuffs and under white sleeves; close-ftting lace cap, lined with pink, having a lace puffing and frill at edge; tray of chocolates in hand; black high-heeled shoes.

CHRISTMAS CARD. Short striped black and gold satin skirt, on the black a row of Christmas cards, printed horizontally, edged with gold braid. At the hem are satin flounces, with gold tinsel and fringe. Red satin paniers and drapery, covered with swansdown pompons; scarlet satin cuirass bodice laced at the back, a garland of Christmas roses across the front, bordered with swansdown, festoons of holly-berries on the arm, below the shoulder, white ribbon epaulettes, holly wreath. Red aigrette, stockings and shoes. A Christmas card in centre of white swansdown fan.

CHRISTMAS CRACKER. (*See* BONBON.)

CHRISTMAS NUMBER. Skirt made of newspapers; in box-plaited flounces, bordered with stripes, on which the titles of various newspapers are inscribed, each stripe edged with a narrow ribbon velvet. Apron formed of Christmas pictures with pink ruches in paper; black shoes, rosettes, with gold and steel pen-nibs; stockings and mittens. Bracelets of pen-nibs; scarlet cap with quills for aigrette.

CHRISTMAS TREE. Dress of green tulle covered with branches of the fir tree, toys, flags, crackers, pieces of swansdown, glittering balls and presents. A tiny fairy surmounts a huge hat bordered with crackers; a white satin placard announcing the tree in front.

CHRISTINE, QUEEN OF SWEDEN, 1633—1654. Long skirt

of brocade, black velvet jacket braided with gold and trimmed in front with blue revers, the sleeves slashed to match the skirt. White cambric fichu, broad brimmed hat trimmed with plumes, hair curled, riding-whip in hand.

CHROMATIC SCALE. Satin skirt and bodice in thirteen semi-tones of color, shading from crimson to white. The hair covered with close set fillets of the same.

CHRYSANTHEMUM. Dress of soft yellow silk with epaulettes and streamers of mauve ribbon. The dress and picture hat all trimmed with chrysanthemums, as also the wand carried in the hand, together with a basket of the flowers.

CIGALE. Short red skirt, with bars and notes of music, black and green satin upper tunic, bordered with gold fringe; Zouave jacket; purple silk vest; colored scarf across bodice, tied under left arm. High riding boots, black silk stockings; round cap of red silk with gold band; a small barrel slung on one shoulder.

CIGARETTE. Short gown of white satin, fluted at the hem to represent a row of cigarettes edged with gold cord. A sash knotted round the waist of many colours. A crossing bodice and puffed sleeves, one side bordered with flutes like a cigarette. An epaulette of the same surrounding the arm hole. The head-dress is a coronet of cigarettes. Sometimes the name of a favorite brand is introduced in front.

CINDERELLA. A short cotton dress and tunic, like Lady Adelina Cocks (now Dowager Duchess of Bedford) wore at the Marlborough House Ball, with long linen bibbed apron, a broom in hand, and a glass shoe at side. Another rendering:—Black and white striped skirt; fish-wife tunic of ash-colored cashmere; high V-shaped cambric bodice; with corselet of red velvet and black velvet bretelles, crossing in front and attached to tunic; elbow sleeves; black and white striped stockings; black shoes, silver buckles; short broom and bellows. **Cinderella** at the ball as follows: Satin gown in style of 17th Century; train of sky blue silk; petticoat pink; square bodice; all trimmed with silver lace and roses; wreath on head; sleeves puffed to wrist, high wired lace collar studded with pearls; the slipper at side, of silver cloth.

CIRCASSIAN. Costume of white satin embroidered with silver, trimmed with ermine, consisting of skirt, long habit, and under-bodice; the face, all but the eyes, veiled with white muslin; white satin Turkish

Fig. 7.—CLASSIC.

trousers; scarlet velvet Greek cap, with gold tassels; hair in plaits, entwined with pearls. Gold coins admissible; dagger and pistol; a **Circassian Slave.** White llama dress, loose and flowing, bordered with rows of gold braid and fringe; scarf and waist-band embroidered in gold; necklace of coins; wrists and anklets united by chains beneath full Turkish trousers; small cap with gold band and coins.

CLAIRE DE LUNE. (*See* MOONLIGHT.)

CLAIRETTE. (*See* ANGOT.)

CLASSIC. (*See* Illustration, Fig. 7.) The dress is made of soft silk or woollen material. The long full robe bordered with gold or silver braid. Deep scarf called diploidia with tassels at each corner draping figure; a brooch (fibula) on one shoulder. Hair in classic knot with pointed classic coronet. (*See* CLEOPATRA, DRUIDESS, ANCIENT GREEK, ETC.)

CLAUDE, QUEEN, French, 1515 (*Wife of Francis I.*) As worn by Princess Augusta of Cambridge, at Buckingham Palace Ball. Skirt of silver tissue, with deep border of ermine, upper skirt of light blue velvet embroidered with fleur-de-lis in silver, one side open and edged with ermine; low full bodice, outlined with diamonds, jewelled girdle, tight sleeves of silver tissue, a row of pearl buttons outside the arm. Crown of turquoise and brilliants; necklace to match. Veil of silver tissue,

CLEOPATRA. This character is frequently dressed in classic garb of white satin or cashmere embroidered in gold. An asp worked in front of the low, loose bodice; wing-like sleeves; jewelled girdle half hidden by fullness; a red toga fastened on the left shoulder with jewels bordered with gold fringe. Serpent bracelets up the arm united by chains. Jewelled diadem. But both Mrs. Langtry and Sarah Bernhardt have treated the character more realistically, and have worn the most beautiful Egyptian dresses (*see* Illustration, Fig. 15; Egyptian.) Sarah Bernhardt's gowns were of clinging diaphanous material, with jewelled belts, necklaces and ornaments encrusted with every imaginable precious stone. The neck and arms ablaze with jewels. The feet encased in pointed jewelled sandals, an unparalleled wealth of opals, topaz, sapphires, rubies, amethysist, turquoise, malachite, sardonyx and scarrabees. The head dresses after the sphynx order or a bandeau with iris in the centre. Her first gown was classic Greek worked in gold and precious stones, jewelled belt; the head-dress a gold band with tasselled fringe of coral and turquoise, the head of the sacred serpent in the centre. The Egyptian dresses were a yellow gauze with an applique of laurel leaves and silver tissue. A tiger skin bound kerchief fashion round the hips; skull cap composed of a lattice crown of pearls edged with large turquoise. Another of yellow crimped gauze was striped with gold spangles embroidered in black, outlined with gold. Black and gold sash, powdered with turquoise. A gold gem circlet in the hair. In another costume a flexible gold serpent two yards long and six inches wide, jewelled, surrounds the bust and waist, it's emerald head with ruby eyes nestling on the right shoulder of a pink gauze gown. Wreath of Persian roses.

CLERK OF THE WEATHER. The back of the skirt formed of a fringe of ribbon in shaded reds, mauves, and yellows, tipped with beads, the front grey satin, which like the low bodice is painted with filmy clouds. One arm has a yellow satin sleeve with the rising sun, the other a grey one with snow flakes. The cap made of silver fringe simulates rain. A thermometer on the front of the gown.

CLIVE, KITTY. Short blue chintz dress with square bodice, elbow sleeves, white stomacher, and white apron. White sun bonnet, standing up well above the face.

CLOCHES DE CORNEVILLE. (*See* SERPOLETTE and GERMAINE.)

CLOTHES, OLD. Thick shoes, under striped skirt. An old redingot of cloth. A red handkerchief tied under the chin. A pair of old trousers over the shoulder. A hat in one hand, hunting boots in the other, and a sheaf of old umbrellas under the arm.

CLOUD. Dress of two shades of grey silver tulle arranged as festooned skirts. The low, full bodice trimmed with silver; silver belt, silver star coronet, silver edging for veil. **Cloud with Silver Lining.** Grey tulle and silver cloth are interblended.

CLOWNESS. Dress of white satin, made with short skirt, a ruche of red at foot, loose full bodice with ruff, short sleeves, all ornamented with grotesque figures in dark red velvet. White shoes and stockings, with red clocks. Comical white felt cap with red velvet band and aigrette. Face painted white with red spots and crescents.

CLUBS, QUEEN OF. (*See* CARDS.)

CLYTEMNESTRA. (*See* CLASSIC. Fig. 7.) Robe of red and gold, gold diadem, gold spangled veil.

COALS. A Phrygian cap with miniature coal scuttle, black silk high bodice, short skirt and tunic all covered with lumps of coal, save the front of bodice, showing a white satin label "100 ton."

COBWEB. A grey tulle gown embroidered with silver cobwebs. A black lace belt with a low full bodice. The arm is bare to the shoulder, but from it hangs a large pendent sleeve worked with cobwebs, one being introduced in the cleft of the wand and on the side of the head.

COCK AND HEN is a good pair of costumes for a married couple or children. The cock wears a bright yellow coat, a jabot of white feathers, knee breeches of fawn brown feathers, silk stockings, black shoes, field-marshal's hat, with cock's crest of golden feathers. (*See* HEN.)

COCKATOO. Short dress of white and yellow satin, white feather wings at the side of skirt, powdered hair, surmounted by a cap in the form of a cockatoo's head.

COCK ROBIN. Short brown pleated satin skirt with rows of Marabout feathers; jacket with pointed basque at the back, like a bird's tail, of feathers and plush; the front of bodice formed of red feathers; high collar, red necktie; head-dress, bird's head with beak.

COD. (*See* FISH.)

COINS. Satin dress, with coins of all sizes arranged round the skirt, paniers, and low bodice; veil of tulle fringed with coins; gold net on head, bordered with coins; ornaments, coins. (*See also* MONEY and GOLD.)

COLETTE. (*In La Cruche Cassée*). White skirt striped with blue, and edged with a deep box-plaited flounce; bodice and tunic of striped blue and white gauze; a pointed waistcoat of blue beneath; the sleeves to elbow; a basket is carried on the arm; a blue ribbon and a rose in the hair.

COLLEEN BAWN. Dark blue stockings, high-heeled leather shoes. Short full petticoat of blue serge. Blue and white striped calico bodice and tunic pinned back kirtle fashion, showing white under-bodice; sleeves tight to elbow. Sometimes the bodice is also blue serge laced with red. Black velvet and cross round neck; hair quite smooth, twisted in coil at back. A red handkerchief may be worn tied under chin. Red cloak with hood.

COLUMBIA. Ruby velvet cap with aigrette and silver stars; low bodice of ruby velvet with blue satin stomacher, embroidered in silver with the words "Hail Columbia." Short sleeves; skirt of striped blue and ruby satin, with silver stars and fringe at hem.

COLUMBINE. White satin full skirt; low cuirass bodice, bordered with roses; rose wreath; wand headed by roses. Or white with blue satin paniers and bodice; Tricorn hat with blue pompons over powdered hair. A pretty French rendering is a short petticoat and bodice of light blue satin, with spangled bertha, ruff at throat, the skirt draped with tulle caught down with a scroll of the several characters in a pantomime; flowers and ribbon floating from the blue felt hat worn over powdered hair.

COMET. Long blue satin train draped with stars, spangled yellow gauze, the front of the lightest shade of gold, trimmed with gold fringe; blue gauze cuirass bodice shot with amber, bordered with stars; hair flowing, a star of electric light in front; star ornaments.

COMING THRO' THE RYE. Poppy-colored short petticoat, dark green bodice and laveuse tunic embroidered with rye; white chemisette, showing sleeves rolled up to elbow; poppy-colored kerchief; straw hat trimmed with rye; poppies and cornflowers slung on arm: wreath of same on one side of the head. Red stockings, black shoes with red bows; sickle at waist.

COMING WOMAN. (*See* NEW WOMAN. Fig. 29.)

COMMERCE. A classic gown worked with emblems of Mercury; his winged cap on the head, the caduces carried in the hand. Drapery of pale sea green trimmed with silver braid. Armlets and bracelets of silver.

CONCIERGE. French muslin cap and light blue skirt, velvet bodice, muslin apron and fichu; broom in hand, key tied with pink ribbon at side.

CONFETTI. Short white lace skirt covered with spots of various colors; black velvet jacket opening over white stomacher laced with pink. At left side a long pointed bag filled with sweetmeats, attached by pink ribbon; white satin cap of same shape.

CONNAUGHT PEASANT. Dressed like Colleen Bawn, with red handkerchief on head, sickle in hand. (*See* COLLEEN BAWN.)

CONSTANCE NEVILLE. (*She Stoops to Conquer*). White satin petticoat, train and bodice of blue and silver; slashed sleeves; powdered hair.

CONTADINA. (*See* ITALIAN.)

COOK. Short white skirt and apron, with white cook's cap and coat; blue ribbon carried across bodice with bills of fare printed thereon; white shoes and stockings; a case with knives hung at side; ornaments, small silver saucepans. Sometimes lobsters, etc., are printed on white coat.

COQUETTE, MY LADY. (*See* POUDRE.)

CORAL. A white satin or tulle or gauze gown draped with red chenille and coral, the flounce round the hem festooned with seaweed and coral; a wreath of coral in the hair; coral epaulettes and coral ornaments.

CORDELIA (*King Lear*). Red or white brocaded over-dress and low square bodice bordered with jewelled band; under-skirt of white cashmere worked with dragons; train from shoulder, with embroidered oak-leaves and pendent sleeves; hair floating on shoulder; gold fillet and sandalled shoes.

CORNFLOWERS. (*See* BLUETTE.)

COSWAY. To represent a miniature in this artist's style, powdered hair with bag wig, standing out well at the side, might be worn. Bodice with collar and full front. A sash round the waist, a short over jacket and a skirt with a frill at the foot.

COTILLON. Ordinary tulle ball-dress covered all over with many-colored ribbon streamers, rosettes, bells, flowers, and the gifts of the cotillon; hair flowing, a pointed cap worn on one side, round Japanese cap; fan; a basket filled with bouquets, and tambourine slung on arm.

COURT DRESS. (*See* GEORGE III. PERIOD, colored illustration Fig. 23, and descriptions of costumes in the several centuries.) Trains, Court lappets, and white feathers are a necessary part of Court dress.

CRACOVIENNE. (*See* POLISH and Illustration Fig. 31.)

CRACKER. (*See* BONBON.)

CRESSIDA (*Troilus and Cressida*). Flowing classic dress of soft, white wool; belt at waist; low under-bodice visible above upper one; helmet-like cap.

CRETAN. Full silk trousers, short Greek jacket and skirt embroidered in gay tints, colored sash round waist; flat cap.

CRICKET, THE GAME. White shoes with leather stitched straps on instep; short white skirt in box pleats and between each at the hem close set horizontal stripes of green, red, and yellow; a wicket with a red ball on either side. Round the hips a scarf of the striped colors tied on left side in bow without ends; white open jacket, a sailor collar bordered with a narrow strip of red with a bat on each corner; a low blue and white shirt with striped tie, and a red plastron to waist with pendent balls; white gauntlet gloves with the three colors, peaked cricketing cap of the same striped colors. Or for **THE INSECT** a brown satin skirt, a gauze tunic fashioned like wings; brown velvet, low bodice, with cricket's feet on the shoulders; the antennae for head-dress; bat in hand.

CROCUS. Skirt of soft mauve silk, cut like the petals of flower, forming points at the hem; edged with silver braid. Bodice of same, the long green leaves used for braces, a bloom in centre of low bodice, a bunch of crocus on the shoulders, one forming the cap.

CROW. Black skirt and feather-bodice and wings; the bird's head as a cap.

CUP. (*See* CAMMA).

CUPID. Dress of blue and silver gauze draped to right shoulder, and left side with roses; bow and arrow, and silver gauze wings.

CURLY LOCKS. This should be adopted by a child with hair in ringlets. She wears a blue frock with white quilted front, and large lace ruff; puffed sleeves.

CYPRUS, QUEEN OF. The Duchess of San Teodoro, as Queen of Cyprus, appeared in the Venetian Quadrille at the Marlborough House ball in a robe of violet velvet, trimmed with gold and pearls, over mauve satin, embroidered in pearls and gold; a gold girdle round the waist. Close and flowing sleeves, jewelled bodice, feathered hat and cap made after the portraits by Paul Veronese and Titian.

DAFFODIL. Dress of yellow satin, draped with yellow tulle, caught down with wreaths of daffodils; head-dress like a man's hat with the petals turning upwards; sleeves fashioned like flower; bodice green velvet; a wand with a bunch of daffodils and bells on the top. **Basket of Daffodils.** The same, only the bodice is of gold basket-work.

DAFFY-DOWN DILLY, "who came up to town in a yellow petticoat and a green gown." The yellow petticoat satin, made full and long; the green gown flowered, looped up on one side; the bodice of the same, opening V-shape, and bordered all round with ermine; tight sleeves with pouf at elbow; high horned head-dress of Edward III. time.

DAGMAR. Long robe of pale pink cashmere, the full classic bodice confined with a gold band at the waist and plaited round the neck. Flowing royal mantle of pale blue trimmed with gold and red gimp and fastened at the neck with a jewelled clasp. Flowing hair bound with gold circlet; leather buskins and sandals worked in gold.

DAHLIA. A ball gown made full with a fringe of dahlias at the foot. The sleeves representing the petal of the flower, made in a darker shade of petunia than the dress. The well-fitting low bodice ends in a satin belt with a pouch formed of lines of garnet. These stones used as shoulder straps and the bandeaux in the hair having an aigrette of dahlias at the side.

DAIRY MAID. Quilted skirt of a bright color; laveuse tunic of chintz; square-cut bodice of the same chintz, with stomacher laced across to match the petticoat; muslin fichu, cap and apron.

DAISY (FIELD), DAISY QUEEN. White silk evening gown, trimmed with fringes of daisies, grass, and leaves; back of skirt tulle, with side panels of painted daisies; dark green silk bodice, bordered at neck and waist with the flowers and leaves; crown or coronet of daisies, with veil; daisy chain round neck. Or a Tam O'Shanter cap made with loops like daisy petals, green tassel in the centre; wand with bunch of daisies carried in hand. (*See* PARQUERETTE.)

DAME SCHOOL DUNCE. A sugar-loaf cap marked "Dunce" held in one hand, birch rod in the other. Black silk gown covered with white letters. A white apron with the multiplication table. A white muslin fichu with elbow sleeves, "C-a-t" on one, "D-o-g" on the other. Mob cap.

DALMATIAN. Long white robe, embroidered apron; short velvet bodice resplendent with gold embroidery, many beads round throat; full long white sleeves; distaff in hand; white cloth about the head, the falling ends edged with gold; girdle round waist. The peasants wear a short red cloth pelisse fastened at waist with girdle. The hair bound round the head in two pleats, interwoven with red braid, covered with a curious helmet head-dress.

DAME DURDEN. Hair powdered, white muslin cap; flowered dress, and bodice of chintz, white muslin fichu.

DAME OF PRIMROSE LEAGUE. Primrose gown, with a bodice plastron bearing the words "Peace with Honour," in violets, and the monogram of the League on one side of the skirt; the badge of the League worn on the bodice; and as many primroses as possible scattered about the dress; primrose-colored gloves and shoes, and fan painted or embroidered with primroses.

DAME TROT. (*See* HUBBARD, MOTHER.)

DANCING GIRL. Three skirts; first, pale blue satin with wide border of gold, the second cerise satin, the third soft cream silk, with medallions and gold fringe; sash tied loosely; bodice of cream silk, fastened round throat with gold band; gold waistband and black velvet Zouave jacket embroidered in gold and fringed with sequins; gold arrow in hair; gay-colored silk handkerchief twisted round head, with sequins; coral and gold ornaments; fan formed of cards, hanging as chatelaine; tambourine with gay ribbons.

DANISH PEASANT. Striped skirt touching the ground; tight sleeves; high jacket coming only to waist, embroidered down the front; large apron almost covering the dress, with embroidery at each side; a colored handkerchief tied cornerwise on head. At Amager the women wear a black velvet sugar loaf head-dress, not erect, but the point standing horizontally and worked in jet round the face. The skirts have six runners at waist uniting it to bodice, a bright sash of ribbon passes round the front, the ends falling either side of front.

D'ARBLAY, MADAME. (*See* ARBLAY.)

DARBY (DARBY AND JOAN). Joan, print dress, white apron; red shawl, crossed in front, just large enough to come to the waist; a muslin frilled cap, white hair, spectacles and stick. Darby in fustian suit, such as an old countryman would wear, or long smock.

DARLING. (*See* GRACE.)

DAUGHTER OF REGIMENT. (*See* VIVANDIÈRE. Fig. 45.)

DAUGHTER OF CHARLES I. (*See* ELIZABETH, PRINCESS.)

DAUPHINE (*Joseph Balsamo*). Light grey brocaded silk with gold-colored flowers; the back long, the front has flounces of the brocade drawn up at the sides with tassels of blue, gold, and pearls. At the Versailles fête, she wears cloth of silver, brocaded with white satin, roses at the side, embroidered with mother-of-pearl; bodice low and pointed, covered with gold and diamonds, trimmed with old English lace; white feathers and diamond aigrette in hair.

DAW, MARJORY. Pretty dress of pink satin, plain skirt, open bodice, bordered with gold; tight sleeves, with puff at the top; hair floating on shoulders.

DAWN. Dress of grey tulle over satin, with pale pink introduced; scarves of grey tulle, and silver stars fastened at regular distances, draping the skirt, looped at the back with narrow pale pink satin ribbon and silver. Low bodice with deep basque of grey satin; short sleeves; a diadem of stars, with a half crescent moon in front, and veil of grey tulle fastened from the head to the shoulders, and again to the skirt at the back; ornaments, silver stars; grey shoes, and fan of pale pink and grey, or grey and silver.

DAY. A white tulle veil and evening dress, with clouds of rose-colored tulle draped over it, rays in gold cloth radiating from the waist. The hair powdered with gold, a gold sun above the forehead. Butterflies on the shoulders. **Grey Day.** A grey tulle gown with diamonds, hair powdered with grey powder, diamond coronet.

DEANS, JENNIE (*Heart of Mid-Lothian*). Scarlet tartan short dress; loose chintz bodice, with basque drawn in at waist by band; hair in curls, bound with a snood; plaid about the head, hanging down on to the dress.

DECEMBER. White holly and tufts of swansdown bordering skirt caught up with a girdle of holly, the fullness drawn upwards to show under skirt. Short bodice draped in falling folds crossed by wreath of holly, short jacket of the Eton shape, very open in front, edged with red berries; the sleeves replaced by holly, bordering the frill. Full red staff with ribbons; necklets of coral; large white hat with white satin bow, and white ostrich plumes curling over the top.

DESDEMONA. White satin flowing skirt, with over-dress and train of silver tissue; pointed bodice and silver cloth stomacher worked in pearls; satin sleeves puffed to wrist; pearled pendent gauze sleeves from arm-hole; pearl girdle with tassels; silver aumonière and round feather fan at side; pearl fillet on head, with silver coronet. Or sometimes the coils of hair are entwined with pearls.

DEVONSHIRE, DUCHESS OF. (Illustration Fig. 10.) Grey

satin gown, blue bow, muslin fichu, curled white wig, large black velvet hat and feathers. This celebrated picture of GAINSBOROUGH was 60 inches high by 45 wide; it was supposed to have been painted about 1783, and is described as "Duchess of Devonshire in a white dress, and blue silk petticoat and sash, and a large black hat and feathers." The figure is shown only to knees. It is said to be a portrait of Georgiana, the beautiful Duchess of Devonshire. In 1876, it was purchased for £10,100 by Mr. Agnew, and shortly after it was stolen. Another rendering is a blue satin flowing skirt; long over-skirt of figured cream silk; long sleeves and belted bodice of same; kerchief, bordered with frill, crosses in front, ends disappear in waist band. Hair powdered, and turned off face in a large roll, larger at the sides than the top, ends curled, floating on shoulders; long strip of muslin entwined with powdered hair forming a turban; almond-colored kid mittens; high-heeled black shoes; very large hat of velvet or satin, with plumes.

DEW. White crystal tulle dress, trimmed with green grass; veil studded with crystal drops. Hair hanging loose, sprinkled with frosting powder; wreath of grasses.

DIABLESSE, DIABLOTINE (*Female Demon*). Short red satin skirt, bordered with gold; black velvet sprites appliqued round low pointed black bodice cut in vandykes, outlined with yellow, black velvet bats appliqued on to front with upright red satin collar, fastened to short yellow satin coat, piped with scarlet, cut like bat's wings. Long pendent sleeves; forks of lightning wired round neck and sleeves; scarf drapery of black satin with firefly wings; black velvet cap with two high horn-like feathers and scarlet lace; gold bracelets as well as armlets worn. Carries forked trident.

DIAMONDS. Short white tulle dress, puffed through silver braid trellis-work closely studded with diamonds; round the hem a full frill of white lace trimmed with silver, diamonds and fringe; silver brocaded bodice studded with diamonds and silver fringe round hips with diamond stars; hair curled and sprinkled with diamond dust; large white feather fan. **Black Diamond.** Short white satin skirt with black boullonnés at the hem. A wheel and crank painted in front with a black diamond on either side and a diagonal band of the same across the front. Black paniers with a miniature shovel and pick-axe attached. Low bodice with leaflet basque, one large black diamond in the centre of the front and a row of smaller ones at the top. Short puffed white sleeve with a diamond on each. Black fan and gloves. Black diamonds in the hair.

DIAMONDS, QUEEN OF. (*See* CARDS.)

DIANA. Short white skirt trimmed with silver, pale green satin over skirt looped up with silver crescents and moons. Green satin hunting jacket, with red satin waistcoat trimmed with silver. A leopard skin attached to the back, with the head resting on the shoulder. Bow and arrows, mirror, and a hunting-horn attached to the side. A crescent of diamonds in the hair. Gold zone round the waist. Green boots and buskins laced with crimson. A classical rendering would be as follows:—White cashmere skirt edged with green velvet and silver, caught up on one side; loose low bodice, sleeves to elbow fastened outside the arm with silver buttons; pointed tunic, silver tassels at points; short green cashmere mantle across left shoulder, fastened under left arm; silver girdle, bow, quiver, and arrows; hair turned off the face in a coil at the back; silver crescent on forehead; silver bangles.

DIANE DE LYS. A white tulle ball-dress embroidered with silver thistles and leaves; bretelles of single leaves carried over the shoulders. Thistle aigrette.

DICKENS (Characters after). The heroines of the great English novelist do not afford much scope for fancy dress. **Sarah Gamp** and **Betsy Prig** appear in print gowns full in the skirt, short in the waist, bright colored handkerchiefs fastened over their ample busts. Large leg-of-mutton sleeves, big aprons and frilled caps with a ribbon bow on the top. Mrs. Gamp carries a pair of pattens. Betsy Prigg has a very visible false front. **Mrs. Nickleby** and **Charity Pecksniff** wear full-skirted gowns with pointed bodices of mousseline de laine. Sleeves of the leg-of-mutton form. Velvet fichus with a bow in front. The hair parted in the centre and again across is gathered in a knot at the back. **Mercy Pecksniff** has a crop of curls. A low bodice and short sleeves and sash at the back. She is also depicted in a pinafore and out of doors in a cape and bonnet with a large veil over the face. **Ruth Pinch** wears grey cashmere, very simply made with linen collars and cuffs. **Mrs. Squeers** a short narrow skirt just reaching the ankles, composed of striped and flounced mousseline de laine. Spenser of the same, made with a short waist and enormous gigot sleeves. Coal-scuttle bonnet of black satin. Corkscrew curls. A birch rod and wooden spoon in her hand. **Fanny Squeers's** dress is made in the same fashion, the skirt white muslin, pink sash tied at the back, and a white satin bonnet. **Mrs. Stodgers,** a hard-featured woman with a row of curls in front wears a black net cap, a crackling brown black silk, and carries a basket. **Miss Wardle's** brown gown has triple flounces. Hair in curls, full bodice and bishop sleeves, and a large old fashioned lace collar. **Mrs. Bardell,** has a striped violet and brown gown, with a deep flounce at the hem, full bodice, large lace tippet and coal-scuttle hat. **Mrs. Nickleby.** Widow's cap; a plain skirted black gown, a pointed bodice cut *en cœur* at the neck, with a turn-down collar and bishop sleeves, a muslin cap; or, instead of the cap, a large old-fashioned coal-scuttle bonnet, with plaited border and large veil, or a close plaited border to a cap with a raised crown. Sometimes she has a shawl about her shoulders; sometimes a pelerine coming to the shoulders with a frill round.

DINORAH. Hair in two long plaits; light blue skirt, with bands of black velvet; lace-edged apron; white chemisette, with long sleeves to wrist; blue square corselet bodice, laced and trimmed with silver and black velvet.

DIRECTOIRE, 1795, COSTUME OF. This is a favorite style of dress at fancy balls, and admits of many good combinations of color. After the great Revolution towards the close of the last century, women launched into all kinds of eccentricities. Wonderful head-dresses were originated. The head-gear stood up boldly from the face, like a spoon. There was the bonnet *a la folle,* with a tricolored butterfly bow at the top; and the casque hat, round without a brim was worn over a Charlotte Corday cap. The hair stood out in large puffs. The following are dresses in the Directoire style:—Skirt of striped silk with one deep flounce at the edge, double-breasted coat having pink cuffs and revers, and two rows of buttons to waist; ruffles and large jabot of crêpe lisse and lace; large hat and feathers; riding whip in hand; eyeglass. Or white satin dress, with paniers formed of loops of ribbon, having two pink satin belts, fastened with enamel buckles; plaited lawn fichu; long Suede mittens; white satin train mounted in box-plaits, lined with pink satin.

DI VERNON. The character is illustrated in Fig. 8, by a flowing satin skirt and bodice of striped velvet with vest and revers of satin, the former handsomely braided in gold. There is a lace jabot and the black velvet hat is trimmed with ostrich plumes. The ordinary rendering is a black or green habit of velvet, cloth, or satin; jacket with postilion basque, double-breasted; mousquetaire cuffs trimmed with a color, such as red satin, sometimes with gold braid and brandenbergs. The skirt is looped up on one side over a plain or quilted satin skirt; lace jabot and ruffles; diamond stars; broad-brimmed cavalier hat, with plume and Stuart rose; hunting whip and horn.

DOCTRESS OF MUSIC. (*See* ACADEMICAL DRESS).

DOLL. As faithful a copy as possible of a Dutch doll; the hair drawn to a bow at the top of the head; red shoes and mittens; cotton or muslin gown made with full plain satin skirt and low loose bodice, short sleeves, large sash. Sometimes a baby doll is simulated. **Doll Pincushion,** a skirt of muslin and lace, plain plastron down front, with steel beads mounted on wire to simulate pins, white on one side black the other; bodice edged with same; on the right side a heart-shaped pincushion; head-dress, a crown made of lace and pins. **Doll Seller.** Short dress and square bodice with elbow sleeves, made of blue satin with lace ruffles. The skirt is flounced round the hem, and caught up in vandykes with dolls hung round in the festoons, and fans of lace intermingled with the flounces; upstanding lace cap with pink ribbon, and an aigrette of dolls; pink shoes; a doll carried in hand. **Doll Paper.** The wearer is dressed as much as possible like a doll baby, but the costume is composed of pink or white crepe paper, instead of silk, cotton, or woollen fabric. Even the close frilled cap is thus made.

DOLLY. Is often represented as a milkmaid, with yoke and pails; large mop cap with red silk scarf tied under chin; green shoes and stockings, and figured cotton short skirt; plain tunic; green fichu tied over low bodice; short sleeves, black mittens.

DOLLY MAYFLOWER. Black satin petticoat; tunic and low square bodice of flowered silk or cretonne, elbow sleeves; muslin fichu and mob cap; pocket outside dress; high-heeled shoes with buckles; black silk stockings.

DOLLY VARDEN (*Barnaby Rudge*). Short quilted skirt; bodice and bunched-up tunic of flowered chintz, the former low and laced across; a muslin kerchief inside; sleeves to elbow with frill; correctly speaking the hair should not be powdered, as she did not belong to the upper classes. Straw hat with cherry-colored ribbons, or muslin cap and apron; high-heeled shoes and bows; colored stockings; mittens.

DOMINO, A. Worn at masque balls and sometimes as a fancy dress. It is made in satin, silk, and brocade, or of plain cotton in the Princess shape, having often a Watteau plait with cape and slender-pointed hood and wide sleeves. It should be large and long enough to slip over the dress easily, and hide it completely. Black is usually trimmed with a color, in the form of a thick ruching down the front and round the bell-shaped sleeves, and are often piped with a color and lined with the same. The newest kinds are made in chiffon and gaily trimmed with flowers. White satin is covered with white chiffon and lilies of the valley are dispersed all over it, falling in a shower; the cape is formed of boullonnees of chiffon; blue satin dòminoes are turned back with pink roses. Handsome velvet and satin brocades are employed on some with no capes, but full bishop sleeves and lace ruffles are gathered from the neck beneath a double frill of lace. The **Merveilleux Domino** is trimmed at the hem with festoons of old lace caught up with pink bows repeated on the shoulders; the large sleeves coming from the plait at the back. Some are parti-colored half black half cerise. A white brocade might have an accordion pleated cape, pink, flame color, black and yellow are effective.

DOMINOES, GAME OF. Short black satin skirt, edged with large white satin ruche, lined with black, and studded with pompons of black silk; a front breadth of white satin with rounds of black velvet appliqued to represent double 6, crossed with a double row of gold braid; paniers of black satin edged with black pompons over kiltings of white satin, and caught up with double 5 dominoes intermixed with ostrich feathers. Smaller dominoes lined with cardboard, form basque to low black satin bodice, the top trimmed with lace and gold cord; shoulder knots of ribbon and feathers; powdered hair; feather aigrette; enamel dominoes and diamonds for ornaments; long white gloves; fan in shape of dominoes; black shoes and stockings.

DORIGEN (*Chaucer*). Sideless gown of 14th century, made of such thick stuff as amber plush, bordered with grebe; beneath côte hardie of rose-colored silk richly embroidered; sleeves also embroidered; small coronet on head; long white tippet, edged with gold; veil of silver gauze.

DOROTHY DRUCE. Black or grey Puritan dress; white bibbed apron; kerchief and Puritan cap. (*See* PURITAN.)

DOROTHY VERNON. Satin skirt trimmed with lace, pointed bodice and bunched-up tunic of brocade. The bodice trimmed with lace, pink bows and roses. Powdered hair and a small cap.

DOVE. Plain grey Princess dress; minute wings on front of satin bodice; cap like the head of a dove; band of red ribbon crosses the bodice from the right shoulder to under the left arm, with a letter attached; pair of wings at back; low bodice, plain; tight sleeves.

DOULTON WARE. A combination of brown and light grey satin. The skirt brown, with a Doulton pattern carried round the hem and up the sides. Tunic of grey satin bordered in the same way. A scarf of grey tulle tied in a bow on the left side of the hips. The brown velvet bodice embroidered like the skirt. Grey tulle puffed sleeves. A coronet fashioned like Doulton ware with veil at the back.

DOWAGER OF BRIONNE. (*See* BRIONNE.)

DRAGON-FLY. Evening dress of green tulle, spangled with green tinsel thread and sequins, trimmed with bulrushes and dragon-fly; a dragon-fly on the head, on each shoulder, and on front of bodice.

DRAUGHT BOARD. White satin gown with draught men in black and leather colored velvet. An apron like a draught board made in white satin and black velvet, ornaments draughts, and these form an aigrette in the hair.

DRESDEN CHINA. (*See* CHINA.)

DRESDEN SHEPHERDESS. An illustration of this character appears in Fig. 9; the skirt is of shot moire with a panier tunic of brocade, the pointed bodice having a jewelled stomacher, the sleeve tight from the shoulder with a triple frill of lace falling to the elbow. A band of velvet threaded through jewels encircles the neck and is tied in a bow at the back, a bow with an upstanding osprey placed at the side of the powdered hair. A crook is carried in the hand entwined with flowers. The pointed shoes which are brocaded on the instep display handsome buckles. This character is very pretty all white.

DRUIDESS. Long flowing cashmere robe bordered with embroidered oak leaves and mistletoe; full low bodice drawn to the neck by a ribbon; no tucker; gold girdle; a scarf with pointed ends floating over the right shoulder fastened with a brooch on left; gold armlets below the short sleeve; a wreath of oak-leaves and mistletoe. A lyre in hand. This may be carried out in white, or in grey, with red scarf; gold necklet; sandals on feet. It is the correct costume for Norma.

DRUM, FOLLOW THE. (*See* F.)

DUCHESSE, GRANDE. Blue satin skirt of walking length, with silver military braiding down the front and bordered with silver; long Louis XV. jacket edged with silver; waistcoat from waist only of red satin, braided to match the skirt; mousquetaire cuffs of red satin; hussar jacket braided and edged with fur, slung from shoulders; white Steinkirk tie; red satin and fur cap, with pendant point and tassel; star on right breast. Second dress, full evening robe with jewels.

DUCHESS OF DEVONSHIRE. (*See* DEVONSHIRE.)

DUCK, WHITE. White satin gown, the front covered with swansdown; feather wings at the side of the skirt. Shoes of the color of a duck's foot. Small cap like a duck's head, with a frog in its beak.

DUENNA. Generally rendered by a modern Spanish dress: a high black silk; the skirt long, the bodice simply made. Spanish mantilla and comb; red rose at side; black shoes and stockings.

DUSK. Dress of grey tulle, or muslin, or gauze over satin, made as an ordinary evening dress, or in classic fashion: a veil of the same material; fire-flies imprisoned in the tulle; bat fastened on one shoulder, an owl on the other; silver and smoked pearl ornaments.

DUTCH. In the illustration, Fig. 11, the character wears a stuff gown gathered on to a full waist-band of brocade, of which the bodice is made, with lapels of an oblong form of red velvet carried over each shoulder. Handsome jewelled embroidery is introduced round the waist and down either side of the front, the white pleated muslin front being crossed by agraffes of gold and silver Dutch jewellery. The upper portion of the sleeves are made of striped velvet or silk multicolored, and this forms the foundation to the head-dress, which mainly consists of the ornaments that Dutch women wear on their heads, in gold and silver. There are many varieties in the national head-dresses peculiar to Holland, which would hardly be suitable for fancy balls. A good **Peasant Dress** is a short blue silk or stuff skirt; short plain over-skirt of yellow satin, or brocade, or chintz; black-velvet bodice laced over a high white chemisette with short puffed sleeves, silver bands on either side of the jacket fronts; white cap with a gathered frill, large silver circles above the ears and a silver band carried across the forehead. The bodice may be made to the waist, square at neck, with kerchief tucked in, a band round the waist and across bust; or with turned-down linen collar. Many pretty Dutch costumes may be copied from Mieris, Gerard Dow, and other Dutch painters. A **Dutch**

Fig. 10.—DUCHESS OF DEVONSHIRE.

Skating Costume of the 17th century is as follows: Short satin skirt, long tunic, turned up all round the waist; long pointed bodice, sleeves with one puff, and then two white satin puffs to wrist; satin fur-lined muff, fur tippets, hood lined with a color, gauze veil, high-heeled shoes, skates hanging at the side. **Dutch Costume worn at Marken:** full short black skirt, bordered with gold; large figured apron; square blue sleeveles jacket bodice, close-fitting, ending at waist, bordered with embroidery, and laced with gold over red; under-bodice high to throat; white tight sleeves to elbow, blue armlets to wrist; round high red head-dress like a busby, with two rows of beads. **Dutch Fish Wife** (*Scheveningen*). Full plain blue skirt, round waist band, 6 or 8 inches deep, red, blue, and white, tied with a ribbon bow in front; short orange bodice, square in front, filled in with kerchief, sleeves rolled up, cape of green, lined with rose color, reaching to below waist; close-fitting cap with lace lappets, over it a large straw hat; carries basket of fish. Linen skull cap, piece turned back at ears, standing out from face with gold ornaments on either side.

DUTCH MATRON (16*th century*). Kilted skirt of brown cashmere, edged with velvet; white linen apron; châtelaine at side, with keys and satchel; close-fitting bodice, with shoulder cape and revers, edged with gold galon, linen chemisette, and linen cuffs to tight sleeves; black velvet cap, with hair hidden. In the 15th century: figured stuffs and brocades over hoops were worn; stiff straight square bodices, all round basque; white chemisette, and close plaited ruff at throat; sleeves with epaulettes; gauntlet gloves, high pointed felt hats. The caps had often two large round gilt plates connected with semi-circle of wire which went round the back of the head, and kept the lace in order.

DUTCH SERVANT. Short chintz skirt, blue serge bodice, with all-round full basque, red kerchief tied over the neck and tucked into front; large muslin lace edged apron; lace cap, silver side ornaments; plain black dress, high bodice, large white tippet, huge turn-back linen cuffs; apron and cap, guiltless of trimming; keys at side.

EARTH. MOTHER EARTH. White satin short skirt with rows of black velvet; red satin tunic, black velvet bodice, laced stomacher, short sleeves; gilt basket on head, with flowers, fruits, and bulbs; ferns, grass, and fruit about dress; a small globe hung at side.

EASTERN QUEEN. Trousers of gold-striped silk, gathered at the ankles; tunic of white and gold broché, bordered with gold fringe;

scarf of Oriental gauze tied at the side, striped with bright colors; loose full bodice made of soft white silk falling to the hips, and confined at the waist by a red silk scarf, powdered with sequins; red silk epaulettes, red silk handkerchief about head with sequins. (*See* ORIENTAL.)

ECAILLÈRE (*viz., Oyster-woman.*)

ECARTE. Short dress of black and red satin, trimmed with gold, and cards. (*See* ROUGE ET NOIR.)

ECLIPSE. Gown with square bodice, divided down the centre perpendicularly, half yellow and gold, half black gauze. Black flowers on one side of the head, gold on the other; one glove yellow, one black; shoes the same.

EDITH BELLENDEN. (*Old Mortality*, 1685). This character should have fair hair, and be playful and arch. She either wears a riding-dress or a simple green cashmere dress, trimmed with white lace and silver braid; black velvet cap with white feathers and pearls, made in the style worn in James II.'s reign; plain upper and under-skirt, pointed bodice high to the throat; plain turn-down collar, full sleeves to elbow tied with ribbons.

EDITH CLINTON. Long maroon velvet dress, quite plain; drooping white hat and feathers.

EDITH PLANTAGENET (*The Talisman*). Long flowing skirt, sewn to cuirass bodice, coming low on hips; cut square at neck, tight sleeves to wrist, pendent ones over them; front of bodice embroidered in blue and silver, bands of same, outlining bodice and sleeves. Hair in two long plaits, braided with pearls; shoes jewelled. A flowing cloak of a distinctive color may be added, but is not essential.

EDWARD I. (*Period of* 1272-1307). **EDWARD II.** (1307-1377). During both these reigns silk gowns were worn with velvet mantles embroidered in gold and furred with miniver. Gold girdles; kerchiefs on the head surmounted by coronets with precious stones. The hair was entirely enclosed in a caul of gold or silver net work, over this a peplum or veil and sometimes also a round hat or cap and natural flowers. Wimples were worn by the matrons unbecomingly wrapped two or three times round the neck and fastened with pins on either side of the face higher than the ears. The long robe consisted of skirt and bodice high to the throat cut in one with extravagantly long trains. The sleeves reaching to the elbows over tight fitting ones of contrasting color. For example, a dress of **Edward I.** White satin skirt, full, reaching to the ground edged with three bands of gold, embroidered with wheat ears. Long violet over dress bordered with gold held up in front, jewelled band at the waist and at the top of the half high bodice. Hanging sleeves to elbow, tight white sleeves to wrist set in gold bands. Green velvet regal mantle attached to shoulder edged with gold. A gold caul on the head, held by a gold band going under the chin with a jewel on either side of the brow. **Edward II.** Full green robe bordered with gold, sewn to a half high bodice with gold band at neck and waist, united by a strip down the centre of the front. Hanging sleeves to wrist bordered with gold, violet streamers from the wrist falling to the hem, and fringed with gold. White veil enveloping the head held in place by a circlet of gold.

EDWARD III. (*Period of* 1327—1377.) This was a time of great extravagance. The gown or kirtle had tight sleeves reaching to the skirt or elbow; it was cut low in the neck, and the bodice was very close-fitting, and so long that it had to be held up in walking. The spenser or short jacket was introduced in this reign, rounded in front and bordered with fur, and the sideless gowns and the côte hardie buttoned down the front like those of the men. The robes were not only furred, but jewelled and embroidered in gold, and sometimes they were parti-colored. For example, short gown of green satin, a band of blue at the hem embroidered in gold, surmounted by gold embroidery. This is gathered to the close-fitting bodice at the waist with a plain band of gold; the sleeves are tight to the wrist, having a close set row of buttons on the outside. Short upper sleeves, red velvet regal mantle lined with miniver fastened round the shoulders with a gold jewelled band. The hair which descends in loops on either side of the face is enclosed in gold network. Pointed gold jewelled collar, two long stoles of white and gold descend from the sleeve to the skirt as far as the knee.

EDWARD IV. (1461-1483). The period is illustrated in Fig. 12 by a simple satin gown with revers of contrasting color, such as ruby with light pink; the head-dress of ruby velvet richly embroidered and jewelled. A veil of lisse depending from each point and floating at the back. The steeple-chase head-dresses were the particular feature of the day. They are described as rolls of linen pointed like steeples, half an ell high, some having a wing at the side called butterflies; the cap was covered with lawn, which fell to the ground, and was tucked under the arm; many chains about the neck; velvet, silk, damask cloth of gold, costly furs, and striped materials, all worn. The period was illustrated in the Health Exhibition of 1884 by a female figure taken from the King Réne Paris Library. The skirt divided in two down the centre, with gold braid, each half subdivided into divisions of pink, or dark blue, gold or white satin, some having diagonal heraldic emblazoning in gold; gold belt round waist where bodice ends; white chemisette with an upright plaiting at neck, and gold necklet; sleeves of pink satin, bordered with gold, tight blue ones beneath, forming a point on either side of the hand; stomacher of white satin crossed with gold; steeple head-dress in gold color, distended with wire, long veil to feet.

EFFIE DEANS. (*See* DEANS.)

EGGS. Yellow satin gown drawn back at the sides over white; low bodice and skirt bordered with white gauze boullonnés like eggs; cap shaped like half an egg. The stomacher in front of bodice embroidered to simulate eggs.

EGYPTIAN. See illustration of a magnificent dress and Egyptian honey suckle; the draperies bordered with heiroglyphics, the ibis a prominent part of the head-dress. (*See also* CLEOPATRA.) The dress of the country is not suited to fancy costumes. Egyptian women out of doors wear a large square of checked cotton thrown over head and figure. A gold ornament is fastened between the eyes, and reaches to the top of forehead, secured to the yashmak of black crape or cashmere passed across the face, falling lower than the waist. A fellah woman wears a loose half high bodice of washing stuff, a necklace round throat, plain woollen skirt, a sash of many colors about waist, and a handkerchief gracefully twisted round the head.

EGYPTIAN LADY. Pale blue cashmere embroidered in silver, with ornate lizard bird; yellow satin skirt, bodice of green tinted jet and open-work embroidery; small richly colored birds dotted here and there over skirt and bodice. Sphynx head-dress.

EIGHTEENTH CENTURY (*Dress of Period.*) Powder was worn until 1795. Large hoops, short skirts, elbow sleeves, and square bodices are distinguishing features. (*See* POUDRE.) The poorer classes had a petticoat and over-dress, opening in front, a pointed bodice and kerchief, muslin cap, and plaited border, tight sleeves, mittens, and long aprons. In 1786, enormous hats, composed of gauze wire and ribbon, were worn,

Fig. 15.—EGYPTIAN.

and turban helmets, high crowned sugarloaf hats from France. In 1794, the waist came below the arm-pits; feathers were perched upright on the head. The vagaries—the high hats, the curious hoods, and the catogan—which originated in the French Revolution found their way to England. (*See* INCROYABLE, MERVEILLEUSE, and DIRECTOIRE.) The following costume was worn in 1784: A full skirt touching the ground, a flounce at edge; high bodice, long sleeves, satchel bag at side, large muff pelerine, edged with a ruche of lace tied at back; muslin cap, a large flap hat over it. In 1727—36, the taste of the day was mock pastoral, and men and women, as Corydons and Sylvias, tried to be mistaken for shepherds and shepherdesses. The hoods of the ladies denoted their politics by their color. The hood was succeeded by the capuchin; long gloves were ruffled on the arm, huge watches and châtelaines hung at the side; the high-heeled shoes had infinitesimal points. In 1760, gaudy brocades and lustring were fashionable materials.

EIFFEL TOWER. Cap fashioned like the Eiffel tower which is painted on the biscuit satin gown.

ELAINE (*Idylls of the King.*) Long golden hair, flowing loosely, encircled by a band of gold with stars round head. Dress of rich gold brocade or cashmere, jewelled in front; the bodice comes almost to the throat, and is cut square; it fits figure to hips closely, where is a jewelled band; sleeves tight, with jewelled epaulette. Lily carried in one hand, and Lancelot's letter in the other; a shield on arm.

ELEANOR OF AQUITAINE. The wife of Henry II., 1154—1189, in Tennyson's play of "Becket," wears most costly robes, the first long and red, worked all over in gold, having pendant sleeves, white muslin wimple and banded head-dress; then a sideless gown of brown velvet, and in last act an over-gown of gold cloth embroidered in jewels.

ELEANORE OF AUSTRIA (1515—1547, *and Wife of Francis I. of France*). Skirt touching the ground, of brocade, satin, or velvet, bordered with gold or silver, opening to show front breadth of silver brocade, a jewelled girdle and pendant falling in the centre; the bodice stiff, coming to the waist, cut as a low square, the front jewelled; puffed sleeves to wrist, over them large hanging sleeves, bordered with ermine; jewelled crown on head. Necklace.

ELEANOR OF CASTILLE (*wife of Edward I. See Period of* EDWARD I.) Dress of green velvet, silk, or satin, richly embroidered, loose girdle at the waist. Regal mantle from the shoulder. Crown and embroidered veil.

ELECTRIC LIGHT IN THE HAIR OR ABOUT THE DRESS. This is now introduced in such dresses as Morning and Evening star, Will o' the Wisp, &c. The lights are attached to a small battery which is hidden in the hair.

ELECTRICITY. Electric blue satin, covered with silver zigzag flashes; silver cords are wound about the neck, arms, and waist, to typify the electric coils. Bodice of blue satin draped with silver and crêpe de chine; wings at the back; an electric light in the hair. A staff carried in the hand with coils encircling the globe which surmounts it.

ELEMENTS. (*See* EARTH, AIR, FIRE AND WATER.)

ELFRIDA, as an Anglo-Saxon Queen, wears a long loose robe of silk or cloth; the bodice and skirt cut in one, confined at the waist by a girdle, and bordered with gold; long hanging sleeves; a wimple or piece of linen wrapped about the throat; hair loose. The dress may be of cloth or silk; gold ornaments.

ELIZABETH OF AUSTRIA (*Wife of Charles IX. of France.*) Robe of velvet or satin, trimmed with gold bands and ermine, the front of white satin, jewelled and embroidered; the bodice filled in with a quilted chemisette; close ruff; large fur sleeves; stomacher coif and girdle all jewelled; tulle veil.

ELIZABETH, DAUGHTER OF CHARLES I. is painted by Van Dyck in a yellow satin gown with Watteau plait at the back, touching the ground. Sleeves to elbow slashed in front showing white satin; lace ruffles. Large apron bordered with Vandyke lace reaching to the hem of the skirt. Lace bib and tippet in one, covering the points of the shoulder. Pearls round the neck; hair square over the forehead falling at the back in curls. Her sister Princess Henrietta, afterwards Duchess of Orleans has a similar dress, but with a close fitting cap like those worn by infants. In the portraits of the family by Van Dyck with a large Newfoundland dog, Princess Mary, afterwards Princess of Orange, is dressed like the Princess Henrietta. Another pretty rendering of this costume is a plain skirt, the bodice cut in tabs buttoned up the front. A large muslin collar opening V shape bordered with Vandyke lace; sleeves to wrist with turned back cuffs; two slashed puffs; a close hood over the hair.

Fig. 16.—QUEEN ELIZABETH.

ELIZABETH OF HUNGARY. Close-fitting under dress of cloth; over this a sideless gown of cream brocade, bordered with fur, crimson above, and heavy gold ornaments. The embroidery on under-dress is worked in gold; the hair hangs in two long plaits, confined by a gold coronet, studded with pearls; tight under-sleeves; loose and large over ones, lined with crimson velvet; long cloak fastened at the neck with antique clasp.

ELIZABETH, MADAME (*Sister of Louis XVI.*) A rich dress of the period. The hair powdered, and turned off the face; long curls on shoulders; pink satin train with roses falling over a satin petticoat trimmed with lace and pearls; the bodice low, bordered with piped satin revers, turning downwards; tulle fichu inside, rose in front; long tight sleeve to wrist.

ELIZABETH PLANTAGENET OF YORK (*Queen of Henry VII.*) In the combined tones of the red and white roses. Brocaded petticoat; red velvet bodice and train, fastened with jewels; long sleeves to hem of skirt, lined with and bordered with ermine; jewelled girdle and crown; white roses in hair. Order of St. Esprit. Diamonds, rubies for ornaments.

ELIZABETH, PRINCESS (*Daughter of Louis XVI.*). **Dress in Prison.** Black stuff gown, with tight plain sleeves to wrist, and full skirt sewn to waist; muslin fichu, with double frills, hemmed, crossed in front, the ends tied at back; hair turned off face in double roll; falling in curls at back. **Dress at Court.** Yellow satin skirt and bodice, the latter a low square, with elbow sleeves; silk scarf tied round the waist, ends falling at back; hair turned over high cushion and powdered.

ELIZABETH, QUEEN OF ENGLAND, AND HER PERIOD (1558—1603. *See* Illustration, Fig. 16). Full skirt, touching ground, of richly embroidered material, often jewelled round hem, gathered to bodice at waist; worn over a hoop. The bodice is stiff, with deep pointed stomacher, low in front and embroidered with serpents, &c., or jewelled; ruff supported on wire at back, the hair frizzed; a small velvet cap and jewelled crown; the front breadth of dress embroidered or quilted with pearls, the sleeves puffed to wrist with ruffles; very pointed shoes. Velvet satin or brocade is suitable. A velvet train bordered with ermine can be worn from shoulders. **Ghost of Queen Elizabeth.** This would be rendered in white with powdered hair. (For dress of Period, *see* AMY ROBSART and LADY BACON). A woman's dress of a lower social grade as follows; full pink cashmere skirt, worn over huge farthingale; dark green paniers; scissors tied to the side with black ribbon; bodice bordered with blue, showing muslin partlet; white collar, stiffened; white cap with black velvet. The **Waiting Maid** of this Period is illustrated in Fig. 17, she wears a simple full skirt of a plain or finely striped woollen of neutral tint, a satchel of the same at the side, a full white apron bordered with lace, tight sleeves with ruffles, long pendent outer sleeves and epaulettes, a close ruff encircling the throat, small coif cap of white muslin.

ELIZABETH WOODVILLE (*wife of Edward IV.*, 1461—1483. *See* Illustration of that Period, Fig. 12). It was a very extravagant age when furs, velvet, and rich material were worn.

ELSA (*Lohengrin*). First dress white cashmere, the square-cut bodice coming down well on to the hips, outlined with a white worsted girdle, the two ends hanging in front; long sleeves caught up at elbow, showing bare arm; this is braided in gold like the tunic, which falls over long plain skirt; fair hair flowing on shoulders. Second dress, white silk Princesse; band of gold embroidery at hem, carried up the front, round the high neck, and wrist of tight sleeves; jewelled girdle about hips; long cloak of silver tissue from shoulders; crown, and gold-spangled tulle veil.

ELSIE MAYNARD (*Yeoman of the Guard.*) Short skirt of cream cashmere trimmed with ruby, ruby velvet bodice worked in gold over white under-bodice, cap of same velvet, with eagle's feather.

EMPIRE, BRITISH. Deep blue silk short skirt with the names of the several colonies; train of satin; blue bodice trimmed with white fur; blue stockings and Indian slippers; aigrette of prepared sea weed; fan painted to represent the rising sun. Necklet of rose, shamrock and thistles. White gloves tied with red, white and blue ribbon.

EMPIRE. (1805-1815) Period of French. Various kinds of dress prevailed during this period. For a while, a classical style obtained: long flowing skirts, with peplums, the sleeves fastened with three buttons outside the arm; the hair dressed with fillets of gold; this was the evening garb. In the daytime, there were the coal-scuttle bonnets, short waists below the arm-pits, and other monstrosities. When Josephine reigned at the Tuilleries more graceful attire was adopted; the court dresses were of gold tissue, and velvets covered with gold embroideries;

Fig. 17.—ELIZABETHAN WAITING MAID.

for example, white under-dress of silk, worked in gold; also the green velvet gold embroidered train from waist, bordered with ermine; gigot sleeves, studded with bees; long gloves hiding the arm. Or pale blue costume worked in cornflowers; gathered bodice of gold gauze, woven with gold, the waist coming under the armpits, and made with a cape; Indian shawl, fastened on shoulder with the gold ornament of the period; large Tuscan bonnet, with bird of Paradise, and blue ribbons carried on the arm like a basket; narrow skirt and very short waisted square cut bodice in one. One puff to the sleeve, a satchel bag at side; a large poke bonnet with soft full crown tied under the chin is suitable for a young girl.

ENCHANTRESS. Skirt of ruby satin, bordered with gold, caught up on one side to show border of mystic characters in black velvet; long black velvet sleeveless robe, opening over ruby vest, covered with gold suns, stars, serpents, and scorpions; striped Oriental scarf round hips; large mantle of dun-colored cloth, bordered with velvet, attached to shoulders; head-dress, an ibis with out-stretched wings, on a scarlet cap, with a band of carbuncles; wand with serpents interlaced; heavy gold jewellery. (*See* SORCERESS.)

ENGLAND. Skirt of cream bunting, the lions of England painted on each of the battlements in which the edge of the skirt is cut; the Union Jack and Standard of Scotland draped over with Prince of Wales' plumes, ostrich feathers; dark blue velvet bodice, made quite plain, and trimmed with gold and small Union Jacks; fan covered with Union Jack; head-dress a helmet; effigy of St. George and the Dragon round neck.

ENGLISH, EARLY. This is generally rendered by a costume in the time of Edward IV. (*See* Illustration Fig. 12, and description.) **Old English.** A Georgian dress suitable to a middle-aged matron, made entirely in satin of one tone or two, such as pink lined with black, or costume of the early portion of 19th century. **English Peasant** (*see* GEORGE II.).

ENID (*Idylls of the King.*) A sweeping robe of gold embroidered stuff, the bodice square, very long and pointed, bordered with fur and gold braid, carried round the neck and down the front in the form of a stomacher; the sleeves hang from elbow; the hair in two long plaits; a jewelled coif or fillet on head. Sometimes the bodice is cut as a low square, showing white chemisette, also low in neck, the trimming bordering the top and surrounding an all-round basque, reaching to hips and up the front; tight sleeves, one puff at top.

ERIN, IRELAND, HIBERNIA. An evening dress of green and white tulle or chiffon, trimmed with dark green shamrocks, a ruche at hem, gold harp; drapery caught up with a wreath of shamrocks; or a white cashmere classic robe, with green peplum, the low full bodice and pendent sleeves bordered with gold embroidered shamrocks; small gold harps on shoulders; wreath of gold shamrocks; gold ornaments. Low bodice; shamrocks on shoes; soft green cap with shamrocks.

ESKIMO. Pretty for children, the girls in woollen stuff skirts, the boys in trousers with a habit and hood in one, of deer skin.

ESMERALDA. A rich gipsy dress in yellow, black, and scarlet satin, made short, trimmed with coins and gold braid; a sash of gold tissue tied about the hips, a tambourine carried in hand; bracelets above and below elbow, united by coins; stay-bodice with coins and gold braid; gold net with sequins: ornaments, sequins. Sometimes the skirt is red, trimmed with gold, and the bodice takes the form of a loose black jacket, with full yellow vest of soft silk. Also yellow satin box-plaited skirt, with lace flounces; black satin jacket, embroidered in gold; large black and gold scarf tied at the side; cap bordered with sequins; tambourine. (*See* GIPSY.)

ESMOND, VISCOUNTESS. Black Velvet dress with flame colored petticoat, lace fichu; many rings on the fingers; spaniel, and snuff box carried; lace cap.

ESTAFELLE. White satin skirt, green satin tunic tied back with various colored ribbons; high jacket of green satin, with white waistcoat and red revers, short sleeves.

ESTHER, QUEEN. Blue satin and silver under-robe bordered with gold and silver, cut low at neck, with sleeves coming from a band at shoulders and flowing at the back; over this a sleeveless dress of moss green velvet, trained, cut heart-shape in front, fastened with a massive gold girdle; beads round neck; red satin trousers embroidered in gold; a silvered tulle veil reaching to feet; sandalled shoes. Hair inter-plaited with pearls; a cap of Oriental material, with a black aigrette and diamond stars, like the one Mdme. de Pompadour wears as Queen Esther, in Van Tor's picture. The train could be borne by a page.

EUMENIDES. Red or black veils, snakes entwined about bare arms, buskins like a huntress, rough chiton of brown, black, or blood-color, girt with skins of snakes; other serpents bind their waists, and their trailing skirts are embroidered with snakes' eyes.

EUROPE is generally carried out by the national dress of some European country, say Italy, Spain, or France. Or by a white cashmere classic robe with appliques of bulls (*see* CLASSIC, Fig. 7) with a battlemented crown, bearing the names of the different countries.

EURYDICE (*Orfeo aux Enfers*). Pink trimmed skirt bordered with fur, as also the loose Greek bodice; hair trimmed with gold fillets.

EVANGELINE. As a Normandy peasant, with blue kirtle or petticoat; the white tunic drawn through the slit at back; low, square bodice with chemisette beneath, or a white fichu over bodice; large ear-rings and cross; white Normandy cap; a rosary hanging at the side. (*See* NORMANDY.)

EVE. Dress of white India muslin, trimmed with apples, leaves, and blossom; fig-leaves for pockets; out of one peeps a serpent's head with emerald eyes, out of the other falls a triplet of white lilies; a wreath of small apples, flowers, and leaves; necklace, a serpent of gold and silver and red and blue enamel.

EVELYN (The Betrothed). Trained white dress open at the neck. Long over-cloak with hanging sleeves brought over the head; spear in hand.

EVENING AND EVENING STAR. (*See* STAR.)

EXPRESS. Trained skirt of steel-colored satin, edged and bound with black velvet, showing a series of rails in steel braid; skirt stiff at back, the hem edged with a row of moveable wheels. The front of the skirt black velvet, striped downwards; steel-colored cuirass; miniature steam engine in the flowing hair, grey feathers issuing from the funnel; wheeled skates for shoes.

FAIR LOCKS (*Fairy Tale*). Long skirt; full, low, banded bodice and short sleeves of gold tissue and white silk, with gold trimmings; hair flowing. **FAIR STAR.** Dress of white satin and silver tulle, cuirass bodice of silver cloth draped with tulle; a star on front. A star over the forehead and flowing veil of spangled tulle.

FAIR MAID OF PERTH. White satin skirt of walking length, with low pointed bodice; stomacher of ruby velvet; sky-blue satin braces; long sleeves gathered perpendicularly to the wrist, with ruby velvet cuffs; short cloak of tartan satin from the shoulders; tartan satin Scotch cap, bound with ruby velvet.

FAIR ROSAMOND. (*See* R.)

FAIRY. Short silver wand; tulle diaphanous dress, with low full bodice, covered with silver spangles; silver belt at waist; wings of gauze on wire attached to back. These are to be had in three sizes made in gauze, silver and gold fastened into a metal groove sewn to the back of the dress; hair floating; a silver circlet on the head. Or, for a **Fairy Queen**, a crown, and a sceptre in addition. Stars should be introduced on the dress and on the satin shoes. **Fairy Godmother.** (*See* HUBBARD, MOTHER.) Short all-round skirt. High bodice with lace stomacher. Huge ruff, spectacles and hat.

FALCONRY. Short skirt of dark cloth, red or brown; long basqued jacket of green velvet; gauntlet gloves; a hawk on the hand. Cavalier hat with drooping feathers; high boots.

FANS. White satin evening dress embroidered with Japanese fans. Small enamel fans for ornaments. An aigrette with fan on the powdered hair.

FANTASIE is generally a dress of the Louis XV. period. A short blue and white striped silk skirt, large passementerie epaulettes; a white satin bodice having blue silk ornaments and festoons of white lace with red roses nestling in it; a black silk hat with gold cockade and tri-colored plumes.

FANCHON. Blue and red gown, with black velvet bands round skirt: muslin fichu on the shoulder; high-pointed hat.

FATES, THE. In antique Greek costume. (*See* GREEK.) **Clotho** bears a distaff in her hand, and wears a crown with seven stars, the robe spangled with stars. **Lachesis** holds a spindle, or is represented spinning; her robe also star-spangled. **Atropos** in black robe and veil; with knife, scissors and threads of various length in the hand.

FATIMA. Petticoat of white satin, striped with scarlet and gold, and edged with deep gold fringe; tunic of blue satin, with gold passementerie, crescents, stars, and pearl fringe; scarf of scarlet cashmere, embroidered in gold round hips; white satin vest, with scarlet and gold; blue velvet Zouave jacket, bordered with ermine. Head-dress, turban of scarlet and blue gauze with chains of pearls; veil of tulle, with gold stars, anklets and armlets of gold; a key hung at side. (*See* TURKISH.)

FAUST. (*See* MARGUERITE, MARTHA, and SIEBEL).

FAVART, MADAME. Short grass-green skirt, red tunic and square stay-bodice, white chemisette, and white elbow-sleeves; red stockings and black shoes; red or black handkerchief about the head, with coins; hurdy-gurdy in hand.

FEBRUARY. Short gown of dun-colored kilt pleated chiffon, cut in scallops at the base and fringed; vandykes of white satin ribbon folded on the skirt; a bunch of spring blooms at the lower points. Panier tunic; low bodice with a bunch of flowers in front, and the short sleeve left open outside the arm.

FEDORA. Madame Sarah Bernhardt in this rôle wore a pale blue embossed velvet, with large moons for bodice and train; paniers and tunic of brocatelle; under-skirt of dark blue velvet, bordered with bouillonnés. Another dress: bodice and train of Pompadour brocade with roses, the front mousseline de soie of a light blue shade, trimmed with lace; elbow sleeves, and épaulettes.

FELICIA, (*Pot of Pinks.*) White muslin skirt and apron and full sleeves, low short-waisted bodice, and blue ribbons in the hair.

FENCING. A skirt with perpendicular stripes of velvet and leather. A leather jacket with a red velvet heart embroidered on the side. A fencing mask forming a head-dress; foils hung at the side.

FENELLA (*Peveril of the Peak.*) Red silk Turkish trousers; short green skirt, trimmed with lace and pearls and Arabesque figures in gold; Oriental scarf knotted round waist, with dagger; green velvet jacket, open at neck, bordered with fur; crimson cap and eagle's feather; white and gold veil; feather fan. Dark hair hanging about shoulders.

FERN. Light green tulle dress with sprays of fern growing up the skirt; three fronds on the front of the low bodice, and a couple on each sleeve; a bunch of ferns carried in the hand, head-dress a fern wreath; ornaments; emeralds or enamelled ferns.

FIAMETTA (*La Mascotte.*) First dress: Riding-costume of scarlet cloth, felt hat, and leather gauntlets. Second dress as gipsy: Short white skirt; tunic and bodice of amber; scarf round hips; square bodice, sleeves to wrists; a scarf of many colours forming a head-dress; hair hanging down; gold ornaments; tambourine.

FIFTEENTH CENTURY COSTUMES. During so long a period there were many changes, but the styles at fancy balls are described under Edward I., II., III., and Henry IV.

FIGARETTE. A pretty mixture of red, black, and yellow, the skirt cut into alternate vandykes, and edged with gold; a white apron, red scarf round the hips, black cocked hat, brilliant yellow sleeves.

FILEUSE. (*See* SPINNING-GIRL.)

FILLE D'AUBERGE. Short sky-blue and crimson-striped skirt; pale blue tunic trimmed with lace; black velvet bodice, laced with crimson; white fichu, high white muslin cap; crimson stockings; ornaments, silver earrings and cross.

FILLE DU REGIMENT. (*See* VIVANDIÈRE.)

FILLE DU TAMBOUR-MAJOR, STELLA. High boots; short skirt of red, blue, and white stripes, with a horizontal band of red just above the hem; black cloth military jacket, with jockey basque at the back, pointed in front; a white cloth plastron covering the chest; red and white facings to the cuffs, and gold buttons; a keg slung across the shoulder; muslin apron: hair curled in front, tied at back *en queue* with black ribbon; cocked hat, with tricolored rosette. The dress of the Fille du Tambour-Major in the first act is a white skirt, with lace-edged flounce; tunic and bodice of grey cashmere with black ribbon; velvet braces; square linen collar coming well down to the bust, back and front; a black velvet bow on head.

FIN DE SIECLE. Green dress with low bodice, a high white hat such as men wear, eye glass, and a masculine coat over the low bodice; cigar in hand. (*See* also NEW WOMAN Illustration, Fig. 29.

FINLANDER. Blue cloth petticoat, the edge embroidered with crimson; full white bodice to the throat; sleeves to wrist, rosettes of red down the front; red sash, knotted at the side; velvet sleeveless bodice bordered with gold. Red handkerchief tied round head. A long embroidered over-dress is also worn by the peasantry.

FIRE. Black tulle evening dress over red silk, with tongues of flames formed of red tinsel at the hem, fringed bodice and skirt covered with red sequins, as also the veil; coronet of tinsel to resemble flames; ornaments, garnets. Torch carried in hand. It may also be carried out with black and crimson velvet embroidered with flames, or in flame-colored and orange lisse. **Fire-Fly.** Under-skirt and jacket of flame-colored lisse, cut in scallops; gold tissue bodice, all ornamented with fire-flies; cap, black and gold, fashioned like a fire-fly. **Fire Brigade.** Dark cloth kilted skirt, a rope round the waist, a ladder embroidered at the side; red velvet bodice with wide revers; a white under-bodice, the word "Fire Brigade" embroidered on front; a gold helmet.

FISH. Costumes of this kind can be carried out in scaly cloth, the fins of gauze distended with wire. The head-dresses representing the head of the fish. The skirts short with high leggings covered with scales. A cod, a sword fish, an octopus can be so represented; for the latter, the various feelers form the head-dress.

FISHGIRLS, FISHWIVES, &c. Boulogne Fishwife. Bayonne Fishwife. (*See* BOULOGNE and the Illustration Fig. 2 of BOULOGNE FISH GIRL.) Red skirt, edged with black velvet; black velvet low bodice, white linen sleeves; handkerchief over shoulders; red handkerchief round head; gold cross and earrings; fish basket. **Calvados Fishgirl.** Blue and white striped skirt, black tunic, and low bodice trimmed with cross-cut bands piped with red and white, over white chemisette; muslin cap; gold ornaments. **Calais Fishgirl.** Plaited muslin cap, close to the face, not standing out in an aureole, as in the case of the Boulogne fishgirl; very dark blue skirt, with light blue stripes, light blue jacket buttoned in front, and apron to match. **Dieppe Fishwife.** Sleeveless jacket and vest of black "bure" or serge made double-breasted and fastened at the side with bone buttons; under-vest of stout linen, long sleeves tucked up above the elbow, a ruching visible along the neck of the bodice; short plain skirt of "bure" with wide stripes; dark grey speckled stockings, high-heeled shoes with buckles; a high Normandy cap of white muslin, supported by a wire frame work; a shallow basket in brown osiers slung round the figure. For festivals she wears a high straight bodice, hooked down the front, with semi-fitting sleeves, black mittens to elbow secured by bows. Gold earrings and chain with saint Esprit. **Fishergirl** (*see* ANGLING GIRL). Skirt of reseda plush draped with a net, and fish attached; the bodice is trimmed with lobsters and crabs, the shoulders covered with seaweed, the whole skirt with crabs, starfish and shells; the silver net tunic, with fish and coral, and a lobster; hair flowing, seagull on shoulder. **Matelotte.** Red and white striped skirt, navy blue tunic *à la laveuse;* muslin lace-edged apron with bib, fichu, with the ends tucked into bib, and sailor tarpaulin hat; the hair down. **Scotch, Edinburgh, or Newhaven Fisherwoman.** Navy blue under-skirt, one of yellow and white above, with three tucks, laveuse tunic of blue and white striped flannel; loose bodice of flowered chintz, the sleeves rolled to elbow; a colored handkerchief round neck; short white linen apron, turned up and forming two pockets; a jacket of duffel, like a man's coat, tied by the sleeves round the neck; muslin cap, with colored handkerchief over it; creel at back. All these dresses are short. Black stockings and shoes with high heels, and colored bows are worn, and mittens or bare hands, gloves are out of place. A basket of fish at the back; a net slung round waist with net attached. **A Scotch Fishwife Dress** (Illustration No. 37) is carried out with a short striped red and white skirt, a navy blue tunic, a flowered cotton bodice, and a red hood and cape; a kreel at the back. **Swedish Fishgirl** wears a sugar loaf hat of black velvet; gay-colored handkerchief with silver necklace; white linen loose bodice, full bishop sleeves to wrist; black velvet belt and shoulder straps; blue skirt, apron striped horizontally; grey stockings; black shoes. **Fisherwoman of Zuyder Zee.** Petticoat of brown or dark blue frieze, red apron with bib embroidered with floral designs pinned in front of a sleeveless jacket, to match the petticoat and hooked at the back; the under-skirt of striped calico, covers the neck and arms; close fitting cap of colored satin, ornamented over the forehead with gold and silver tinsel cloth. (*See* HONFLEUR.)

FIVE-O'CLOCK-TEA. Short blue satin skirt and bodice embroidered with cups, saucers, and teapot; muslin fichu and apron, with dial of clock pointing at 5, embroidered teapot beneath; head-dress, a tea-cosy or a close-fitting cap like a cup with aigrette of sugar tongs; spoons forming necklace; silver chatelaine, with tea-spoons and sugar-tongs; ornamented silver spoons, and cups. Instead of embroidery, chintz cups and saucers may be gummed on.

FLAG, BRITISH. Tricolored skirt, draped with Union Jack, the bodice ornamented with a flag to match. Or, brown dress looped with white flags; white sash across the bodice, the name of vessel, and burgee in hair.

FLAG, PILOT. Two flags on one side of black tulle skirt; the head-dress a pilot flag of navy scarlet, and white silk; two smaller flags in front of bodice, two carried in the hand.

FLAGS OF ALL NATIONS. A white gown covered with a

Fig. 18.—FLEMISH COSTUME.

variety of flags, the British ensign in the centre. White sailor hat with a band interwoven with flags, red shoes with parti-colored rosettes. A banner carried in the hand.

FLAME. (*See* FIRE.)

FLANDERS, FLEMISH. The illustration Fig. 18 shows a very rich style of Flemish dress adapted to mediæval ages. It can be carried out in velvets and satin or in handsome watered or brocaded materials. The front of the bodice is embroidered and so are the bands which surmount the shoulder. The double collar is wired and the hat is bent to the face and surmounted by ostrich plumes.

FLEMISH FLOWER GIRL. Black velvet short skirt and pointed bodice laced over a muslin stomacher. It has an upstanding collar edged with silver braid; puffed sleeves to wrist, with a shaped band of velvet covering the fore-arm. Over-skirt, pink satin; embroidered muslin apron; high felt hat, velvet brim, and pink feather; pouch bag at side, slung by cord; pretty pleated lace caps are also worn. (*See* also VIERLANDER.)

FLEUR D'ÉTÉ. (*See* FLOWERS.)

FLEUR DE CHAMPS. Petticoat of striped silk, rose and white, trimmed with rows of velvet, edged with gold; a green satin tunic looped up with wheat ears; on the right side a bouquet of wild flowers; velvet bodice in the Louis XV. style, trimmed with gold; a collar of green satin, forming revers; apron, with lace pocket and bib; a coquettish hat, with wild flowers placed on the side of the head.

FLEUR DE LYS. Brocaded skirt over a farthingale, silver lilies embroidered on satin tunic, bertha studded with lilies, and fastened with silver lily; hair powdered, diamond lily in the hair.

FLEUR DE THÉ. (*See* Illustration of JAPAN IN SPRINGTIME, Fig. 26.)

FLORA. White tulle gown striped with silver. White silk shoes embroidered with various flowers. The entire dress from waist to feet covered with roses, lilac, sweet peas, violets and narcissus. The bodice a la Grecque trimmed with silver. Bands of eglantine on each shoulder. Garlands of flowers looped across the bodice. The hair loose and garlanded with flowers and diamond eglantine. Necklets and bracelets formed of flowers. A maypole carried in the hand. Or a classic dress with floral insignias. A cornucopea in hand.

FLORA MACDONALD. White satin dress, made with a plain skirt and half-high bodice; hair in curls; plaid of Macdonald tartan (Clan Ronald) over shoulders, a ribbon snood with rose at side; buckled shoes; long mittens.

FLORA McIVOR *(Waverley).* Plaid skirt and black velvet bodice; tartan scarf draped loosely across, secured with Scotch brooches on shoulders; hair in curls; black velvet Scotch bonnet with plumes.

FLORENTINE LADY *(from Taddeo Gaddi's picture).* Dress of rose-colored satin over a peacock-green skirt; bodice square and close-fitting, bordered with gold braid; tight sleeves, with pendent ones from shoulder, trimmed with ermine, also carried down the side of skirt, made as a train, open half a yard from edge, on both sides showing under-dress; skull cap of green velvet, embroidered in rose and gold color, with tulle veil; hair flowing.

FLORIAN SHEPHERDESS. Red velvet Louis XV. coat, pale lemon lisse skirt, straw hat wreathed with flowers and red ribbons over powdered hair. Large crook.

FLOWER-GIRL. To be carried out in various ways. An evening dress besprinkled with all kinds of flowers, and straw hat with flowers. A poudré dress with flowers. The most general style is a short bright-colored skirt, velvet bodice, laced stomacher, muslin apron with or without bib, a bunch of flowers on bodice; a basket of the same in hand, or hung to side of skirt, a straw hat with ribbons, or a wreath of flowers, (*See* VIERLANDER). Sometimes a chiffonier's basket is carried at the back filled with flowers, and a Normandy cap worn. A Vaudois flower girl wears a wheel-shaped lace cap under a straw hat, woollen skirt; square bodice; low under-bodice; velvet yoke, and ribbon streamers. Sometimes bright colored silk handkerchiefs are draped about the head. (*See* FLEMISH and LOUIS XV).

FLOWERS. An evening dress trimmed with any flower, and called after it, is the easiest rendering of a flower costume, and a tulle veil with wreath and floral china ornaments; a basket of the blooms carried in the hand. Sometimes the flower is imitated, such as Lilac, Snowdrop, Pansy. Sometimes the dress is the color of the flower, viz., a violet evening gown made up with silver gauze and green leaves, for a **Violet;** or **Forget-me-not,** skirt formed of festoons of blue tulle; baby bodice of same, with short sleeves, all bordered with forget-me-nots; hair loose; head-dress of blue silk like large inverted forget-me-not, with green

Fig. 19.—FOLLY.

stalk, blue shoes; or if more of a fancy costume is desired, the lower part of skirt is gathered in diamonds, and outlined with silver or gold braid, or leaves and flowers; the bodice made *à la* Louis XV., and trimmed with gold or silver; an apron with bib, and a coquettish hat at one side of the head entwined with the particular flower. (*See* APPLE-BLOSSOM, BLUETTES, BLUEBELLS, BULLRUSHES, BOULE DE NEIGE, BUTTERCUPS, CHRYSANTHEMUM, CONVOLVULUS, DAISIES, DAFFODILS, BASKET OF VIOLETS, FLEUR DE CHAMP, FUSCHIA, HEARTSEASE, HYACINTH, and HELIOTROPE; or the dress is embroidered with any bloom required. For WATER-LILY, *see* WATER-NYMPH; for ROSE, *see* R.

FLY. Black tulle dress, veiled with dark blue gauze; wings of the same; low bodice; a cap representing the head of fly.

FOG. Smoke colored net, with silk bodice, and tulle scarf bound round figure; long grey gloves; shoes, hose, and fan, all deep grey. **Fog, Yellow.** Deep orange tulle, with one skirt of grey tulle thrown all over it; a veil of grey over orange tulle falling from the one shoulder; hose, shoes, and gloves all orange.

FOLLOW MY LEADER (*Storey's Picture*). Red coat bodice, with revers; wide silk band and sash about the waist; cocked hat and feathers; short blue skirt.

FOLLOW THE DRUM. Short dark blue skirt and jacket, braided with gold, red facings; three-cornered hat and long white feather; drum carried at side. (*See* VIVANDIERE).

FOLLY, FUN. Folly in Illustration Fig. 19 is arrayed in red, yellow, and black or blue, or pink and blue, or blue and red satin skirts, the three upper ones edged with gold cord, tipped with balls which reappear on the double points of the bodice, and on the falling points of the sleeve, cap with three points; bauble in hand. Sometimes the bodice is square with a square collar and streamers, bordered with bells; and high boots are worn. **Goddess of Folly,** white satin dress made *en sacque,* decorated with discs of black velvet; a fool's cap to match. **Priestess of Folly** wears a white satin sleeveless robe and the black velvet Phrygian cap; silver snake ornaments; powdered hair. (*See also* POLICHINELLE.)

FOOTWOMAN OF THE FUTURE. Black satin quilted skirt; maroon double-breasted tail-coat, brass buttons; black waistcoat showing beneath the jacket in front, and lace ruffles; hair powdered; tricorn black and gold hat; gold-headed cane in hand.

FORD, MRS. *(Merry Wives of Windsor).* Pink silk skirt of walking length, with rows of black velvet, worn over hoop; a black velvet train bunched up; low black pointed bodice, pink bows down front; a muslin fichu edged with lace over neck, with bow in front; five rows of pearls tight round throat; sleeves to elbow, with ruffles; hair turned off face in double roll, and powdered; black hat, with pointed crown and pink ribbons, bound with pink; pink stockings and black shoes.

FORGET-ME-NOT. (*See* FLOWERS.)

FORTUNE AND FORTUNE-TELLER. White cloth gown with the several games, cards, dice, roulette, &c. appliqued on in black velvet and gold, long pendent sleeves lined with blue. Phrygian bonnet with wheel of fortune in front. (*See* GIPSY.)

FOUNDLING DRESS. (*See* CHARITY GIRLS.)

FOURTEENTH CENTURY COSTUME. The distinguishing features are: flowing skirts; bodices coming well down on hips, with stomachers; cloaks from shoulder; head-dress a veil. Sumptuary laws prevented the wearing of costly fur by any but noble ladies or their attendants. This period includes the reigns of Edward II. III., Richard II., Henry III. (*See* Descriptions.) It was a time when very extravagant materials were employed. The spencer or jacket bodice was bordered with fur; hanging sleeves to wrist, and often pendent ones over. The Côte-Hardie was also worn. Parti-colored dresses were adopted; and the sideless gown faced with fur; long streamers from the elbow. The reticulated head-dress towards the latter part of the century showed the hair gathered in a caul at side, a veil at back.

FRANCE is represented by a short white satin dress with stripes of red, white, and blue, emblazoned with arms in gold, &c.; low bodice draped to correspond, gold filigree eagle on the shoulders, and on the red satin cap. Square fan covered with red, white, and blue, pockets in front of skirt with tricolors escaping therefrom, festooned at side, joined to sash end at the back; scarlet satin shoes; white stockings with red clocks. (*See also* REIGNS OF LOUIS XIII., XIV., XV., XVI. INCROYABLE, EMPIRE, REPUBLIQUE, FRANCAISE, FRENCH PEASANT, MERVELLEUSE, &C., &C.)

FRANCIS I. 1515-1547. *(Time of.)* Costume worn by the late Duchess of Leinster at the Marlborough House Fancy Ball. Green satin petticoat, with three rows of gold embroidery beneath scarlet gown, opening in front, jewelled on either side, the whole covered with gold; close-fitting low square pointed bodice, jewelled girdle, and pendant rows of jewels at top of bodice; full slashed and puffed sleeve to wrist, of white and green; open hanging sleeves of red satin, lined with sable, fastened with jewelled clasps at elbow, lace ruffles; head-dress, a coronet of jewels. At this time very handsome stuffs were worn; it is identical with the Tudor period in England, and Charles V. of Germany.

FRANCIS II. (1559-1560.) Is identical with the Medicis period. A grande dame of the court would wear an under-skirt and sleeves of white satin, embroidered at the feet; bodice and skirt of blue velvet richly wrought down the sides; the square bodice pointed at the waist; outlined with a jewelled band and festooned with gems; wired lace ruff from shoulders; sleeves one puff to elbow, three puffs to wrist; Marie Stuart jewelled coif, jewelled girdle hanging in front; veil of gold and gauze floating at back.

FREEMASON, FEMALE. Black velvet dress; white satin Watteau sacque, trimmed with swansdown; swansdown ruff at throat; hair powdered; quaint velvet hood, studded with pearls and Masonic emblems; a Master Mason's apron and collar of office, with pendent gauntlets and Masonic jewels; clock at girdle.

FRENCH PEASANT GIRL. Pink and white striped petticoat, short blue and white over-skirt; black velvet basqued, low square bodice laced in front over white with blue cord, and shoulder straps; low white chemisette and short sleeves; white apron, with pink and blue bows; dainty muslin cap; a tiny bouquet on cap and apron; pink stockings with blue clocks; gold ornaments of Normandy type. (*See also* WHITE DRESSES, BOULOGNE FISHWIFE, NORMANDY PEASANT, &C.)

FRIESLAND PEASANT. This costume is characterised by a large flat circle of straw with ribbon which forms the hat, worn over a close-fitting cap, both tied under the chin. The women wear shoes with buckles, short crimson skirts of wool closely pleated to the bodice, with large silk aprons and silver-mounted bags hanging at the side. The dress is of the XI. and XII. centuries. There are two bodices, one of cloth with gay-colored sleeves, over it another interlaced with yellow ribbon having pendant silver tags. Girls wear a tag of silver on the left side, married women on the right. Out of doors, a short open jacket is embroidered with gold and silver thread, and indoors a head-dress of fine linen of a helmet shape covers the head.

FRIBOURG PEASANT OF THE XVI. CENTURY. Short blue woollen skirt, red and white striped silk apron, black velvet bodice with a red satin stomacher laced in front and a white chemisette.

FRIQUETTE (*Les Prés St. Gervaise*). Short blue silk skirt, with white muslin lace-edged flounces; muslin apron having forget-me-nots and roses on pockets; muslin kerchief and high Cauchoise cap, with forget-me-nots; hair in long plaits; high-heeled shoes, blue stockings.

FROST. Gown of satin broché, trimmed with frosted tulle and frosted snowdrops, the front arranged as an apron, of ribbon and lace insertion, with long garlands of snowdrops at the left side. The bodice laced with cord over frosted tulle, sleeves like apron; snowdrops on shoulders; powdered hair; aigrette and necklet of snowdrops. (*See* HOAR-FROST.)

FROST, MRS. JACK. Poke bonnet for head-dress; white dress and cloak.

FRY, MRS. Grey quaker dress. White muslin kerchief folded closely about the neck. A white quaker cap with black and grey ribbons fastened under the throat.

FUCHSIA. Dress of red satin, made in the form of a fuchsia, and laced up the back; sleeves also like fuchsias, with pearl and other pendent beads; cap of fuchsia form; small fuchsias attached to bracelet and necklet. Or, a fuchsia bodice made with no visible fastening, an effect produced by turning up the two back leaves and having them laced together after the dress is on; sleeves in the form of fuchsia with the stamens made of pearls and other beads falling on the arm to elbow; cap a complete fuchsia; necklace and bracelets formed of several pendent fuchsias.

FUN. (*See* FOLLY.)

GABRIELLE D'ESTRÉES. (*Mistress of Henry IV.*) 1589. She was dazzlingly fair, with brilliant dark eyes, and had abundant hair worn brushed back from the forehead and temples in a double roll, and encircling the head in coils, entwined with pearls. Rich brocades; Flemish or English point lace should be worn. Bodice long-waisted, close-fitting, high to neck, with Elizabethan ruff. Her dainty silk stockings and high-heeled shoes were famous. Violet velvet over skirt and bodice; sleeves with fine Indian muslin to wrist; plain white satin under-skirt with gold lace, and gold cord worn over a farthingale; violet velvet head-dress and white feathers; large ruff of pointed lace. She was fond of black satin embroidered with pearls and precious stones.

GAINSBOROUGH (*After*), generally represented by the famous Duchess of Devonshire. (*See* Illustration, Fig. 10.) A simpler style after this artist is a soft, scanty, white muslin dress, with a flounce round the edge, blue sash with large bow at back; muslin fichu and cap bordered with frills; tight sleeves to wrist. **Lady Barbara Yelverton** (after Gainsborough) wears a plain white muslin gown with short sleeves; ruched at the neck and elbows with bows of rose-colored or blue ribbons; a large tied sash of corresponding color round waist; an elaborately-trimmed lace cap. A **Grey Gainsboro'**, 1775. Upper skirt and bodice of pale grey ottoman silk; petticoat, pale coral broche velvet; hat of grey silk, with pale coral feathers.

GALATEA. Long white classic robe of Indian muslin embroidered with a Greek scroll. A peplum of the same coming from the shoulders, forming points at the side, bordered with gold fringe, terminating in tassels; armlets and bracelets united by chains; gilt band round the head and waist; hair flowing. (*See* GREEK and Illustration of CLASSIC style, Fig. 7.)

GALICIAN MATRON. Skirt of dark colored brocaded cloth in plaits a quarter of a yard wide; bodice buttoning in front, with a double turn-down cape, edged with narrow plaiting and buttons, showing white under-bodice, with two up standing frills, and many beads; head-dress of same material with white lining in front, and revers to match dress; tight sleeves to elbow.

GAMES. A short low gown of blue and pink striped silk with chessmen, dominoes, cricket bats and balls, tennis net and racquet in gold, draped from the waist and introduced on the shoulders and head-dress; a chess board forming the stomacher.

GARDE CHAMPETRE. Short brown skirt draped with dark blue velvet; bodice of the same, high, and jacket-shaped with brass badge on the sleeve; high hat covered with birds; red necktie.

GARDENER, A LADY in the Illustration Fig. 20 has a white satin skirt covered with a lattice work of light green ribbon, flowers clustering at the hem and brought up the skirt. The black velvet bodice has a lisse fichu and sleeves tied with green and pink ribbon as is also the rake. A bunch of roses appear on the right shoulder, and the large hat is trimmed with pink and green ribbon. **Gardener's Daughter** *(Picture by Mdlle. Achilles Fould).* Chiffonier's basket slung at back, with flowers therein; lace fichu tied carelessly round the neck; red woollen skirt; white muslin apron; black bodice loosely buttoned in front; white sleeves peeping below tight long ones; a bunch of flowers in the hand.

GALEUSE DE POMME. Short blue petticoat; over-skirt and bodice of white and chocolate stripe, with blue waistcoat cut low in front; white muslin short sleeves, paysanne cap of muslin, with rosette of two colors, black shoes, striped stockings. Basket of apples carried in the hand.

GEM OF THE OCEAN. (*See* AQUARIUM.)

GENERAL *(Lady).* High leather boots, kilt-plaited red cloth skirt, green cloth pointed bodice fastened at the side; field glass slung round figure; cocked hat.

GENEVA SISTER, AMBULANNCE NURSE, RED CROSS NURSE, SISTER OF CHARITY. (*See* AMBULANCE NURSE.)

GENEVIEVE DE BRABANT. Mediæval skirt of gold brocaded tissue, trained over-dress, bodice one side pink the other white, trimmed with hearts and caught up with a girdle; gold brocaded sleeves, tight to wrist, pink satin pendent ones, lined with amber; steeple head-dress of pink satin bordered with ermine. A gauze spangled veil.

GEORGE I., II., III., IV., *(Time of).* The ladies wore powder up to 1795. In **George Ist's Reign,** 1714-1724, women wore hoops, and the sacque was introduced from 1711 to George IV.'s reign. The hair dressed low and covered with frilled caps; aprons were universally worn. **George II.,** 1727-1760. Long trained skirts; powdered hair, which was continued till 1795; fichus; large hats and feathers; sashes about waist; lace ruffles; long gloves; large gold watches and chains showing at side. The taste of the day was mock pastoral, and men and women of the court figured as Corydon and Sylvias—dressed as shepherds and shepherdesses. The hoods of the ladies denoted their politics by the color. The *Spectator* writes, "I took notice of a little cluster of women sitting together in the prettiest colored hoods I ever saw: one of

Fig. 20.—LADY GARDENER.

Fig. 22.—ENGLISH PEASANT OF GEORGE II'S. TIME.

[See page 113.]

them was blue, another yellow, another philomel, the fourth was of a pink color, the fifth of a pale green. I am informed that this fashion spreads daily, inasmuch that the Whig and Tory ladies begin already to hang out different colors, and to show their principles in their head-dress." The hood was succeeded by the capuchin; long gloves were ruffled on the arms; huge watches and châtelaines hung at the side; the women's hoops, however, grew and grew; they were made of whalebone, and rendered life a struggle. How to get in and out of a room, and how to get into a sedan, occupied thought and attention, and the satirists of the day hurled their shafts without mercy. In the Georgian period the prettiest shoes found favour; high heels, pointed toes, diamond buckles, and embroideries.

GEORGE II's. TIME, AN ENGLISH PEASANT OF, in illustration Fig. 22, wears a striped woollen gown, muslin apron, fichu, and ruffles to elbow; felt hat over white cap. It might be rendered in cotton or satins.

GEORGE III., 1760-1820. In this reign flounced petticoats, long trains, square bodices, and wide open elbow sleeves were worn; older women had lace hoods. The powdered hair was drawn off the face over a very high cushion, and formed into chignons at the back with marteaux; long buttonless gloves, often embroidered on the outside of the hand, painted vellum fans; bracelets, jewelled necklaces, such as the esclavage with rows of gold chains; beads or jewels falling in festoons, covered the neck; the Maccaroni head-dress was in vogue (*see* CHARLOTTE, QUEEN), all curls, puffs, and flowers, with long side curls; hoops, and paniers, bodices with long waist. (*See* 18TH CENTURY.)

GEORGE III., COURT DRESS OF THE PERIOD OF. The Illustration, Fig. 23, shows a white satin petticoat embroidered with roses, wheat ears, and garlands. The train and bodice are of yellow bordered with a large ruche, a frill headed by jewels falls from the top of the neck, a belt with jewelled clasp encircles the waist. There is a coronet of jewels in front of the erection of white ostrich feathers tipped with yellow. Long lappets of lace were then worn and one falls over the shoulder in front, the train is carried on the left arm.

GEORGE IV., 1820-30. During this reign short waists and plain short skirts prevailed, together with huge flap hats. The Georgian dress for fancy balls is generally a satin skirt, plain or quilted, over-dress of brocade, velvet, or silk, with colored embroidery. Sometimes there is a train and front breadth trimmed with lace, flowers, pearls, and diamonds; the bodices pointed, cut as low or high squares, with trimmed stomachers. Elbow-sleeves, and ruffles; jewelled necklaces, or floral ones, made with a puff of ribbon and a flower alternately, tied tightly round the throat. Sacques were worn (*see* WATTEAU). Feathers, pearls, and flowers on the powdered hair; also flat caps and gipsy hats.

GERMAINE (*Les Cloches de Corneville*), Brown stockings, high-heeled black shoes; short skirt, with two box-plaited flounces of cerise and white silk; plastron waistcoat of the same; white scarf tunic, brown velvet low square jacket-bodice with striped pockets; transparent sleeves from shoulders; cerise silk cap. Second dress: Short skirt, tunic, and low square bodice of brown, bordered with yellow; muslin fichu inside; brown cap and tassel.

GERMAN HOUSEWIFE, XVIIth CENTURY. Stiff skirt touching the ground, bordered half a yard up with velvet, a wide band of the same above; long white apron worked in cross-stitch; low square velvet bodice, high white chemisette, sleeves tight but puffed and slashed at shoulders and elbows; satchel bag and keys at sides. Sometimes a large linen cap and veil are added, and a stiff ruff like a collar, of the same material as bodice. In the upper classes much profuse embroidery was introduced on the front of bodice and throat band. **German Peasant.** Short green or red skirt, plaited to waist, bordered with gold; large square apron, white chemisette, and long sleeves; low velvet bodice, laced across with silver; round velvet cap with streamers, worn at the back of head. This is the ordinary German peasant dress. **German Peasant Brides** appear in georgeous raiment. A Mecklenberg bride, for example, has a high tapering silver coronet, rows of beads round the neck, a red sash about the waist, a skirt of brocaded silk, the stockings red, and rosettes on the shoes. At Starnberg the wedding garb is a large white embroidered apron, almost covering the dress, and a fichu of the same tucked into the laced velvet bodice, a wreath replacing the usual fur-shaped busby. (*See* STARNBERG, BAVARIAN, BLACK FOREST, AUSTRIAN PEASANTS, &C.

GHOST OF QUEEN ELIZABETH. (*See* ELIZABETH, QUEEN.)

GILLE. White silk short skirt, trimmed with flounces; blue silk tunic; coat bodice cut as a low square; vest of blue silk; revers, cuffs, and collar of the same; short sleeves and long gloves; white hat; black shoes; blue stockings.

GILPIN, MRS. JOHN. Short white or brocaded dress, with paniers and fichu, trimmed with lace; large satin hat, and hair poudré, or mob cap.

GIPSY, QUEEN OF GIPSIES, FORTUNE, FORTUNE-TELLER, PEDLER, BOHÉMIENNE, AND ZINGARI. For the pedlar and fortune-teller order or Gipsies, a short red, black, or print skirt, loose red bodice, with belt; yellow neck handkerchief, red cloak, straw bonnet, and basket stocked with laces, clothes-pegs, cheap jewellery, and pack of cards. Gipsy Queens wear such dresses as a red satin petticoat, with black velvet and gold hieroglyphics, trimmed with coins and gold fringe; gold satin upper-skirt, covered with a gold trellis-work, and vandykes with coins, Spanish balls, and fringe; silk scarf of many colors round waist, stay bodice of black velvet, trimmed with gold, short sleeves; gold crown with coins, bracelets and armlets united by chains, coin ornaments; a tambourine in hand. This is equally applicable for a Zingari or Bohémienne, except that a gold net and coins is best for the head, or a red handkerchief with coins. High black satin boots with gold trimmings, or black shoes embroidered in gold, and sometimes a white chemisette above the low bodice, black gloves, black stockings; another rendering is a short black satin skirt edged with black grelots and gold fringe and coins; bold gold design worked up the front and sides; above this a scarf of black lace, almost covered by a tunic of scarlet and gold; Oriental silk tunic, pointed on one side, and knotted on the other; low black bodice cut square, trimmed with gold chains and coins; handkerchief of the same red and gold material, tightly tied round the head; black stockings embroidered with gold spangles and shoes *en suite.*

GIRL GRADUATE. (*See* ACADEMICAL and Illustration, Page 2.

GIRL, OLD FASHIONED. Long white satin frock, with full low bodice, short sleeves in one puff, coral necklace, hair curled on each side of face, with large loops stand up at the back. Satin reticule hung on arm; sandalled shoes.

GIROFLÉ, GIROFLA. White skirt, trimmed with gold braid; draped tunic, embroidered in gold and confined by gold girdle; bodice low, trimmed with gold lace; ruffles; festoons of pearls about bodice Spanish comb and veil.

GIROLA *(Manteaux Noir).* Black satin dress with gold braid and gold butterflies; gold and white scarf across the skirt; black satin bodice embroidered with gold, sleeves of gold beads; toque of black satin and gold braid; red and white bouquet.

GISMONDA. A long flowing gown of richest golden or velvet brocade cut all in one. A handsome jewelled belt high up beneath the arms, forming an artificial waist and descending in one end down the front. The sleeves slashed at the top the upper puff defined by a pointed band and then tight to the wrist, worked all over with gold and jewels. Jewels encircle the neck and are encrusted on the gold band surrounding it. One plait of hair falls between the shoulders, entwined with pearls. Madame Bernhardt's costumes in Sardou's opera were of barbaric splendour.

GITANA. (*See* GIPSY and PORTUGUESE.)

GLEANER. Short yellow skirt; red tunic; black velvet low bodice, laced across the front, cut in tabs at waist; short sleeves and low chemisette; hat with flowers, sometimes a colored handkerchief wound about the head; costume trimmed or embroidered with wheat, cornflowers, and poppies; a sickle at the side; wheat-sheaf and wreath. **Rachel the Gleaner:** orange-colored handkerchief loosely thrown over the hair and tied in front; grey bodice with cream fichu, quite plain without frills; over-skirt grey with wheat ears in the lap; orange-colored petticoat; grey stockings or tanned shoes; sickle in hand, and bunch of corn poppies and bluettes.

GLEE MAIDEN, THE. White satin dress, trimmed with blue satin and silver lace, blue satin ribbons hanging from the waist, with silver bells round the skirt; jacket of blue satin and silver, ornamented with bells, under which are worn three waistcoats of different colored brocade; head-dress, gold and silver net, and silver bodkin: boots, blue satin and silver.

GLOAMING, IN THE. (*See* DUSK.)

GLOWWORM. Dress of light brown satin or tulle with an electric star in the hair.

GOAT GIRL. Red and white striped skirt, with red tunic; black velvet bodice, faced with red; straw hat, with flowers.

GODDESS OF FOLLY. (*See* FOLLY.)

GODMOTHER FAIRY. (*See* HUBBARD, MOTHER.)

GOOD LUCK. White satin skirt dress of gold spangled tulle; skirt short, bordered with a plaiting, a horse shoe fastened with a nail to each fold. Tulle, draperies and deep bands of satin from the waist, fastened with horse-shoes, as if nailed down; white satin cuirass bodice; diadem in form of horse shoe.

GOODY TWO SHOES. Short terra cotta woollen gown much patched, leather bodice laced in front, full low white chemisette beneath it. Flowing hair and no shoes.

GOOSE GIRL *(Fairy Tale).* A white satin dress covered with silver tissue, lace, and silver trimmings. Short skirt, low full bodice with silver belt, cap of silver tissue.

GOLD. Dress of gold tissue, with fringe, gold lace, and coins. Gold head-dress, fan, and ornaments; hair powdered with gold dust, shoes and stockings embroidered with gold. (*See* MONEY and COINS.) **GOLD, A SHOWER OF.** Short white satin petticoat, draped with lace, the whole skirt entirely covered with gold sequins; round the hem a full frill of white lace sequins and gold fringe. Bodice of gold tissue with short sequin sleeves; wide band of pale blue satin, tied under the arms and across the front, matching another band about the head. The whole body trimmed with chains of sequins. **GOLD MINE.** Dress of white and gold brocade or tulle, made as an evening dress, trimmed with sequins; a painted panel let into one side, with a sketch of a gold mine.

GOLF. Grass green satin skirt studded with golf balls and clubs, fringe of grass and gorse; scarf of sand-color draped round waist, and ornamented with balls and clubs. Bright red cap and coat with swallow tails and white satin facings held back with golf buttons Suede shoes, white gauntlet gloves, a golf club in hand.

GONERIL, (KING LEAR). Long flowing robe of red and gold brocade, with pendent sleeves, jewelled girdle, wimple and gold crown.

GOUT wears a Georgian dress of a port wine color with silver buttons, Colchicum pill bottles at the side, porous plaisters on one leg, bandages on the other. Watch and long gold chain hanging at the side.

GRACE DARLING. Short skirt, striped bodice and tunic in one, belt at waist; sailor collar and tie; a red silk sailor's tasselled cap on head. Wide sleeves lined with white and rolled up. A life-buoy fastened to back of dress, a small lighthouse and anchor as a châtelaine, ropes round the waist, a lighted lantern in the hand, a fishing net on shoulder. This may be carried out in navy blue and red and white cotton, or serge; or more prettily, in red, and red and white soft silk or satin. Hair curled, a coil at back.

GRACES, THE (**Aglaia, Thalia and Euphrosyne**). Dressed in similar classic dresses, but of different color; Thalia in chiton and under-dress of pale blue and silver; one white and gold; the other pale green. When intended to represent statuary: robed in white; faces powdered; batting over the hair.

GRAHAM, MRS. Festooned petticoat of rose pink just clearing the ground, with old lace turned up all round; the skirt in points; sacque of old brocade. pink stripes and bouquets on cream ground; the bodice folded over, fine puffs of white muslin trimmed with old gold, tinsel roses; vandykes of pink ribbons and pearl cabochons; a high wired pointed lace collar, loose muslin sleeves with lace ruffles; black beaver hat with white feathers and diamonds. This was worn at the fancy ball at Warwick Castle, 1895.

GRAND MADEMOISLLE, PERIOD OF THE FRONDE (1647). White dress, immense black hat, and cane in hand. (*See* LOUIS XIV).

GRANDMOTHER, MY GREAT GRANDMOTHER, or the **Ghost of my Grandmother,** is generally rendered by a poudré dress of brocade, with large cap, sacque, fichu, quilted skirt, high heels, and stick; lace mittens. Another style is a black dress with folds of muslin crossing the bust, large cap, spectacles, and white curls. For the Ghost of my Grandmother it must be all in white.

GRAPES. (*See* SOUR GRAPES.)

GRAPE GATHERER. Dress of red satin and purple; the short under-skirt red, bodice and tunic purple, with a panel on one side completely covered with green and white grapes; a basketful of the fruit carried in hand. Hat crowned with grapes.

GRASSHOPPER. Short green tulle dress over satin, with green gauze wings on the side of skirt; low bodice; cap of green velvet, close fitting, with the horns of a grass-hopper at the top; fan, a gauze leaf, veined.

GREENAWAY, KATE. Reproductions of little people's costumes after this charming artist are much in favour at children's Fancy Balls. The girls often wear narrow skirts with one deep flounce and puffings, showing the sandalled shoes; very short waists; turn down frills at neck; sleeves, with one puff. Boys, long trousers, buttoning over the jacket; large linen collar frilled, &c.; or plain short skirts; tunics open in front, and looped up at the sides; square bodices, elbow-sleeves, and powdered hair.

GREEK. Ancient Greek. Chiton or under-garment of linen or wool girded round the waist; over this the diploidia which was wrapped round the shoulders and fastened on one side with a brooch or button serving for a cloak. In later days this was superseded by the chitonion, a sort of jacket joined on the shoulders and falling in points at the side, hiding the bodice; and also by the himation, also draped about the figure; the whole displayed beautiful borderings of Greek designs. Only wool or linen are correct materials. At Fancy Balls the costume is rendered by a flowing skirt of cashmere, the hem braided in gold; chitonion, or sleeveless jacket to match. Gold belt, armlets, bracelets, and fillet on head. (*See* CLASSIC Illustration, Fig. 7.) **Alcestis** (*Euripides*) wears a sleeveless robe of soft silk, draped in straight folds over a loose falling under-robe of the same, caught up high at the side and again below the waist. Hair in Greek knot, high at the back of the head, encircled by a band of gold braid. Sandals on feet. **Modern Greek.** (*See* Illustration, Fig. 24.) Rendered in velvet and satin, handsome gold embroidery on the front of the bodice, the under bodice white; long pendent over sleeves of white Algerian material; cap of velvet with thin gauze veil, white embroidered apron. It is often rendered with the hair in two long plaits, interwoven with gold; round velvet cap and tassel; silk trousers to ankle; short skirt. Long embroidered velvet paletot of green, red, or blue, trimmed with gold—it can hardly be too richly embroidered; an Oriental scarf round waist, loose sleeves, and veil of gold-spangled gauze.

GREENMANTLE. (*See* WALTER SCOTT.) Plain skirt of yellow satin, slightly distended with hoops; loose green jacket, with deep basque and hanging sleeves; lace ruffles; long gloves; fan; black quilted hood, lined with yellow.

GRETCHEN (*Faust*). Plain pink short skirt; blue flowing over-dress; square bodice, coming well down on the hips; long skirt sewn to it, bordered with gold; white chemisette; sleeves with white puffings at shoulder and elbow; hair in plaits; rosary. Or, hair covered with striped handkerchief, and one long plait; grey stuff dress looped over scarlet petticoat, edged with dark blue, on which are rows of blue, scarlet, gold, and brown braid; grey bodice with brown velvet braces; sleeves large, puff at shoulder, upper portion plain, slashed at elbow, tight to wrist, falling over the hand in a cuff of a pointed shape; chemisette fastened round neck with pale blue buttons.

GREY, LADY JANE. Generally represented in grey and white satin, or black velvet and white satin. The surcoat opens over a jewelled stomacher and kirtle, and is bordered down the sides and bodice with ermine. The bodice is pointed at waist, square at neck, has a chemisette of satin, quilted with pearls; close honeycomb ruff at throat, a velvet coif, like Marie Stuart's, less pointed, bordered with pearls; gauze veil. Long hanging velvet sleeves, tight under-ones of satin, with ruffles. Jewelled girdle, often pearls. The skirt or surcoat is full, and touches the ground. The kirtle is embroidered or quilted with pearls.

GRIGNAN, MADAME DE (*Louis XIV. reign*). Quilted skirt and sacque, trimmed with lace, flowers, and pearls; high-heeled shoes; powdered hair; wreath. Rose and ruby, white and pink, yellow and violet, are suitable combinations.

GRISELDA OLDBUCK (*The Antiquary*). Train and bodice of old-fashioned brocade, over satin-quilted petticoat, and pointed stomacher; sleeves to elbow with large ruffles; lace apron; antique gold ornanents, large eyeglass and chain; long embroidered gloves, high-heeled shoes, buckles; hair powdered, lace cap, patches.

GRISETTE DE LA VENDÉE. Short grey dress; white apron; low bodice made with a cape and revers, and full short sleeves; cap pointed back and front forming a pouf over the face, bordered with lace.

GRISSETTE OF LOUIS XV. PERIOD. Brocaded petticoat, tunic and pompadour bodice of contrasting shade, hair powdered, small muslin cap and apron, high-heeled shoes, and mittens.

GROTTO. A green gown covered with green moss, and shells; the head-dress in the form of a grotto lighted with the electric light.

GUARDIAN ANGEL. (*See* ANGEL.)

GUINEVERE (*Idylls of the King*). Costly dress of gold tissue, velvet, and brocade; the skirt long and flowing, fastened from neck to hem with jewelled clasps, an emerald in each; square-cut bodice, with jewelled bands round; sleeves tight at lower part, of a distinct color to the bodice, the upper portion slashed, and jewels introduced; coronet of pearls; hair in plaits. A long brocaded cloak enveloping the figure may be added. Miss Ellen Terry in King Arthur at the Lyceum in 1895 as the Queen, appeared in a robe of pale green crape with gold flames forming a deep border of embroidery round the hem. The crape above studded with stars of gold. The girdle high up on the figure. Sleeves of transparent green gauze interlined with gold. A vest of gold embroidery and jewels was seen in front and a veil of gold tissue studded with topaz fell from the crown of may blossom about the figure. The regal robe had a mantle covered with a thick net work of tinsel chenille, with bluish-green turquoise and dull gold blended. The bodice was a straight corselet of gold tissue and above it was a white mediæval chemisette richly embroidered. The cloak of jewelled chenille was embroidered with birds and peacocks in tones of blue and green with clasps of turquoise and pearl, heavily bejewelled. A gold crown was worn over the golden wimple with a peacock of turquoise and enamels, and tasselled cords of pearls and turquoise. In the fourth act, her gown was of violet-hued crepe, shot with blue and brown, the girdle high and jewelled. An over-dress was studded with sequins of dull purple like the scales of a serpent. The final robe was of milk-white satin, curiously crinkled and embroidered with diamonds; the short-waisted bodice hidden beneath gold passementerie. The sleeves puffed, terminating in close-fitting armlets of cloth of gold.

GYMNASIA. Red velvet short gown, with trapeze, dumb bells, parallel bars, and other gymnastic paraphernalia festooned about the bodice and skirt, and introduced as ornaments. Crossed dumbbells form the head-dress.

GYNETH (*Scott*). Long skirt of soft white woollen stuff; bodice and tunic of grey satin bordered with gold; jewelled girdle; quiver slung round waist, bow in hand; green cap with jewels and eagle plume.

HADES, QUEEN OF. (*See* DIABLESSE.) She brandishes fiery weapons, and her dress is entirely red and gold, in the mediæval style, with a crown of flames.

HAGAR. Long Jewish robe of grey, with hanging sleeves, over yellow silk; head enveloped in white muslin, hung with coins, or a loosely twisted turban of muslin, with a veil depending therefrom. (*See* JEWISH.)

HAILSTORM. Short dress and long veil of white spangled tulle, with earrings, white chenille spots and flashes of lightning appliqued on to the skirt in silver cloth.

HALL. The figure made to represent a hatstand with pegs, candlesticks, etc. Skirt of black and white checks to resemble oilcloth; a lamp in the hand. One of the realistic characters so much in favour of late.

HALF-AND-HALF CHARACTERS, such as **Which shall it be:** an angel on one side, Diablesse the other. **Church and Stage:** The figure dressed half in ecclesiastical raiment, the other half as a ballet dancer. **Black and White:** Half of one half of other, one glove and shoe of each. **Romeo and Juliet:** The two characters united. **Full and Half-Pay:** One half is arrayed as a peasant in a coarse suit of frieze with a peasant hat, the other half as a court lady in powder, patches and handsome brocades. **United Service:** One half a parlor maid, the other a postman.

HAMBURG FLOWER GIRL. (*See* VIERLANDER.)

HAMILTON, MARY. (*See* MARIES, THE QUEEN'S.)

HAMILTON, LADY. A gown of ruby velvet with a picturesque ruff at the shoulder, the lace trimmed with yellow pearls. A soft silk scarf of a yellow tone twisted about the head.

HARDANGER PEASANT. Red skirt with two rows of black velvet, linen apron with a couple of bands of embroidery across it. White chemisette with close ruche to the neck and full sleeves to wrist. Over bodice with shoulder straps of red woollen with embroidery. White linen head-dress fastened with pins.

HARDCASTE, MISS (*She Stoops to Conquer*). When the piece was acted, in 1773, the first dress was white figured with black; a silk scarf folded round the shoulders and tied behind the waist; hair in ringlets; large flat straw hat trimmed with ribbons. The second: plain silk dress, neat apron, small cap and mittens. Mrs. Langtry in the character appeared as follows:—First dress: pale lemon satin petticoat puffed and trimmed with embroidery; pointed bodice, cut low; elbow sleeves with old point; satin train, brocaded moss rosebuds and leaves on gold ground; point lace ruffles; diamond buckles. Second dress; cream embroidered India muslin and Sicilienne square bodice, pointed in front, Watteau back, and elbow sleeves, trimmed with marigold ribbons and marigolds; lace ruffles and fichu; brown velvet hat and cream plumes; Suède gloves. Third dress: short skirt of blue grey cashmere; tunic at back, pointed bodice, elbow sleeves, fichu and apron, ruffles of muslin, cap of muslin and lace, with revers, trimmed with colored ribbons. Bunch of keys, scissors, needlebook, and pincushion attached to side by red ribbon; grey stockings.

HARDCASTLE, MRS. Plain satin skirt, chintz over-dress; pointed bodice; elbow sleeves; fichu; powdered hair; cap.

HARDY, MISS LETITIA (*Belle Stratagème*). In first scene: wears a grey brocaded satin gown made short; high-heeled black shoes; pink stockings; white muslin hood fastened under chin with pink ribbons, and over it a hood of grey cloth, with rose lining; carries a grey pink lined muff. In the next act: a white muslin and lace dress with sacque of lemon-colored satin brocade; pattern and brown foliage and blue blossoms; wreath of yellow flowers knotted with blue ribbon.

HARLEQUINETTE ARLEQUINETTE. Short skirt of orange, blue, and scarlet, arranged in diamonds; jacket, bodice and tight sleeves, opening over a white waistcoat, a red scarf round the hips; black cocked hat, powdered hair, black cloth gaiters, black mask, and black wand, or wooden bâton in the hand. Or, short pleated black, red and yellow satin skirt draped with red satin; tunic meeting cuirass bodice, copied from harlequin; tight fitting coat; short black satin shoulder cloak, with straight upstanding collar; lined red ruff at throat; cocked hat; powdered hair. This character is suitable for children as well as adults.

HARVEST. Maize or brown tulle dress, trimmed with silver or gold lace and fringe, and châtelaines and garlands of poppies, wheat-ears, silver or gold oats, cornflowers, marguerites, and bunches of wheat tied with ribbon. A small wheatsheaf carried in the hand, a sickle at the side; a wreath and gold scythe on shoulders; flowers on fan. (*See* AUGUST and CERES.)

HAWKING. Petticoat of dark claret velvet; over-skirt green velvet, caught up at the side; long basqued jacket, with gauntlet gloves; cavalier hat and drooping feather; high boots; hooded falcon on wrist. **XVIth-Century Hawking Costume:** Long plain cream dress; cream velvet over-dress; bodice and skirt in one, with gold embroidery round hem and square bodice; rolled epaulette; hanging sleeves bordered with gold; caul cap; white under-chemisette; hawk on hand. Dress of cream woollen worked in gold, a flowing skirt with an over-dress bodice and skirt in one, cut square, bordered with gold satin, which appears on the hanging sleeves, and as epaulettes; close-fitting cap like a bonnet, made of gold and white lattice work; a hawk on the hand.

HAYDÉE. In modern Greek costume. Under-dress embroidered in pearls and gold; over-dress lined with a contrasting color, edge trimmed with gold, cut in one with bodice; trousers of striped silk or gauze; folded turban with ornaments in front; long veil and sleeves of gauze; Oriental shoes, suitable colorings: blue and gold, red, green and gold. (*See* GREEK.)

HAYMAKER. Sage green petticoat, salmon-color turned up over it and embroidered with grasses, buttercups and daisies; loose chintz jacket with belt; red handkerchief or sunflower hanging from the shoulder; basket at back, rake in hand, miniature rakes and pitchforks at side; a sunbonnet tied round the neck.

HE AND SHE, THE LITTLE *(Molloy)*. Dressed as Dresden China figures. (*See* DRESDEN CHINA.)

HEARTS, QUEEN OF. (*See* CARDS.)

HEARTSEASE. Short skirt of pale mauve tulle trimmed with a thick purple ruche at hem, lined with moss green, edged with silver cord, caught down here and there with yellow pansies; over-skirt, of shaded tulle, the lightest tint at the top, covered with pansies; long loops of purple velvet lined with moss green at side; pointed mauve satin bodice, laced at back, the basque bordered with gold fringe, front covered with a large purple heartsease; elbow sleeves; pansy fan; pansies forming an aureole round head.

HEBE. Classical dress of white soft silk or cashmere trimmed with gold; loose peplum with gold belt, the sleeves short, fastened outside the arm with three buttons; a gold fillet about the head; classical ornaments.

HEBREW WOMEN. (*See* JEWISH.)

HELEN MACGREGOR. (*See* MACGREGOR.)

HELEN OF TROY. Classic under-dress of white woollen stuff, sleeveless, and just resting on the ground; the bodice full, clasped on the shoulders with gold ornaments, a gold zone at waist; over it a tunic, set in a band at neck and ending below the hips, open at the sides, with tassels at the points; Etruscan gold ornaments; gold armlets; hair fastened in Hebe knot, with curls escaping, three fillets of gold braid; long veil; sandals, etc. (*See* GREEK.)

HELENA *(Shakespeare).* Mediæval robe of pale blue satin, cut square at neck, trimmed with silver gimp or embroidery, the skirt draped with silver cord; a peacock fan; Girard de Narbonne's prescription in the satchel pocket; wreath of ivy-leaves; veil of silver gauze.

HELENA FORMAN. Rubens's second wife. (*See* RUBENS).

HELIGOLANDAISE. A red skirt and bodice sewn together at the waist and trimmed with rows of black ribbon. The stomacher embroidered in green and gold, with a close fitting black skull cap.

HELIOTROPE. Heliotrope crêpe draped with gold brocade; the flowers introduced on to a skirt, bodice, and headdress.

HELOISE *(from Heloise and Abelard).* Petticoat of white satin; blue satin over-dress trimmed with black velvet and gold braid; a black velvet satchel pocket on a band, loops up the skirt over the petticoat; the bodice is cut square, and filled in with folded muslin; long sleeves with muslin puff at elbow; head-dress of blue satin and white muslin trimmed with velvet; veil of white muslin.

HELP, LADY. Neatly-made print dress such as domestic servants wear, high to the throat; sleeves to the wrist; linen collar and cuffs, linen apron, a dust-pan and broom suspended from the waist.

HEN. Bodice, wings, and tunic made of brown feathers to resemble the body of the hen; flounced skirt of gold-colored chiffon; belt and shoulder-sash of soft lace; eggs in basket; lace mittens outlined with gold; hen's head for head-dress. (*See* COCK.)

HENRIETTA MARIA. (*See* CHARLES I.)

HENRY I. Period of (1100-1135). The sleeves, trains, and veils, at this time were of great length. The robe long with a shorter garment over; the hair hung in plaits; the period has been illustrated by two figures from the Aschaffenburg library; one wears a white printed cotton under-garment; a yellow, red, and black parti-colored habit over, called the super-tunic or surcote, divided back and front, lacing in front; one half a figured stuff of yellow, black, and dark blue; the other green, mauve, etc., the sleeves *vice-versâ*, fitting the arm closely to wrist; the hair hangs in one long plait encased in a woollen cover, and entwined with braid. The other figure was a woman of higher rank, wearing a white woollen under-dress trimmed with green, white, and grey, bordered with braid; over-dress green, bordered with yellow, opens at side to show belt; bodice round at throat, showing white under-habit; veil at back; band beneath chin.

HENRY II. Period of (1154-1181). (*See* ELEANOR OF CASTILLE.)

HENRY III. OF ENGLAND. Period of (1216-1272). The hair was worn in a coil, encased in gold thread; the under-dress was confined by a waist-band; the sleeves to wrist had a turn-back cuff of lace; the bodice was laced, and the over-dress reached to the feet. For example, a red robe fitting the waist, trimmed with gold appliqué; short sleeves bordered with gold, the hem also; white head-dress with wired wings at side; long veil; green mantle lined with white, fastened with a gold clasp; handsome materials were worn.

HENRY IV. Period of (1399-1413). The Côte Hardie with flowing skirts fitting the figure closely at hips. Strange head-dresses were the leading features. For example, long skirt of pink cashmere; grey bodice, trimmed with fur, forming a stomacher or surcot; tight grey sleeves; turn-down collar; huge reticulated head-dress with the hair gathered at the side into a caul of pink and white muslin, with veil. These head-dresses met with much ridicule; the women were compared by satirists to horned snails, harts, and unicorns; slit coats showing the under-dress through the apertures, and the sideless gowns, were also objects of popular derision.

HENRY V. Period of (1413-1422). In this reign the horned head-dress assumed enormous proportions, great horns were added to the cauls, with the veils stretched to their fullest extent; the waist of dresses became short, and the sleeves covered the hands.

HENRY VI. Period of (1422-1461). The trains grew longer, and were tightly girdled; turn-down collars, of fur or velvet, came to a point over a distinctive stomacher. Horned head-dresses were still worn; turbans were carried up in a peak over the face; the Hennin, from Flanders, was in vogue, made of muslin with horns, ornamented with precious stones.

HENRY VII. Period of (1485-1509). This reign has been illustrated as follows: **Maid Servant,** from picture at Oberwesel: Grey cashmere skirt, bound with white, edged with black; bodice to waist, cut low in front, outlined with a band of white, edged with black; white chemisette, showing close horizontal plaits; white turban-like head-dress, black braided star in front. And by a costume from the tapestry at Orleans: Brown under-dress and bodice with the belt and skirt trimmed with white; the other robe loose and distinct, with turnback collar; over-dress brown, and reddish leather color; printed velvet, bordered with a strip of white; sleeve in one puff to elbow, and then tight to wrist; cap like a turban in the two shades of the dress.

HENRY VIII. Period of (1509-1547). (*See* CATHERINE OF ARAGON; ANNE OF CLEVES; ANNE BOLEYN; CATHERINE HOWARD; JANE SEYMOUR: CATHERINE PARR, and Illustration of TUDOR PERIOD, Fig. 43). Lady of the period: Under-skirt and sleeves of a light yellow green satin, with an arabesque design in gold thread; over-skirt, or kirtle, and bodice of violet velvet, embroidered with gold; the kirtle lined with green, like the under-skirt, showing where the dress is looped up; ruff of pleated cambric; head-dress of violet velvet, encircled with pearls, and ornamented by a long white plume at the back.

HERALD OF SPRING. Short full skirt of pale grey tulle, the lower part covered with swallows in silk appliqués, holding violets or primroses in beak; round the skirt, scarf of silver gauze tied behind and fastened on one side with apple blossoms; pointed laced bodice of pink satin, or pink and silver brocade, cut low and draped round the neck with silver gauze, trimmed with cordons of violets, primroses, and leaves; short sleeves of silver gauze, across which are festoons of violets; powdered hair; wreath of apple blossoms on one side; on the other a stuffed swallow, in its beak a diamond heart; wand, with spring flowers tied with pink ribbon; chain of shaded violets round neck; pale pink shoes and hose; fan of pink marabout, swallow in centre.

HERMES. Classic dress with a serpent twined round the short blue tunic.

HERMIONE (*Winter's Tale*). White cashmere or long loose red silk robe, made low and sleeveless, with belt. Over it a cloak of the same, all trimmed with gold fringes, crossed in front and draped; diadem on head, flowing veil; the whole as statuesque as possible.

HERNANI. Cream-colored low square dress with train, trimmed with gold braid and Spanish lace, the sleeves slashed with crimson velvet; hat of crimson velvet, and feather.

HERODIAS. Is represented by Carlo Dolce in a soft satin gown, the over dress opened in front and looped back. The coloring green and gold. The low bodice is made of green velvet and the waist is clasped by a jewelled band with a large centre ornament carried up the front. The low neck is draped with soft silk of which the full sleeves are made. Hair in curls.

HERO *(Much Ado About Nothing).* Dress of white satin, the skirt touching the ground, wrought in pearls, with gold and white; over-dress of the same, forming a high square to low bodice; the stomacher worked in pearls; there is a wired ruff starting from the front of bodice widening at the back; tight sleeves entwined with pearls on shoulder; lace ruffles at wrist, and puffed epaulettes, and coronet, band, or coif of pearls; the hair hanging in long ends, interplated with pearls; pearled shoes.

HESTER GLAZEBROOK *(She Stoops to Conquer).* Grey cashmere dress, square bodice, and ruffles, fichu, and cap of soft muslin and fine lace.

HIBERNIA. *(See* ERIN.)

HOGARTH *(Dress after).* As shown in the Illustration is a pretty satin gown with frills on either side of the front breadth, loose over-dress bordered with frilling, small frilled cap, hanging sleeves. The Illustration is from "Marriage à la Mode" and other works of this well-known painter; can be easily carried out. The full skirt, kerchief, elbow sleeves and hoods are the distinguishing features.

HIGHLAND LASSIE. *(See* SCOTCH COSTUME.)

HINDOO LADY. (*See* INDIAN.)

HOARFROST. White crystal tulle dress, the front of the skirt looped across with beads and crystal over silver tissue; veil of tulle, spray of frosted flowers on one side; bodice, silk with silver tissue and crystal; aigrette of frosted twigs. (*See* FROST.)

HOLBEIN, STYLE OF. (*See* HENRY VII. and HENRY VIII., and his several wives.)

HOLLAND. (*See* DUTCH.)

HOLLY. (*See* WINTER.) Low sleeveless bodice and short skirt of pale green muslin trimmed with branches of holly and red berries, the latter form the zone and bracelets. Rod of holly in the hand.

HONFLEUR FISHERWOMAN. (*See* F.) Wears sabots and woollen stockings. A short woollen dress with plain bodice and a white kerchief. A cap of bright red, like a fisherman's without the point.

HOOPS. (*See* Periods of ELIZABETH, GEORGIAN, &C.)

HONOUR. (*See* MAID OF HONOUR.)

HOP GARDEN. A gown of green tulle with rows of hops carried perpendicularly up the skirt and round the low full bodice on strips of fawn colored velvet. Hops in the hair.

HORNET. (*See* BEE.)

HORTENSE, QUEEN. Dress of pink satin and silver embroidery, large bunch of natural violets on left shoulder; round the short waist a zone of diamonds; hair raised high; diadem of pearls and diamonds.

HOURS. Long flowing cashmere dress, with loose low bodice and pendent sleeves; scarf draped on shoulders; round the skirt a band, half blue half gold, with the hours upon it; the hair flowing; a crescent coronet of gold. Veil of spangled tulle; gold armlets and necklet; sandals.

HUBBARD, MOTHER, Mother Bunch, Mère Michel, Mother Shipton, Nance Redfern, Dame Trot, Enchantress, Witch, and **Fairy Godmother** are dressed much alike. Mother Hubbard in a quilted petticoat touching the ground; a chintz tunic open in front, bunched up; muslin apron; low velvet bodice with deep point, laced across the front; sleeves to elbow with ruffles; muslin kerchief, close ruff; tortoiseshell rimmed spectacles, mittens, and stick; loaf of bread, bottle of red wine, and bone are other insignia. A lace mob cap, and over it a high-pointed velvet sugar-loaf hat with peacock's feather; high-heeled shoes with rosettes; a small white dog; the hair may or may not be powdered, and a red cloak can be worn. She is sometimes accompanied by a boy dressed as a dog in a white skin with large tail and mask head. Mère Michel is the French Mother Hubbard. She wears a flowered chintz gown, white linen apron, checked handkerchief, white muslin cap, spectacles, blue stockings, feather broom. Mother Bunch is always *poudré*; the same in other respects. Dame Trot wears a pointed hat not so high. Nance Redfern, Mother Shipton, and the Old Woman who Swept the Sky (*see* O), being witches, carry brooms, and on their skirts are toads, cats, serpents, curlews, frogs, bats, and lizards in black velvet; a serpent twisted round the crown of hat, an owl in front, a black cat on shoulder. Sometimes a scarlet cloak is attached to the shoulders, and the velvet bodice is high, with pendent sleeves.

HUGUENOT (*after Millais*). Black skirt and close-fitting bodice, with gathered basque of figured velvet, the sleeves to wrist, with lace cuff, slashed with white satin at shoulder; close plaited ruff at throat; hair waved and rolled from the face; round velvet cap with row of pearls and white feather. Or, satin dress, bodice to waist, and high to throat, the front with silver cloth let in; ruff, sleeves with six puffs to wrist, slashed; hat of satin; bordered with silver, and a feather. **Huguenot Period.** Long plain skirt of velvet; low sleeveless bodice of the same, with white lace berthe, and white muslin sleeves, coming below the elbow; a band of velvet round the head; the hair dressed in a coil, with curls depending from it.

HUMMING-BIRD. Dress of white tulie scattered all over with feathers and jewels; the train composed entirely of feathers, ending in a point like a humming-bird's tail; four little wings fastened between the shoulders; a small bird on the head.

HUNGARIAN. Short white or red satin skirt, with rows of gold braid and ermine; blue or ruby tunic, with ermine; low satin bodice, bands of ermine and velvet; jacket of velvet bordered with fur slung from shoulder; round fur edged cap; high patent leather hunting boots bordered with fur. Or, sometimes a long pelisse high to the throat replaces the jacket tunic and low bodice; a gold and red scarf round hips; ornaments, glass beads of different colors; the hair hanging in plaits, plain in front. Gold and silver embroidery admissible. **Hungarian Lady's Military Dress.** White and blue gown over black

Astrachan petticoat; black Astrachan and blue busby; sleeves embroidered in silver; blue and silver cord across chest; blue mantle attached to left shoulder, trimmed with fur. **Hungarian Peasant.** White woollen skirt with rows of green velvet and red satin edged with gold; low square red velvet bodice, braided in gold across the front, and cut in tabs, each ornamented with an Hungarian knot; a watch hangs at one side; the Parta (head-dress) is of striped red, white, and green ribbons, the national colours; white lace fichu; red leather boots. The Hungarian peasant in the Bukowina wears a curious head-dress of silk, gold braid and feathers, and fur, fixed to a card-board foundation; sleeveless leather jacket with the soft bunda, the hairy surface turned inside forming a furry edge; linen sleeves, with Oriental embroidery; sash, bright colored silk, with bright velvet band. Another peasant costume has a head-dress formed of two bright colored kerchiefs shaped like a fez; plaited skirt of dark cloth trimmed with red and green ribbons; silk apron of contrasting color with bow and streamers.

HUNTING COSTUME *(Louis XIII.)* Close fitting bodice of peau de Suède; skirt of emerald satin looped with gold braid; boots and gauntlet gloves of grey kid; grey felt hat; green and white feathers. **Time of Louis XIV.** Short plain full skirt of pink satin laced with gold; waistcoat of white brocade, square pockets; mousquetaire coat of blue satin, braided with gold; three-cornered hat with feathers; powdered hair in a queue; ivory whip, jewelled handle, and horn. Point lace cravat and ruffles. Or, short satin skirt of chamois color; blue velvet bodice and tunic caught up with gold cord. High untanned leather boots, a horn slung at the side, a peaked cap like a naval officer's; powdered hair.

HUNTRESS OF THE BLACK FOREST. A green velvet dress, quite short, trimmed with gold fringe; high boots and gloves edged with fur; bow and arrows slung across, and hunting-knife in the girdle; cap of gold and green velvet; or, dark green trousers meeting the top of the boots; green cloth petticoat with velvet hem; dark green velvet coat with old gold satin cuffs and revers; bag netted with gold cord; the high hat has green feathers.

HURDY-GURDY GIRL. Short petticoat of light blue satin with band of Havana brown; tunic of Havana brown; loose white jaconet bodice, open at neck; full sleeves to elbow; braces of black velvet united by three straps across back and front; blue and brown striped handkerchief on head; brown shoes; blue stockings; a hurdy-gurdy slung round neck. Or, white folded head-dress, red bodice, yellow skirt, imitation sabots, miniature organ, stuffed monkey.

HUSSAR. Short blue velvet skirt and bodice with silver braiding, a hussar jacket fastened on the left side by silver cord, and trimmed with sable. Blue velvet cap with white ostrich feather; high boots trimmed with fur; military gloves. For **Polish Hussar** the Polish cap is worn. (*See* POLISH.)

HUSBAND AND WIFE. Evening dresses suitable for a married pair are Kings and Queens, Cock and Hen, &c.

HYACINTH, WHITE. White satin and tulle gown covered with sprays of the flower. Cap shaped like one of the single blossoms turning downwards and the stalk upwards. A large bouquet of the blooms carried in the hand.

HYPATIA. Long trailing skirt with an over robe of soft diaphonous stuff fringed and draped about the figure iike a shawl. The sleeve with three buttons on the arm draped in classic style. A scarf falling softly over the shoulders. Hair bound with a fillet.

ICE, ICICLE, ICE MAIDEN, ICE QUEEN. A short white satin dress, draped with crystal fringe, icicles, silver tissue or swansdown, and tulle; spangled silver veil. Hair covered with powdered glass; icicle wreath; shoes and stockings embroidered with crystal beads. Long gloves; bracelets and chains of icicles, girdle of same. Tiny silver bells, frosted holly, and a robin redbreast nestling on shoulder may be added. (*See* WINTER.)

ICELAND, COSTUME OF. Black cap with long silk tassel on one side, the hair flowing loosely; black jacket and skirt with apron of variegated stuff. The holiday attire is a white helmet-shaped cap, a golden diadem round the temples, wide over the forehead, narrow at the ears, tied behind with a silk bow; thin white veil; black cloth bodice embroidered from the neck with gold to the waist; golden belt with pendants to knee. The black skirt is embroidered round the hem. **ICELANDIC BRIDE.** High black cloth dress, with long sleeves; the stomacher embroidered in fine gold-work; high white horn-shaped cap, with gold embroidered band; lace veil; large silver belt.

IDA, PRINCESS (*Tennyson*). Cassock of yellow brocaded silk, over flowing robe of white silk; yellow stockings with white clocks; academical cap. (*See* PRINCESS.)

IDYLLS OF THE KING. (*See* ELAINE, ENID, &C.)

IGNOTA (*detta La Bella di Tiziano*). (*See* VENETIAN.)

IMOGEN (*In Shakespeare's Cymbeline*). A long robe of soft white silk, made high to the throat, but without sleeves; the full bodice girded in at the waist with a dead-gold band; a gold band round the neck, and a circlet of the same, or a chaplet of pearls, in the hair, which might be left flowing; on the right arm a gold band bracelet; shoes of white wash-leather; no gloves.

IMOINDA (*Tragedy of Oronoco*). A silver brocaded gown made very full and distended by wide hoops. The low bodice has a narrow basque bordered with gauze boullonnées carried up the centre of the front and round the top. Sleeves to elbow and then pendent and plaited, like the bodice of white satin. Under sleeves with embroidery at the wrist. The neck is filled in with a soft lisse fichu; a lace ruche at the throat. A small close fitting cap with an aigrette and pendant veil.

INCROYABLE. The dress of the Revolution 1789. Skirt of rose pink satin, the front white, veiled with lace. Jacket double-breasted, ending at waist in front, forming coat tails at the back. The double lapels of old brocade match the double points of the waistcoat appearing at the waist, and are held down with large diamond buttons. The lace cravat and collar band also fastened with diamond buttons. A black velvet tricorn hat with a bordering of ostrich feathers and a bird of Paradise osprey, starting from a tricolored cockade. A gold headed stick, a bouquet of roses on the front of the lapels, an eye glass, large seals suspended fob fashion at the side; powdered hair. Or, Triple cape of green satin, just reaching to the shoulders; the hair dressed in marteaux in front, and in a long plait at the back; the conventional black felt hat with tricolor cockade.

INDIAN DRESSES. (*For* NORTH AMERICAN INDIAN *see* AMERICA.) A **Nautch Girl** has bare feet, short muslin full plaited skirt, bordered with gold; tight-fitting long-sleeved under-dress; silk drapery over one shoulder and under one arm, bordered with embroidery; hair in two long plaits; flowers and gold and silver ornaments on head; many beads about neck. A cloak of gold and white mnslin from the head and entwined about the figure may be added; anklets and bracelets of gold. **Begum.** Full plaited skirt of fine Indian muslin, the edges bound with silver braid, long drapery from the head of the same; belt round waist; slippers embroidered in silver. **Indian Queen** at a fancy ball might wear short skirt of Indian material intersected with gold; violet velvet bodice trimmed with gold; shoulders covered with Indian gauze; full trousers to ankle of soft silk; Indian scarf round hips, Indian fan and ornaments; Oriental shoes, pink stockings. **Indian Woman, East.** Full trousers of thin silk to ankles; tunic of printed cotton; silk scarf draped round the waist as a petticoat, and carried round the back over left shoulder and head, just covered with a white handkerchief, bordered with band of embroidery; silver bangles; necklace of sequins; embroidered slippers. The cholee is a short under-bodice with tight sleeves coming half-way to elbow, bordered with embroidery. (*See* LAKME, LAHORE REINE DE, AND RANEE.)

INFLUENZA. Dress of grey tulle with a hot water bottle on one side and a packet of mustard leaves on the other. A pair of scales in the hair attached to a bandeau on which appears the word "quinine."

INSECTIFUGA. This can be represented by every variety of insect, dotted over a black or white tulle evening dress intersected with gold; fireflies imprisoned in the veil.

IONE (*Last Days of Pompeii*). Classic robe of delicate tone. (*See* GREEK or CLASSIC Illustration, Fig. 7).

IOLANTHE. First appears in a dress all seaweed and grasses, and then in a classic white gown with long sleeves, wings at the back; the bodice low and clasped on the shoulder, just bound with a girdle at the waist, a diamond band crossing the bust from shoulder to shoulder; a wand in the hand; sandals. She has six **Attendant Fairies** wearing antique Greek dresses made in mauve, laburnum, coral, pink, cream, and green, soft Liberty silk with silver wings and stars. Phillis, the Arcadian shepherdess and ward in Chancery, has a most harmonious combination of blue, pink, and white; long bodice with paniers; stomacher, and bows of ribbon in front; short striped skirt with lace and ribbons round the edge; powdered hair, blue satin hat with roses and ribbons. The **Queen of the Fairies** wears the cap of Mercury, with wings on either side; a long cashmere skirt bordered with gold embroidery, a gold scaled cuirass bodice, wings at back, golden hair, a trident in her hand.

IPHIGENIA. A soft flowing classic dress; the diploidon pure white, bordered with Greek honeysuckle; bare arms; embroidered veil wreath; cloak from shoulders; sandals.

IRELAND. (*See* ERIN and IRISH PEASANT.)

IRENE (*Rienzi*). Square-bodied close-fitting blue under-dress; over it a white juive robe, embroidered in gold; diamond crown; regal mantle of blue satin embroidered in gold.

IRIS. (*See* RAINBOW.)

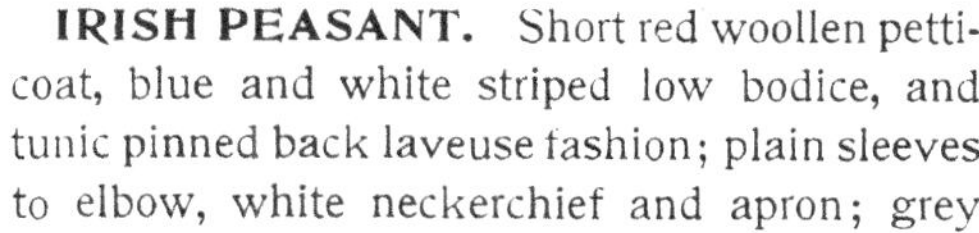

IRISH PEASANT. Short red woollen petticoat, blue and white striped low bodice, and tunic pinned back laveuse fashion; plain sleeves to elbow, white neckerchief and apron; grey stockings, high-heeled shoes. (*See* COLLEEN BAWN.)

IRISH POTATO GATHERER. Wears in accompanying illustration a striped red, black and white petticoat, with a long white apron. Her pretty chintz bed gown jacket is drawn into the waist with the apron string, the red shawl is lightly draped over the shoulders and knotted in front. Her dark tresses are hidden beneath a red 'kerchief. She carries a potato hoe, and a basket.

IRISH QUEEN. Dress of light blue and amber; petticoat trimmed with gold shamrocks; low square bodice, long blue satin basque, gold-colored stomacher worked with shamrocks; crimson scarf fastened on shoulder with gold harps; crimson velvet cap, a blue velvet coronet and shamrocks; massive gold ornaments.

ISABELLE OF BAVARIA. (*Married Charles VI. of France, 1385.*) Rich pink satin petticoat embroidered with gold and jewels; white satin train worked with gold and bordered with ermine; black velvet plastron also worked with gold. Bodice and sleeves bordered with ermine; gold crown and muslin veil.

ISABELLA DE CROYE (*Quentin Durward*) Costume of Louis XI. period. White satin flowing skirt, tight sleeves, loose bodice and girdle, all worked in gold fleur-de-lys, bordered with ermine; horned head-dress and veil.

ISABELLA OF NAVARRE. Long white satin dress, embroidered with fleur-de-lvs and other heraldic devices; bodice and train of ruby velvet, bordered with ermine; plastron of white satin, worked in gold; long sleeves with ermine; gold crown and muslin veil.

ISABELLA QUEEN OF SPAIN. (A.D. 1512.) As worn by Lady Blake in Jamaica, 1891, when Sir Henry was Governor. Narrow underskirt of gold and white brocade; long sleeves and train of ruby velvet, bordered with jewels; under sleeves of plaited white muslin, caught down at intervals by jewelled bands; jewelled crown and belt.

ISABELLA, WIFE OF PHILIP AUGUSTE (1180). Gold crown with fleur-de-lys in gems; velvet hood with jewelled bands falling on either side of the face. The robe cut low at the neck, bordered with gold and precious stones; a handsome pearl ornament in the centre; a regal mantle of gold brocade with the same jewelled band.

ISOLDE. (*Tristram and Isolde*). A dress of barbaric splendour. A gold turretted crown starting from a band of emeralds confines the flowing tresses; a long red and green classic robe; a red mantle fastened to the shoulders of the low bodice with jewelled clasps, attached with chains to a centre ornament matching the clasps. Pendent sleeves; heavy bracelets above and below the arm.

ISTHMUS OF SUEZ. Short skirt of white satin, bordered with gold; green satin tunic embroidered at the edge with palms and Oriental figures; low round bodice of cloth of gold, richly worked; gold and red turban with flowing veil; blue shoes, red stockings.

ITALIAN PEASANT. As illustrated in Fig. 25, wears a blue skirt, a multi-colored apron, red cloth bodice over white linen under-bodice trimmed with Italian lace and embroidery, long sleeves. The flat Italian head-dress made of linen, bordered with lace. This is the garb of the Roman Peasant. The **Neapolitan Peasant** at a Fancy Ball is mostly clad in lighter colors, such as pink and green, or blue and maize; the sleeves to match the corselet, coming often to the wrist; the tunic of Algérienne; the head-dress satin or silk. A **Lombardy Peasant** has a scarlet and white embroidered petticoat; blue bodice and

Fig. 25.—ITALIAN COSTUME.

tunic trimmed with gold; white kerchief on shoulders; blue silk handkerchief about the head; belt of black and silver. A **Sorrentine Peasant.** An amber satin skirt, edged with scarlet, over-skirt of scarlet; black velvet bodice; white silk chemisette; scarlet silk head-dress, with gold clasps.

ITALIAN STATE DRESS (1497). Long skirt of bright-colored brocade; tunic of another tone, opening in front, and caught together with three festoons of pearl fringe, tunic bordered with same; bodice low and long waisted, with jewelled stomacher; sleeves to wrist, leg of mutton shape; crown and veil.

IVY. White tulle evening dress, trimmed with ivy; basket of ivy in hand; ivy wreath.

JACOBITE INNKEEPER'S DAUGHTER. Dress of soft grey cashmere; full plain skirt; short waisted bodice; elbow sleeves, piece of muslin turned up for cuffs; muslin cape and cap without lace, bordered with hemmed frills.

JACOBITE LADY. Dress of old-fashioned brocade; short-waisted square bodice; plain skirt, looped over cream-colored petticoat; cambric kerchief; mittens; lace cap.

JACKMA. White skirt with a band of green; white jacket with green revers opening over a horizontally striped green and white vest; white fisherman's cap and green tassel, and an awl carried in the hand.

JAMES I. (1603-1625). Short skirt, panier train; high bodice with close ruff; tight sleeves with puff at top and pointed head-dress. The Holbein style was continued with large farthingales; the ruffs were stiffened with starch and a panier puffing appeared round the waist like a short upper skirt; velvet and rich stuffs were worn; the hair rolled from the face.

JAMES II. PERIOD (1685-1688). A colored satin petticoat made walking length and embroidered. The bodice is square, stiff and narrow, with high stomacher covered with jewels; the sleeves are ample, and come to the elbow with ruffles; a satin train of contrasting color, bordered with the same gathered flounce, falls from the shoulder in box plaits; the hair is curled, not powdered, and over it is the *commode* head-dress made of row upon row of lace on a wire frame; two or three stories high; lace lappets, hanging at the back; shoes with very pointed toes; long gloves; a fan in the hand. The dress of **Princess Louisa**

Maria, Daughter of James II. (*after N. de Largillière*) also illustrates the quaint and formal costume of that time. The hair, which under Charles II. had been permitted to fall in natural ringlets upon the shoulders, was covered with a tower *commode* head-dress; the waist was confined in a pointed bodice of silk, cut square, with a lace stomacher in front; short sleeves, with a cuff and lace bow at the elbow, leaving the forearm bare; the black silk petticoat was covered in front with a lace apron, and an ample over-skirt with long train made of colored damask, fell from the shoulders.

JANE GREY, LADY. (*See* GREY.)

JANE SEYMOUR. (*See* SEYMOUR.)

JANE SHORE. (*See* SHORE.)

JANUARY. A light grey and white kllted soft short skirt; over this a shaped tunic, leaving the under-skirt visible at the sides. Full bodice with *boules de neige* falling in front. Over the shoulders, grey capes bordered with swansdown, single puffed sleeves; long grey gloves; grey stockings and shoes. The head-dress, a cap with three points like Folly, one on each side, one in the centre, a pompon at each tip; long staff with a Christmas tree laden with presents on the top.

JAPAN (*Spring Time in. See* Illustration, Fig. 26.) The robe is made of Japanese silk and bordered with apple blossoms, introduced also on the shot velvet bands which surround the waist, and border the neck. The Japanese parasol is also edged with flowers, which likewise ornament the pins placed on either side of the head. The coloring should be bright for Japanese costumes, and the dresses trimmed according to the season of the year. The loose outer robe crosses in front, and only fastens with a broad soft silk belt; wide hanging sleeves, the edge wadded. Two under-skirts, plain and bright colored. (*See* MIKADO.)

JAVANESE DANCER. Black satin pointed hat descending over the ears with an aigrette of feathers at the back, and bordered with gold galon. Low black satin bodice to match. Skirt of Javanese printed cotton made short. Scarves of golden yellow silk gauze. Gold embroidered slippers.

JAVOTTE (*La Cruche Cassée*). Short dark blue skirt, with rows of black velvet and orange-colored ribbon; black and white striped overskirt; yellow apron, with bib and heart-shaped pockets; black velvet sleeveless bodice open at neck; large hat set at back of head; blue stockings, black shoes with orange rosettes.

JEALOUSY. (*See* PASSIONS.)

JEAN, MISTRESS. Quilted silk petticoat; yellow satin upper skirt, trimmed with old Irish point; bunch of keys, pin-cushion, and large white satin pocket embroidered with gold, hung at side; powdered wig; mutch, with red ribbons; blue stockings and shoes.

JEANIE DEANS (*Heart of Midlothian*). (*See* DEANS).

JEANNE D'ALBRET. Dress of crimson satin made long, trimmed with ermine, under sleeves slashed with white satin; pendent sleeves over high close-fitting bodice with ruff; crimson cap, with pearls and white feather.

JENNY JONES. In Welsh dress. (*See* WELSH COSTUMES.)

JESSICA (*Merchant of Venice*). Long plain stuff or velvet skirt; large apron; velvet bodice, white slashed sleeves; keys hanging at side; pointed head-dress.

JESTER'S WIFE. Cardinal satin skirt with silver bells; pale blue satin over-skirt and cuirass bodice, with red sleeves; small satin cap of two colors, with bells, fan, etc., to match.

JEWISH COSTUME. Full silk trousers, dress cut in a V shape in front; an over-jacket with pendent sleeves; the hair in plaits; a soft silk handkerchief wound about the head with gold ornaments; long white drapery floating from it; a girdle about the waist. Loose under-dress; sandalled shoes. **Judith the Slayer of Holifernes** Illustrates another style. A woman of great beauty and commanding figure in robes of gorgeous colour and picturesque draping; a soft falling skirt; the bodice opening at the neck, with pendent sleeves turning back to the shoulders. Around the waist, forming a tunic, is a drapery of magnificently embroidered Oriental silk, caught up to the bust with an Eastern jewelled brooch, having a fringe of sequins, which are repeated on the wide jewelled band bracelets; her dark hair flows freely on her shoulders; a sword in her hand.

JILL (*Jack and Jill*). Flowered cotton bodice and tunic, over a short petticoat; small shawl; poke bonnet, or hat tied under the chin; she carries a pail. The name is often embroidered on the pockets. Another rendering: Brown and yellow striped petticoat; yellow silk bodice laced over white chemisette; brown silk tunic; yellow stockings; brown shoes; straw hat with wreath of poppies and cornflowers. (*See* JACK in Appendix.)

JOAN. (*See* DARBY.)

JOAN BEAUFORT, WIFE OF JAMES I. OF SCOTLAND (1357). A sideless gown of gold-colored plush, edged with brown marabout, a wide border of the same round the hem of the trailing skirt. The under-dress should be a spun silk of a golden-brown tint, and the fur trimming of the over-dress should be clasped with golden "owches" down the front. The hair is confined within a net-like coif of gold wire or thread and pearls; while a wide gold kirtle, low on the hips, supports an embroidered pouch of brown and gold. The shoes, of brown velvet, are worked with gold, and made with very long, peaked toes. No gloves, but a book, bound in white vellum and clasped and edged with gold, in the hand. The ruby heart on throat. The costume, as worn at the Queen's Ball, 1842, by the Duchess of Roxburgh, was a skirt of red and blue satin, embroidered with the arms of England, and bordered with ermine; cuirass bodice of ermine with jewels down the front; tight red satin sleeves to wrist; embroidered blue velvet cloak bordered with ermine, fastened on shoulders; badge of St. Andrew on left shoulder; hair in gold, side nets, with crown.

JOAN OF ARC. White plaited cashmere skirt; a suit of armour, with helmet and plume, mailed feet, gloves; red cloak on shoulders. Or, as she appeared at the coronation of the French King, skirt and tunic of blue satin, spangled with fleurs-de-lys; silver helmet with white plume; coat of mail, mail on arms, gauntlets, feet encased in long boots; sword with cross on hilt, and shield; the hair floating on shoulders. The suit of armour may be of silver, burnished steel, or what is called scale armour. But it can also be made by cutting out in strong brown paper the various pieces required, copied from any illustrated history, or from Knight's "Shakespeare," pasted over with silvered paper, and strips of linen inside strengthen them, so that tapes may be sewn with which to tie them on. The hair should be rolled under, after the manner formerly called Joan of Arc; and a cloak of cashmere to match the skirt should float from the shoulders. **As a Village Girl** she wears a skirt and bodice of grey cashmere; a tunic of blue sateen bordered with black velvet; square bodice and short sleeves; small muslin cap.

JOAN, JUMPING. Suitable for a child. Tall and pointed cap with flying streamers, pink and white stripes carried round; soft pink silk dress with honeycomb yoke and linen chemisette to throat; a skipping-rope round waist; sleeves with puff at shoulder, slashed puffs at elbow, cuffs falling over the hand; a girdle about the waist.

JOCKEY, (LADY). Short bright-colored satin skirt, striped, with cards of the races printed or tacked on it, and bunches of coins between; bodice to match; jacket to waist, buttoning down the front; jockey cap of two colors. Orange and red, brown and blue, red and green, are good mixtures of color.

JOCRISSE. Short skirt of dark blue satin, with a gold wand; crimson satin jacket with long gilet of yellow, bound with gold, cut square in front, flap pockets; elbow sleeves with Louis XV. cuffs; the jacket has revers of blue satin, and a lace ruff; tricorn hat.

JOKETTE. Short skirt of lemon-colored muslin flounced to waist; cuirass bodice of brown velvet laced at the back, with elbow sleeves, bordered with yellow lace, fastened with silver horseshoes; brown velvet boots; jockey cap of brown and yellow; whip in hand.

JOSEPHINE, EMPRESS. (1805-1810), and her time. Scanty skirt of white satin, embroidered round and down the front in double rows; very short-waisted bodice with jewelled girdle, puffed sleeves with low upstanding frills of lace, rounded to top of shoulder; necklace of pearls; hair curled; large jewelled coronet and comb. **Lady, of Period.** Clinging dress, short-waisted bodice beneath arm-pits, with short puffed sleeves; full ruche at the edge of the skirt; hair arranged in small curls with rows of pearls.

JUBILEE. Gold diadem and veil. Bodice of dark blue velvet with Union Jack in front surmounted by the Crown of England. The blue ribbon of the Garter on the left side. Skirt formed of the Union Jack. The British lion worked on the gold cuirass bodice having a border of rose, shamrock and thistles in silk applique. Blue velvet train powdered with roses and fleur-de-lis. The portrait of the Queen on one corner with 1837-1887.

JULIA MANNERING *(Guy Mannering).* An amber stuff dress, short-waisted, with puffed sleeves and large hat; or in an "arriving" dress, a sort of princess pelisse with treble cape made of pearl grey satin; large hat of same with white plumes.

JULIET *(Romeo and Juliet).* Flowing dress of silk or satin, with golden girdle, the bodice cut low in front; pointed elbow sleeves caught up inside with gold ornaments, and trimmed with gold lace; gold girdle; pouch at side; pearl and velvet or satin head-dress; long veil. Miss Terry in this character wore, first, a sleeveless gown of creamy white satin, bordered with blue, under-sleeves of soft woollen stuff; hair on shoulders, crowned with wreath of yellow marguerites. Second dress: Large patterned blue and gold brocade; hem bordered with band of cinnamon brown, embroidered in gold; a square-cut bodice and long open sleeves; tight under-sleeves; blue girdle. Third: Woollen under-dress made plain and full, gathered at the waist, over it a loose white silk gown, open in front, with square sleeves to elbow. Miss Anderson wore a long cloak from shoulder embroidered in pearls; satin dress with bands of pearls; puff at each shoulder, muslin peeping in at elbow; satchel bag; flowing hair, with filet and jewelled hand.

JULY. White Empire dress, lace frill, widening on shoulders; wreath of flowers at foot of scanty skirt, and under it, with butterflies hovering, streamers from under arms with insects at end. Large white hat; Japanese parasol.

JUNE. Blue short tulle dress, the lower portion gathered together at intervals in front, with bouquets and a bird hovering over bunch of flowers at the side, fullness caught up on hips with blue ribbons. Short full bodice crossed with three straps of ribbon, puffed sleeves to elbow, large round upstanding ruff diminishing towards the front, edged with close-set roses without foliage.

JUSTICE. Short white satin dress, scales in black velvet appliqué upon it; black velvet jacket with policeman's badge on one arm; a leather belt; a truncheon in hand, and policeman's helmet.

JUST 100 YEARS AGO. A favorite name for a pretty *poudré* dress. (*See* POUDRE.)

JUTLAND PEASANT GIRL. Green, black, and red striped petticoat; large black and green apron with border; green velvet bodice, tight sleeves trimmed with bands of embroidery across front to imitate square bodice; red and black handkerchief about head, with revers of lace turning up from ears.

KATHARINA (*Taming of the Shrew*). Plain satin skirt touching the ground; low pointed bodice with basque all round formed of loops of ribbons; a ruff from shoulder widening at the back, supported by wire, edged with pointed lace, the sleeves tight to wrist, with lace cuffs;

puffed epaulette, and over-sleeves, which button at elbow and hang therefrom in a straight piece; a velvet head-dress, bordered with pearls of Marie Stuart form. A satchel bag attached to girdle falls loosely round hips.

CATHARINE OF ARRAGON, CATHERINE HOWARD, CATHERINE PARR. (*See* C.)

KITTY CLIVE. Dress of blue cashmere; plain skirt; bodice square cut with white stomacher and black velvet bands; sleeves turned up a elbow, with square cuffs, full muslin sleeves beneath; muslin apron trimmed with lace; cap of same, with black velvet bow; powdered hair.

KITTY, DUCHESS OF QUEENSBERRY. Petticoat of brocade, trimmed with lace; black velvet sacque, lined with crimson satin, velvet, and pearls; stomacher of amethysts, rubies, and pearls; diamond ornaments; hair powdered. A crimson velvet and lace head-dress.

LABURNUM. A white gown and upstanding collar to a low bodice, puffings at elbow, and all trimmed with bunches of laburnum.

LA VALLIÈRE, MADAME DE. (*See* V.)

LACE COLLECTION. Red satin petticoat; up the front a plastron formed of short lengths of different kinds of lace, narrower towards the top; flounce of red satin and a band of lace round. The black satin paniers bordered with short lengths of lace secured by red bows. Round the black tunic a band of red with tassels of lace upon it. A low black square bodice with lace scraps carried up the front and on the sleeves. A black band round the top with the names of old laces worked in gold. A lace lappet above, lace at the top of the gloves, on the red cap, with powdered hair, and on the fan. A lace pillow with bobbins at one side, and a parchment with a piece of lace begun upon it. Ornaments bobbins.

LACE MAKER. This could be represented by a Dutch Frau, with the lappeted cap and stuff gown. Or, by a woman of Louis XIV. period, with bunched-up dress; long lace edged apron; lace cap; half high bodice cut in points and elbow sleeves. Or, by a woman of the Louis XIII. period; the bodice with long basque cut up into tabs; full plain skirt; sleeves puffed inside the arm with linen revers edged with lace on bodice and sleeves.

LADIES' BATTLE. Leonie de Villegontier. Short muslin dress; short-waisted bodice with fichu; wide striped lavender sash;

necktie of white muslin; hair curled; long mittens tied with ribbons above elbow. As the **Countess d'Altreval,** Mrs. Kendal wore a grenat satin made as a train, with short-waisted Empire bodice, large bow of the same at back of the waist, tight sleeves to wrist, slashed with figured silk of a violet-grey tinge, which forms the front of the dress; a white tulle fichu fastened with a bunch of flowers at the side; muslin Steinkirk tie round neck; hair curled and parted at the side, on it a close muslin cap.

LADYBIRD. Suitable for a child. Skirt of brown tulle, in three thicknesses. Low square orange velvet bodice, the sleeves of tulle, with tawny red silk wings for epaulettes. The tunic in the form of two wings of orange red silk, with black velvet spots. Tiny wings as a coronet, orange stockings, black shoes, red rosettes and red sash.

LADY BURLEIGH. White satin under-skirt trimmed with old lace, caught up with loops of pearls on wire in large festoons; tunic of a bold patterned brocade; pointed bodice cut low; powdered hair; pearl ornaments. Or, short-flowered skirt, simple striped over-dress opening in front, gathered on to pointed square-cut bodice; muslin fichu inside, sleeves to wrist with ruffles; high muslin cap.

LADY HELP. XIXth century. (*See* HELP.)

LADY JANE (*Patience*). Long close-fitting Japanese robe of dark blue silk embroidered in gold, with design of scrolls and peacock's tail; light blue scarf at the back.

LADY OF THE LAKE (*Sir Walter Scott*). White muslin dress flounced to waist; low black velvet bodice, with white stomacher, laced with silver; tartan scarf of satin fastened with Scotch brooch on shoulder; hair in curls; light blue snood. Or, skirts and bodice of silver tissue trimmed with water lilies and any water plant.

LADY OF THE LAST CENTURY. (*See* POUDRÉ.)

LAHORE, REINE DE. Train of white satin, draped with red India cashmere, richly embroidered in gold; head-dress, a jewelled coronet, tulle veil with gold tassels. (*See* INDIAN.)

LAITIÈRE DE BAGNOLET. (*See* LOUIS XIV.)

LAKMÉ (*Delibes' Opera*). An Indian dress; pointed jewelled cap with fringe of beads; many beads round the neck. Long soft falling white dress bordered with gold; over it a species of Senorita jacket with short sleeves all jewelled; gold cloak; a scarf of many colored Indian cashmere crossing left shoulder, under right arm; a jewel on the shoulder; bracelets like serpent.

LALLA ROOKH. A rich Oriental dress. Petticoat and trousers full to ankles, of gold tissue over pink; long green satin skirted paletot with over-sleeves trimmed with gold, girded round the hip with orange and heliotrope scarves, ending in pearl tassels; the front of bodice pink, embroidered in gold, silver, and jewels; pink under-sleeves. Green satin cap with heron's plume like a fez, fastened with jewels; gold-spangled veil; green satin pointed shoes; the hair in two plaits entwined with pearls, fringe of pearl and emeralds round the neck; pointed sandals for shoes.

LAMBALLE, PRINCESS DE *(As worn at Marlborough House).* Pale blue satin over-skirt fastened to white satin petticoat with a bouquet of roses, the front breadth sprinkled with shaded roses. The bodice comes to the waist only; a low, double lace edged pelerine drapes the shoulders; the sleeves are of a bell shape; the hair turned over a large cushion and powdered; wreath of roses on one side, with pearls and ribbons, veil at the back, falling over curls. (*See* LOUIS XVI.)

LAMP PEDESTAL. Head-dress formed of a shade made of lace and amber silk surmounted by an owl with the electric light in the eyes. Low bodice of amber silk edged with lace, short skirt of the same color. A lamp carried in the hand. **Lampshade.** Short red silk skirt with lace flounce at waist and hem. Low rounded bodice bordered with a ruche and lace, sleeve puffed to elbow and ruffled. A red silk wired lampshade bordered with lace forming the head-dress.

LANGE Mdlle. *(Madame Angot).* An Oriental striped dress with coins; afterwards a long beflounced cream colored silk with low bodice and sleeves; and in the duet scene a black and red-striped petticoat; a large blue serge apron and velvet bodice and a huge cap.

LAPLANDERS. Heavy boots turning up at the toes. Thick woollen stockings. A short robe with long sleeves and roll collar, a fur habit banded at the waist, long sleeves. A woollen cap bordered with white trimming fastening close round the face, hiding the hair, but standing out from the head at the back in a point, like a Normandy cap.

LASS OF RICHMOND HILL (1760). Blue and white satin skirt; bodice and paniers of white brocade; powdered hair; hat with streamers. For style, *see* GEORGIAN PERIOD.

LAURA *(Petrarch's)*. Long white flowing robe embroidered in silver; bodice cut low, edged with gold braid, two rows round neck, one round arm-hole and elbow sleeve, beneath this a red and white under-sleeve, fitting to wrist; hair in coil; black shoes, pointed toes.

LAVENDER, FRESH. (*From C. E. Perugini's picture*). Suitable to fair, slight girl; a simple colored cotton dress, with elbow sleeves; mob cap; tray of lavender carried in the hand.

LAWN TENNIS AND BADMINTON. Sometimes for these only an ordinary lawn tennis dress and pouch are worn, with a bat attached to the side. A better representation is a short plain skirt of grass green satin, gathered at back, trimmed round the edge with two rows of grass fringe, headed by a flat band of white satin an inch and a half in width, to represent the boundary of the court; six lines of the same round the skirt at intervals; a gold tennis net draped from waist, edged with scarlet and white worsted balls; miniature tennis bats hold up the drapery; bodice of green velvet, long sleeves to wrist, all bordered with gold braid and scarlet and white balls; epaulettes of scarlet and white satin ribbon; red and white satin peaked cap, with daisies and leaves beneath the flap; Suéde gloves, and black shoes; scarlet stockings; ornaments, gold tennis bats; fan like a bat, in red. For **Badminton Shuttle Cocks** replace the balls.

LECZINSKI, MARIE (*Married Louis XV. for his first wife*, 1725). Pale pink robe of state, the train scalloped round and richly trimmed with lace; fine diamond crown, and diamond ornaments; snuff-box carried in the hand. (*See* LOUIS XV. Period.)

LEE, THREE YOUNG MAIDS OF. Blue and chintz dresses with large hats. **Three Young Maids of Lee, and Three Old Maids of Lee,** are sometimes represented by one side of the hair and face to represent old women, the other side young ones.

LEEK, A. Accordion plaited frock of green silk, bordered with silver leeks; full bodice with hanging sleeves; a pointed green cap ruched at the edge, an upstanding leek at the top. A leek carried in the hand.

LEMONS. (*See* ORANGES and LEMONS.)

LEONIE DE LA VILLEGONTIER. (*See* LADIES' BATTLE.)

LEONORA (*Il Trovatore*). Satin skirt, with tunic caught up on one side; low black velvet bodice, puffings of muslin at the top;

the long all-round basque, cut in tabs; elbow sleeves, with treble rows of lace; ribbon bandeau in hair.

LIBERTY. Short red, white, and blue striped satin skirt, made plain, with perpendicular stripes; low red satin bodice, with coat-tails; plain muslin fichu tucked inside, lace frill and cravat in front; cap of Liberty, tri-color at one side; dagger stuck in leather belt; sleeves to elbow and rolled. Classic cashmere dress embroidered in pearls; pearl girdle; the red cap of Liberty studded with pearls; a white satin banner, embroidered with the word "Liberty," carried in the hand. The dress is made with a long skirt, loose, low, full bodice, pendent sleeves. (For style, *see* CLASSIC.)

LIGHT OF HAREEM. (*See* ORIENTAL COSTUME and LALLA ROOKH.)

LIGHT, ELECTRIC. (*See* ELECTRICITY.)

LILAC. Mauve satin dress, the front embroidered with lilac on crêpe lisse; bunches of the flower on dress and head.

LILY (*Arum*). A white satin gown draped with tulle; large white velvet arum leaves falling on the skirt from the waist; an upstanding ruff to low bodice formed of the same; arum fan; powdered hair, with head-dress like an arum, stalk upwards.

LILY OF THE VALLEY. Short green satin skirt with a row of lily leaves and flowers above the hem. A scarf drapery of spangled tulle festooned from the waist, and falling in one end at the sides, caught up with lilies of the valley. The low bodice is cut and plaited to resemble lily leaves in gold satin; green satin ribbon at the waist tied in long falling ends at the front; stiff folds of silver tulle from the shoulders disappear beneath the bodice in front; the short puffed sleeves are of the same tulle, with a row of leaves and flowers round them; a bunch of lilies of the valley on each shoulder in the centre of the front; a wreath of the same flowers.

LILY OF LEOVILLE. White cambric head-dress, goffered all round, and trimmed with falling ends at either side of gold silk; brown velvet bodice opening *à la Brèton* over white chemisette, trimmed with gold braid and beads; Swiss belt of brocade; lace collarette and elbow sleeves; blue satin skirt with bands of brown plush; very large apron of light blue silk bordered with insertion; gold cross round neck.

LITERATURE. White flowing robe worked in gold, a manuscript scroll in front. Head-dress composed of white blotting paper, quill pens and gold pendant pen nibs.

LISMORE. (*See* MAID OF.)

LITTLE BUTTERCUP. (*See* PINAFORE.)

LIZARD BIRD. Yellow satin skirt; bodice of green jet; lizard birds on the head, and perched on the shoulders.

LOBSTER. Rows of lobster carried round a green dress. The head-dress resembling a lobster's head; enamelled lobsters for ornaments.

LOHENGRIN. (*See* ELSA.)

LOMBARDY PEASANT. (*See* ITALIAN.)

LORELEI. Dress of watered silk, shot with silver, draped with green, and caught up with water lilies, coral, and diamonds; veil to match; sometimes soft muslin is draped in classic fashion; the hair flowing; a coronet of silver on the head; an old fashioned lyre carried in the hand. (*See* WATER-NYMPH.)

LORN, MAID OF. White muslin dress, with scarf of the clan tartan. Lady Elizabeth Campbell appeared thus in the character at the famous Waverley Ball at Willis's Rooms.

LORRAINE PEASANT. Mob cap of fine muslin, a cockade in front; short brown peasant dress; bodice opening in front, the revers plaited like the frill; ruffles at wrist of long sleeves; white muslin fichu; lace ruffles.

LOUIS XIII. Period of (1610-1643). A petticoat of satin or brocade, an over-dress either fastened down at the side or loose and flowing; the bodicc cut in one with the skirt or pointed; gauze sleeves puffed from shoulder to wrist, and pendent ones above, lined with a contrasting color; the bodice high at the back, and square in front, with either a falling collar of lace, or a ruff supported on wire; the hair is not powdered. The following is a good rendering: Grey silk skirt, with lace flounces; cardinal tunic, trimmed with white lace, and caught up at side; round bodice of grey silk; stomacher of gold; tight sleeves, with epaulettes; grey paniers and rich cardinal sash; muslin and lace fichu, and boa round the throat, the ends fastened at back; large white hat, trimmed with cardinal satin and three white ostrich feathers, the whole costume trimmed with gold.

LOUIS XIV. Period of (1643-1715). In this reign ladies wore the hair powdered over high cushions; hoops were in fashion, and sacques; also patches, and very long gloves. The following is the usual style for fancy balls: Satin petticoat, plain or quilted with pearls, or with rows of lace across headed by tulle puffings and roses; a velvet, brocade or satin train rounded in front, coming from the waist or *en sacque* (*see* WATTEAU), trimmed with lace, headed by ruchings and pearls, carried up the sides, and bodice which should be cut as a low square; the stomacher pointed, wirh rows of ribbon across, a bow in the centre; the sleeves to the elbow, with ruffles; pearls and flowers on the powdered hair. A lady's hunting dress of this reign is made with a plain skirt, a very deep satin waistcoat with square pockets, and a longer basqued jacket with mousquetaire cuffs and ruffles; a lace tie and frill at the throat and a three-cornered hat over powdered hair. **Laitière de Bagnolet.** Blue short skirt embroidered round the edge; yellow bunched-up upper skirt, red-pointed, low, square-cut bodice bordered with gold, white under-bodice; sleeves with turn-back cuff at wrist; white cap with a red and yellow handkerchief tied over it. **Marquise.** A red plush coat, with silver buttons and braid, showing a vest of cream satin; a cream satin dress; a cloak of red plush, lined with cream satin, fastened to the shoulders with silver cord and tassels; three-cornered hat of red plush, with cream feathers and silver cord on the powdered hair; riding gloves with gauntlets, and a riding whip. **Peasant of Period.** Short cream dress of cashmere, embroidered with roses; moss green apron and white fichu crossed on the bust. (*See* BERCEUSE).

LOUIS XV. Period of (1715-1774). A similar dress is worn to that described in LOUIS XIV.'S time. **A Marquise.** Pink silk skirt bordered with a lace flounce, caught up in vandykes, with pink roses and silver tassels; long upper-skirt of silver gauze, with strips of pink satin ribbon, and silver tassels and roses, keeping it in its place; low stiff bodice with gilet of silver cloth; powdered hair; blue silk skirt with lace flounces, headed by bands of pink silk laid on in double gatherings; pointed stomacher of the same, with pink bands and bows across; skirt and bodice of pink silk, bordered with the same plaiting in blue, elbow-sleeves and ruffles; powdered hair. Or, dress of embossed velvet broché with bouquets of roses on a ground of oyster-grey satin, the hips padded as worn at that period. The front of the skirt vieux rose silk with flounces of antique point de gaze; bouquets of variegated roses to match the broché, loop up the drapery; bodice of the broché trimmed with the lace; the hair powdered; patches. A young girl might wear a muslin dress with silk sacque, train and bodice. **Waiting Maid.** Short silk skirt, two flounces gathered at edge; square bodice, and bunched-up tunic in contrast; bibbed muslin apron; powdered hair. **Peasant Girl.** Linen striped skirt, blue, red, and white; red tunic caught together, high at the back; square, sleeveless, blue cashmere bodice with velvet bows and trimmings; loose linen under-sleeves, flat muslin cap, black velvet bracelets, and band round neck. **Flower-Girl.** Pink and blue costume, covered with garlands of small roses, draping the Pompadour skirt; pink tunic, ruched with pink satin; bodice to match; white muslin apron with pockets, trimmed with pink and blue ruches; large flat basket suspended from a garland of flowers passed round the neck and filled with real flowers; hair powdered; white muslin cap; at the side tufts of roses and loops of blue ribbon. **Bourgeoise.** Grey silk skirt, having lace flounces; pink over-dress and mantle, showing grey stomacher; pink shoes, with diamond buckles; grey stockings; head-dress of Brussels lace and pink ribbons diamond ornaments. **Barmaid.** Red silk skirt bordered with black velvet band; tunic of Pompadour chintz; white muslin apron and fichu; black velvet bodice with lace revers on the sleeves; muslin coif, stiff, and trimmed with black velvet.

LOUIS XVI. (1774-1789). (*See* LAMBALLE, PRINCESSE DE; MARIE ANTOINETTE; ELIZABETH, MADAME; POUDRÉ COSTUMES, and SHEPHERDESS.) The rich gown opens over a chiné petticoat of lighter tone, with three rows of lace at the hem, the bodice has a pointed white stomacher, overlaced with cord, soft lisse draped as a fichu is caught up with flowers and a double ruche of the same encircles the arm. The head-dress is a singularly becoming one, white lisse with colored flowers. The reigns of Louis XV. and XVI. were chosen for the costume ball given by the Countess of Warwick, January, 1895. Among many lovely costumes worn were a petticoat of rose-petal satin, bordered with a flounce of lace headed by roses. The pointed bodice showed a pink vest, laced across; ruffles and fichu of Mechlin; the hair powdered and dressed high with roses and diamonds on one side; shoes with paste buckles. And a yellow satin draped with white muslin, edged with pink roses; over-dress low, double-breasted, of blue velvet with paste buttons; ruches faced with blue brocade and lace; a velvet toque on the powdered hair. The following illustrate the style. White silk long skirt, and jacket of striped gold and red silk, long sleeves and low neck, finished off with a cambric fichu, showing the neck, a rose in front; the jacket is cut away in front, has gold buttons, and displays a full white under-bodice with straps of red across. The hair is powdered, and a small toque of red silk is bordered with the stripe, a diamond aigrette and bunch of flowers worn on one side. A curious costume *d'apres* Debucoure, 1787, is as follows: Light blue under-skirt with a flounce round the edge, blue train bordered with gold, red bodice terminating at waist with gold belt, large blue revers at neck; white tie and chemisette; tight sleeves to wrist, blue cuffs; enormous hat with floral wreath over powdered hair; stick in hand. Large picturesque hats were worn.

LOVE. White satin dress with low cuirass bodice, out-lined with red velvet, displaying white hearts; red velvet hearts appearing on the skirt; wings at the back; coronet head-dress with a red heart in centre; the skirt is caught up with an arrow and quiver. (*See* CUPID.)

LOVE BIRDS. The skirt a series of scolloped green silk flounces, with plumage fashioned like the bird's tail for tunic; the cap made to resemble the head and beak; the veritable birds perched on the right shoulder of the bodice which is covered with green feathers.

LUCENA, QUEEN OF THE MOON. (*See* MOON.)

LUCIA. Striped green skirt caught up in the front; low white chemisette and embroidered sleeve; jacket of striped pink, green and yellow; yellow necktie; kerchief fastened about the shoulders.

LUCY (*The Rivals*). High-heeled shoes, with plain buckles; stockings, with silk clocks; quilted satin under-skirt; bodice, and bunched up over-skirt; lace tucker round bodice; small mob cap; black lace apron.

LUNA (*See* MOON.)

LURLINE. Dress of frosted or silver spangled tulle, over white or green, caught up with crystal and aquatic plants, such as water-lilies and grasses; a veil of tulle to match dress, falls over the floating hair, which should be covered with frosting powder; bodice of silver tissue; diamond ornaments. (*See* WALTER NYMPH.)

LUTIN. Short white muslin skirt with two flounces; satin tunic, caught up at side by bands of black velvet; corselet bodice of black satin, embroidered with gold, double braces of the same, worn over muslin; under-bodice open at neck, with elbow sleeves; cap and mittens.

LUXURY. A black or white evening dress covered with fruit, flowers, shells, seaweed, gems, birds, &c. Head-dress of fruit, necklace of cherries.

LYDIA LANGUISH. Dress of white India muslin, trimmed with lace; sash and bodice bows of dark violet ribbon; hair in curls, pearls round neck. Or, as in last scene, a silk hood, black silk scarf, long gloves. Or, handsome red and white brocaded silk dress, looped up over a white satin petticoat; hair powdered.

LYONS, LADY OF. (*See* PAULINE, and MELNOTTE, WIDOW.)

MACAIRE, MADAME ROBERT. Man's tall hat smashed in, torn lace tie, chintz chiné waistcoat, man's coat of shabby blue velvet. Brown and blue short skirt with high boots, eyeglass, gloves with torn fingers.

MAB, QUEEN. A diaphonous dress with elbow sleeves; cloak attached to shoulders; crown and veil; flowers heading a sceptre.

MABEL (*Rob Roy*). Plain skirted plaid dress; bibbed apron; fur edged hood.

MACBETH. LADY MACBETH. First dress: A long velvet robe, having a narrow velvet tunic fastening down the front, with brodequins; low bodice, showing white chemisette slightly at the neck; plaid scarf flowing loosely; short sleeves; massive bracelets; long hair; a velvet cap secured by a broad ribbon passing under the chin. Second dress: White satin trimmed with silver; scarlet mantle with ermine; silver coronet surmounted by cross. Third dress: White wrapper trimmed with lace. **Witches.** Short skirt with frogs and toads appliquéd in black velvet on quilted satin skirt; chintz tunics; black velvet bodices laced in front; ruffles at elbow; cats and owls on shoulder; short cloaks with square collar at back; high black velvet hats, entwined with serpents.

MACGREGOR, HELEN. Short Macgregor black and red tartan skirt; high velvet bodice, laced across the front; a plaid fastened with a brooch on one shoulder; Scotch bonnet of black velvet with an eagle plume and cairngorm, hair flowing, sword and pistol at girdle. Heather collarette and belt; plaid stockings, black shoes with buckles; sword and shield in hand.

MACINTYRE, MISS (*The Antiquary*). Crimson velvet bodice, flowered petticoat and sleeves; dress turned up *à la laveuse;* broad

Brussels point collar; crimson stockings, with white clocks; black shoes, with crimson heels and bows, diamond buckles.

MACONAISE (*Peasant of Bourg-en-Brise*). Brown cashmere dress, with blue silk bibbed apron; low bodice, shawl and elbow-sleeves; large round black hat, with a huge knob atop in centre, trimmed with gold cord, tassel and net streamers; black stockings and shoes. Or, short striped red woollen petticoat; red corselet bodice; muslin chemisette; small red cape slung round shoulders; round flat cap with an upstanding tail like a rat's.

MADALENE (*On the Eve of St. Agnes*). Skirt of white satin, bodice blue velvet with pendent sleeves; a white chemisette, trimmed with bands of blue velvet and pearls; a blue girdle and aumonière bag at the side; the hair hanging about the shoulders; and a chaplet of pearls.

MADAME DE MAINTENON. (1643-1679.) Black velvet skirt, open in front, showing under-petticoat of brocade, trimmed with lace or plain satin, richly embroidered; the bodice should be low, cut high on shoulders, pointed in front, sleeves to elbow, with ruffles; gloves without buttons; high-heeled shoes, pointed toes and diamond buckles; missal hanging at side; hair in flat curls, and head-dress of many jewels; veil flowing at back.

MADAME LE DIABLE. (*See* DIABLOTINE.)

MADEIRA PEASANT. Striped petticoat woven in bright colors. A low embroidered stay bodice lacing across the front over a high white chemisette with short sleeves, fastened with gold link buttons. A blue or scarlet baize cape with scalloped falling collar bound with a contrasting color is worn out of doors, and a peculiar cap which fits the head closely, and has a sharp point in the centre.

MADELINA (*Rigoletto*). A short Spanish costume; red satin skirt, with gold braid and fringe; blue upper skirt; black Spanish jacket, laced across the front, over white loose bodice, which forms a puff at the waist; long sleeves slashed inside the arm, showing white muslin through; gold betrimmed epaulettes; gold net with sequins.

MADELINE (in *Belphegor*, Scene 3rd). Short crimson cashmere skirt trimmed with black velvet, tucked up over a petticoat of pale blue cashmere; crimson vest, with bodice of black velvet strapped over it; small white apron, with pockets and scarlet bows; French cap, period of

Louis XVIII.; shoes same reign; antique French cross fastened round the neck with black velvet; earrings to match.

MADELINA (*Rigoletto*). Red and yellow striped skirt; black bodice opening in front; flat round head-dress of red puce coloring.

MADOLINATA (*From Wagner's Picture.*) Front gold brocade; over-dress velvet bordered with gold; bodice low, square jewelled stomacher; high stiff ruff standing up at the shoulders; full puffed sleeves to wrist; hair curled on forehead, rolled above and entwined with pearls.

MAGDALEN MAGPIE. Miniature boating hat with black and white streamers on powdered hair. Black silk jersey, scarf, sash, and satin kilted skirt striped white and black, with pompons of the same color. Black stockings with white rosettes on the shoes. Shield of Magdalen College, Oxford, fastened to bodice.

MAGPIE. Half black, half white dress; hair powdered on one side and not on the other; one glove and one shoe black, one white; short satin skirt, covered with gauze; basque bodice; gauze fichu; satin ribbon tied in a bow at the throat; gauze cap. All half black and half white, so that the wearer seems on one side all black, on the other all white; a magpie on the right shoulder. **La Pie Voleuse** has a magpie on the shoulder with a diamond ring in its mouth.

MAHOMEDAN LADY. Loose trousers of striped silk, tunic of gold-spangled muslin; bodice and sleeves of crimson satin striped with gold; pendent sleeves of crimson gauze; bangles round ankles and arms; pointed shoes; many beads about neck; pointed head-dress of gold and beads.

MAID MARIAN. A brown satin short skirt, bordered with dark fur; a pelisse of Lincoln green velvet, the skirt gathered to the bodice, with revers of red satin, and red and brown on the cuffs: the sleeves long, bordered with fur, light brown satin ones beneath, and leather band and knife at the waist, with quiver at back; round velvet cap bordered with fur. This costume looks well in green satin and black velvet. Pelisse with green revers, the green carried down the front; green cuffs and sleeves; the velvet cap has a brim turning up in battlements. A horn is carried at the side; boots bound with fur; hair in plaits.

MAID OF KENT. White satin gown trimmed round neck and skirt with silver chiffon, caught up on shoulders with hops and cherries. The skirt covered with Kentish horses in silver, one of which appears in centre of silver crown. Cherry silk sash falling on the side of the skirt with the Kentish motto "Invicta."

MAID, MY PRETTY. ("My face is my fortune, sir, she said.") Plain yellow satin skirt, antique over-dress of cream print, pattern wild flowers; sacque back; bodice square in front; bibbed muslin apron; mob cap trimmed with yellow; black silk stockings and satin shoes. Or, short colored petticoat; an open tunic of blue flowered chintz, pointed bodice laced across the front; muslin kerchief; straw hat bound with black velvet, and tied under the chin; yoke and milk pails.

MAID OF ATHENS. (*See* ATHENS.)

MAID OF HONOUR TO QUEEN MARY OF ENGLAND. Black velvet skirt with lace down the sides, quilted satin front; square low bodice of black velvet, pointed at waist; epaulettes, a puff of velvet trimmed with pearls; tight sleeves between arm and wrist, puff of white to wrist, frill of white inside; ruche round neck; black velvet pointed head-dress edged with pearls.

MAID OF LISMORE. Long plain skirt of satin; half-high bodice, front fastened with pearls; sleeves full to wrist, with turned back cuff of lace; Tudor head-dress of velvet and pearls.

MAID OF OLDEN TIME. White satin petticoat, quilted with pearls; paniers and bodice of brocade with crimson roses, old lace and pearls; powdered hair.

MAID OF SARAGOSSA. Short blue woollen skirt trimmed with red; upper skirt of red, drawn through the placket-hole at the back; a low bodice, made stiff and firm, lacing across the front, displaying a low white under-dress; the hair drawn from the face, and gathered in a knot at the back, a dagger thrust through it, and a red handkerchief wound about the head.

MAID OF THE MILL. Short dress of white muslin or silk; muslin apron; bag of flour at side; cap with windmill.

MAID WAS IN THE GARDEN, THE. Short scarlet petticoat, with flowered polonaise; muslin fichu; cap, and mittens; clothes-pins hung on cord round waist, basket with clothes in hand, and blackbird on the shoulder.

MAIDEN ALL FORLORN. Pretty figured cotton dress; the petticoat of pink and white stripes; jacket of blue and white tied round waist; sleeves rolled to elbow; white apron all in holes pinned to left side with gold-headed pin; white sun-bonnet; brown stockings and shoes; milking stool under one arm, milk pail on other; hair dishevelled.

MAIDENS, LOVE-SICK (*Patience*). Loose flowing skirts half-high classic bodices with ribbon belts tied in a looped bow in front, forming braces at the back; the long drooping sleeves fasten with three buttons on the outside of the shoulders, and spring from the fulness of the dress at the back. The best colorings are, dark blue serge and sun-flowers, white with daffodils, sickly green and passion flowers, terra-cotta with gold, light blue and claret. Lyre in hand; fillet round head.

MAIDS, THREE LITTLE. (*See* MIKADO.)

MALAPROP, MRS. (*School for Scandal*). Brocaded sacque, caught back with bows, over quilted petticoat; peaked stomacher, laced with ribbons; hair rolled over cushion; lace cap; black mittens; black velvet round neck and wrist; high-heeled shoes, muslin kerchief tucked into bodice; old-fashioned fan.

MALTA. A black satin gown with Maltese crosses. An academical head-dress. A key carried in the hand.

MALTESE. With a black silk dress, touching the ground, the black silk head-dress called Faldelta should be worn. It covers the head and the figure like a cloak, and has a piece of whalebone, half a yard long, sewn into one side; the gathered part comes a little in front of left cheek, and the whalebone forms an arch over the face. At a recent ball a Maltese country dance was given. The dancers wore Maltese colors, red and white. The ladies white brocade with broad red ribbons on left shoulder, hair poudré. The gentlemen red satin trimmed with gold gauze, white ribbon bows on the shoulders, and perruques.

MAMIE ROSETTE. Grey cashmere dress, with white muslin apron caught up with pink ribbons here and there; a becoming muslin cap.

MANETTE, LUCY (*Tale of Two Cities*). White muslin dress, with square bodice, single flounce on skirt; wide blue sash; hair drawn up over cushion and curled, *à la* Gainsborough.

MANON (*Massenet*). Flowered brocaded gown, opening over a white satin petticoat magnificently embroidered with roses and silver filagree; pointed bodice draped with lace; elbow sleeves and powder.

MANON LESCAUT (*Opera by Signor Pucchini*). Flowered dress, black scarf mantle, with hood attached.

MANOLA. Dress of amber and blue satin, trimmed with sequins and gold braid; dark blue senorita jacket and satin cap. Or, large felt hat, trimmed with red; grey silk skirt with scarlet garnitures; amber merino over-skirt embroidered; bodice red, trimmed with grey silk, black beads, and lace; gold over-skirt trimmed with gold silk fringe.

MARBLE BUST. The head and bust draped with white, and powdered; the skirt simulating a flower decked pedestal.

MARCH. A combination of yellow and light peach; under-skirt primrose; upper-skirt peach, caught up round the hips with a wreath of primroses and leaves, which also border the hem. The sleeves fall over the elbow in three puffs edged with primroses, and are divided by bands of yellow ribbon, tied in a bow; yellow ribbon round the waist and brought from under the arm and tied in front; low square bodice headed by primroses; a weathercock in the hair.

MARCHANDE DE BALAIS. (*See* BUY-A-BROOM.)

MARGARET, LADY (*Lay of the Last Minstrel*). White satin dress, embroidered with jewels, veil at back, wimple of clear muslin reaching to elbow; a knot of plaid ribbons fastened on the left side; wreath of white roses round head.

MARGARET OF ANJOU, 1422-1461 (*Wife of Henry VI.*). Hair hidden by the curious head-dress of the period, or gold coronet and gauze veil; shoes broad over instep, and pointed and embroidered; blue velvet square bodice, filled in with lisse, quilted with gold; front breadth gold brocade: jewelled girdle.

MARGARET TUDOR, QUEEN. (*Daughter of Henry VII.*, 1485-1509, *and Wife of James IV., Scotland*). Black bodice over low black plastron, turning back with a high wired collar having an inner collar band attached to the bodice passing under the plastron. Hair turned back in a roll with black velvet; Marie Stuart head-dress; sleeve with slashed cuff tight to the wrist, perpendicular bands of trimming. Bodice opens to the waist with the sloping Holbein collar and soft crepe puffings. The muslin chemisette is embroidered with black stripes; an organ pipe ruff round the throat. (*See* also TUDOR, Illustration Fig. 43.)

MARGERY DAW. Grass green dress, made with plain short skirt; low bodice, large, short puffed sleeves; round cape, mittens to elbow.

MARGERY, MISTRESS. Petticoat of rose-colored silk; rose-colored train lined with pink; bodice laced over muslin stomacher; fichu of lace; hair powdered; lace cap.

MARGUERITE (*Faust*). Short skirt of cashmere, bordered with rows of black or contrasting velvet; long skirt over this, trimmed in same way, and caught up by means of a satchel or pocket, and girdle on left side. The skirt is sewn to a long close cuirass bodice made of the same cashmere, coming well on to the hips, where it is trimmed with bands of velvet or tabs of velvet. It is cut square at the neck, over a linen chemisette; the sleeves are made with horizontal puffs to the elbow, where a close-fitting portion of the sleeve meets them, and falls a little over the hand. The hair is worn in two long plaits. Grey cashmere with black velvet; white with blue can be used. Miss Ellen Terry wore a full white chemisette to throat, hanging sleeves, and bodice of brownish velvet, front of dress a lighter shade, train at back; close cap; satchel pocket attached at side; pointed brown shoes.

MARGUERITE DE VALOIS. (*Married,* 1572, *to Henry of Navarre, subsequently Henry IV. of France*). Long skirt of satin or velvet, of contrasting color to petticoat which is trimmed with bands of gold at the hem; a jewelled girdle encircles waist and falls down centre of skirt; square bodice, trimmed to match, with a high ruff on wire from the shoulders; the hair turned off the face in a double roll, not powdered; a jewelled crown; the sleeves in longitudinal puffs to the wrist, with bands of gold between; lace cuffs; feather fan; pointed satin shoes.

MARGUERITE. (*See* DAISY).

MARIA (*School for Scandal*). White muslin frock with sash; in last act ivory satin cape and pelisse trimmed with white-fox; a white beaver Gainsborough hat, ostrich plumes.

MARIA, INFANTA OF SPAIN. A skirt touching ground, large close ruff and hanging voluminous sleeve caught together above the wrist, and showing under-sleeves. Bodice slashed over white muslin shirt, crinkled and brought up to the throat with a band of small jewels.

MARIANA (*Measure for Measure*). Plain flowing tulle skirt; velvet bodice, open, heart shape, with low chemisette; sleeves to wrist, with puff at elbow; fur round neck of bodice; hair in coif of gold and pearls.

MARIE (*Cinq Mars*). Under-skirt of yellow satin, brocaded in gold; over-skirt of blue velvet, embroidered, to match; gold waistbelt;

Fig. 28.—DRESS OF MARIE ANTOINETTE PERIOD.

hat and feathers; bodice low, with Medici collar; short upper sleeves, under sleeves slashed with white.

MARIE ANTOINETTE AND HER TIME. (1774-1789). In Illustration, No. 28, this beautiful period is displayed in a gown after the well-known portrait of the Queen by Le Brun. The skirt is made in white satin bordered with a band of brown fur carried up either side of the narrow front breadth, which has a scroll of fine embroidery just at the hem, the swathed satin bodice is fastened by three diamond buttons, and is surmounted by a lisse fichu fastened on the shoulders by fur tails. The toque is blue velvet with a rouleau of white satin round, diamonds fastening the ostrich plumes and the white aigrette. The sleeves form one puff to the elbow met by the long gloves. The Countess of Warwick at the ball given by her, January, 1895, at Warwick Castle appeared as Marie Antoinette in a cream brocade with pink and blue roses, the foliage worked in gold thread, the skirt plain, the bodice forming two paniers on hips. The neck and sleeves trimmed with gold flecked lisse. A regal train of sapphire blue velvet from shoulders, embroidered with large gold Fleur de Lis caught across from shoulder to shoulder with rivieres of diamonds. Powdered hair, cap of white muslin and blue velvet; ornaments, diamonds; pink, white, and blue plumes at the side. In her prison days (after Paul Delaroche), the Queen wears a plain, long-skirted, short-waisted black silk dress, the sleeves short and turned up with a band of muslin; a long muslin scarf fichu over the neck, the ends falling in front of the skirt; the hair white, and tied with a black ribbon at the back, turned off the face in front; no ornaments; a black bow and band of velvet round the neck. The noted dress worn at the Trianon was: A short quilted skirt; square bodice; elbow-sleeves, and train of brocade; powdered hair; large velvet hat and feathers. Another lovely dress: Pale blue satin skirt, trimmed with festoons of pale yellow lace, looped up all round with small wreaths of pale pink "pompon" roses; upper skirt of pink brocaded satin, exactly matching the roses in color, looped rather high upon the hips *à la* Watteau; square bodice of pink brocade, trimmed with the same lace as skirt and roses; tight elbow-sleeves, with falling lace and roses; hair dressed high and powdered; aigrette of pink roses and a mass of most magnificent diamonds and pearls, which were also profusely scattered over the bodice and other parts of this beautiful costume.

MARIE DE MEDICIS (*2nd Wife, Henri Quatre*, 1589–1610). Wears a full skirt of rich brocade, just touching the ground, with or without a distinct embroidered jewelled front; pointed bodice; stomacher jewelled and embroidered; large upstanding ruff coming from back of shoulder; folds of muslin and lace laid on top of bodice, meeting in front with brooch; sleeves to wrist in graduated horizontal puffs, cuffs of lace; hair turned back from face over cushion, powdered, and covered with gold dust.

MARIEE, LA, DE VILLAGE. Short white silk skirt, with blue and orange bows; blue satin apron trimmed with guipure lace; white lace cap fastened with gold pins.

MARIE STUART (*when Wife of Francis II., King of France*). The Princess of Wales, as Mary Stuart, at the Waverley Ball, wore a petticoat of cloth of gold embroidered with pearls, a dress of ruby velvet with point-lace, the bodice made with a satin habit-shirt quilted with pearls; the sleeves with a puff at the shoulders coming to the wrist; the bodice ruby velvet, the stomacher worked with precious stones; head-dress of ruby velvet studded with diamonds and pearls; veil of lisse, jewelled girdle, and fine parure of jewels. Costume worn by the beautiful Countess of Bective at one of her own fancy balls: Satin dress, front of gold brocade covered with jewels, high bodice jewelled, jewelled ruff, sleeves with puffings at the shoulders of gold brocade and red velvet; train of ruby velvet bordered with ermine, embroidered with fleurs-de-lis, etc.; white satin pointed cap of the Marie Stuart form, covered with jewels. As Schiller's heroine, Marie Stuart wears white. As Mary Queen of Scots, she is generally represented in black velvet and white satin. The velvet robe opens straight down over the satin petticoat, at a little distance from the centre; the velvet bodice is a low square over a satin quilted habit-shirt; the sleeves have one puff at top, and are straight to the wrist with lace cuffs turning upwards; a close ruff about the throat; the black velvet Stuart cap bordered with pearls, a clear muslin veil edged with lace hanging at the back; a rosary at the side, and a medallion or cross hung round the neck.

MARIE THERESA (*Empress of Austria*). Robe of gold brocade over distended hoop. Puffed elbow sleeves and a cape fichu of lace, bordered with frilling. Jewelled and embroidered train from shoulders, of purple velvet bordered with ermine. Rows of pearls for bracelets, crown and long veil, orb in hand. Or, Costume de Chasse, black trimmed with gold; red velvet waistcoat; scarlet petticoat with gold band; cocked hat and white feather; Brussels lace cravat; diamonds.

MARIES, THE QUEEN'S; viz., Mary Beton, Mary Seton, Mary Hamilton, and **Mary Carmichael,** all wear dresses of the Marie Stuart order. **Mary Beton,** the eldest, handsomest, and haughtiest, a petticoat of pale blue satin festooned with pearls; a train of white satin embroidered with gold and draped with roses; a square bodice slashed with blue; stomacher and girdle of diamonds and pearls; lace ruffles and Marie Stuart cap and veil. The laughing, roguish, irregular-featured, dark-eyed **Mary Seton,** a ruby velvet train trimmed with silver; a white satin under-skirt and stomacher, with lattice pattern of silver and pearls; and a black velvet coronet with pearls; a white veil spangled with silver. **Mary Hamilton,** beautiful, pale, dark-haired, and melancholy; a blue velvet train over a canary bodice, blue velvet slashed with canary, trimmed with gold braid and pearls; coif and veil; ruff and girdle, with pearls; and **Mary Carmichael,** a dress of cramoise satin (between crimson and plum color), with white satin petticoat, trimmed with gold and pearls, silver brocaded front; satin head-dress to match; the dress also trimmed with pearls; veil and ruff; pearl ornaments.

MARION DE L' ORME. Hair in curls, low chignon at the back. Pink satin dress, veiled with soft silvery diaphanous lisse, round waist and square cut bodice. High Medici collar, full sleeves slashed with pink; gathered skirt.

MARIOTTE (*La Famille Trouillat*). Yellow cashmere skirt with rows of black velvet; scarlet cashmere tunic; black velvet square bodice; leg-of-mutton sleeves; blue silk apron and bib; Normandy cap, trimmed with lace fastened with gold pins; long gold earrings; gold chatelaine; blue silk stockings, black shoes tied with scarlet.

MARITANA. Rich Spanish dress and veil; red satin skirt, yellow sash, and black bodice; red cap; the whole trimmed with sequins and gold trimmings; ornaments, diamonds, sequins, and corals; a tambourine carried in the hand.

MARJOLAINE, LA (*Rôle Jeanne Granier*). A short, striped brown and white petticoat, bordered with blue; high-heeled shoes, with blue bows; brown stockings; yellow tunic, lined with blue, forming a pouf at the back; a blue bodice with a double basque—one all round, one cut up in front and at the side. This bodice is laced across with brown and shows a white chemisette beneath. The sleeves are bell-shaped, and made of brown and white, like the petticoat; a coachman's white cape, with yellow revers, collars, and silver clasps, covers the shoulders; a high-pointed hat, with blue feathers; a yoke across the shoulders, with four Dutch clocks suspended, completes this dress. The other is even more piquante: a short white skirt, bound with pink; white shoes and pink rosettes; pink tunic; white apron; high jacket opening in front to show a waistcoat; both white, bound with pink and trimmed with gold; a close-plaited ruff about the throat; a white silk hood lined with pink.

MARMITON. Short skirt of brown satin; white linen over-dress and bodice with rows of red braid, cut low and edged with lace; apron, one corner tucked into waistband; blue scarf on shoulders; belt, with knife at side.

MARQUISE. (*See* LOUIS XIV., XV., XVI., and POUDRE). **Marquise, French.** Petticoat of rich blue brocaded satin, trimmed with rose point; train, ponceau velvet, rose point and floral trimmings; bodice blue satin and lace, with diamond stars; flowers, feathers, and diamond ornaments; tiara and necklace of diamonds. Hair powdered, sometimes surmounted by a black velvet tricorn hat, plume of white feathers.

MARSEILLAISE, LA. Long black skirt and Marquise coat, mousquetaire cuffs, flap pockets, two revers of white satin edged with gold; long white satin waistcoat; tricorn hat of black velvet, with tri-colored plumes, lace ruffles; tri-colored scarf knotted loosely below waist, whip in hand.

MARSETTA (*Madame l'Archiduc*). Pink satin skirt, trimmed with gold and diamonds, and white cashmere tunic embroidered in gold over pink satin; corselet with white bodice; square Italian head-dress, and veil of gold-spangled tulle.

MARTHA. Short skirt of red merino; bodice of grey trimmed with cerise and black velvet; coronet of black velvet; gauze veil. Or, cloth under-skirt, with long over-skirt caught up with girdle and satchel; long bodice, sleeves puffed at shoulder and elbows; white linen chemisette; suited to middle-aged woman.

MARY, QUEEN (1553-1558). Long pointed plain bodice, the high collar turning from the neck in double points, showing a necklace of beads and a jewel in front. The sleeves are tight at the shoulder, with a broad band of the fur descending to the knee. The large under-sleeves are slashed. A jewelled girdle encircles the waist, the front is richly embroidered and the full distinct skirt touches the ground. Over the costume is a black brocaded velvet gown trimmed with ermine and studded with precious stones. White crepe ruffs edged with gold. Coif of black velvet studded with diamonds. Long white veil.

MARY II. OF ENGLAND, 1689-1702 (*Wife of William of Orange*). Petticoat of orange poult-de-soie with medallions of black velvet, pearls, and diamonds; tunic of light blue satin trimmed with ermine and gold; bodice and sleeves to match; the former low, the front studded with jewels; manteau de cour of light blue satin bordered with ermine and gold, fastened with diamond stars; coronet of diamonds; order of the Garter.

MARY OF MODENA (*2nd Wife of James II.*), 1685-1688. Black velvet cap bordered with diamonds, diamond crown in centre; bodice of dark velvet made low; high ruff at back, a quarter of a yard deep, on wire; blue satin carried round the front and neck, the puffed sleeves slashed with it; velvet train showing satin front, worked in pearls.

MARY, MARY, QUITE CONTRARY. Pink quilted petticoat edged with colored pictures of "pretty girls all in a row," bordered with silver cord; pink satin tunic with silver bells, having garlands of cockle-shells and primroses; the bodice a low square, with long sleeves trimmed to match; satin hat with primroses, bells, and cockle-shells; silver châtelaine of spade, hoe, rake, and watering-pot; tiny watering-pots for earrings; cockle-shell necklace; mittens; high-heeled satin shoes.

MASCOTTE. Dress of cream cashmere, bodice and skirt slashed with crimson silk and gold, having epaulettes of the same, tunic embroidered with gold, edged with gold fringe, looped with gold girdle and tassels; toque of crimson and gold; vivandière's barrel and gauntlet gloves. The gipsy costume worn in the third act of *La Mascotte* is composed of a drapery of crimson and gold, shorter on one side than the other, but nowhere reaching the ground. Colored silk stockings and shoes, with sandals of gold reaching to the knee; a handkerchief of red and gold tied over dark flowing hair; tambourine; no gloves or mittens worn. (*See* BETTINA and FIAMETTA).

MASHERETTE. Black satin tail coat and skirt, with white waistcoat; black embroidered stockings; crimson silk handkerchief;

opera hat and crutch stick; high Wellington boots; shirt front; high collar; eyeglass in eye; buttonhole.

MASKS AND FACES. (*See* PEG WOFFINGTON.)

MATCH GIRL. Short costume of blue and white cotton, with low bodice of cherry-colored muslin; kerchief; hair in long plaits; muslin cap; basket with matches.

MATELOTTE. (*See* FISH-GIRL.)

MATHILDE, EMPRESS (*Daughter of Henry I.*, 1100-1135; *Wife of Henry V., Emperor of Germany*). Dress, pale blue and cream brocade; long flowing drapery of cream cashmere and jewelled girdle; head-dress of Indian muslin fastened beneath chin, and jewelled crown. (*See* PERIOD HENRY I.)

MATILDA (*Wife of William the Conqueror, of* 1100). Tunic of crimson velvet, with gold border; blue mantle; gold châtelaine; cream satin robe, with blue velvet fleur-de-lys; jewelled crown, veil; blue and gold girdle and tassels.

MARTON. Large full red stuff gown, made to touch the ground; stay bodice of the same, laced with gold, muslin kerchief tucked inside; large linen sleeves in one puff to elbow; becoming muslin cap.

MAUD, LADY (*Ages ago*). White silk petticoat; bodice and tunic trimmed with gold lace and fringe; XVth century head-dress of white satin and pearls; veil spangled with gold; red rose in bodice; diamond and pearl ornaments.

MAY, MAY QUEEN. Flowered brocade trimmed with may blossom. Or, green and white striped satin skirt, pink satin tunic, and low square bodice festooned with may flowers; a maypole, surmounted by flowers, carried in the hand; a crown of hawthorn, primroses, and marguerites, and a tulle veil. Sometimes a simple village girl's white muslin dress is worn, with floral trimmings, for this character. (*See* ROSIÈRE.)

MECKLENBURG BRIDE. (*See* GERMAN PEASANT.)

MEDEA. Blue velvet robe, bordered with gold, made in classic style; dagger in the hand; flowing hair, gold bracelet.

MEDIÆVAL. This term for fancy costumes has a very extended meaning. It is applied to almost any dress worn during the middle ages. The following are a few descriptions; Corselet and sleeves of bright red velvet, epaulettes, and plaited chemisette of pink crêpe or gauze; the sleeves tight to wrist with gold embroidered cuffs, matching the stomacher on the low square bodice, made with belt; short skirt of striped red and white silk, front breadth of gold embroidery, satchel pocket, close plaited ruff at throat; large silk or velvet hat with feathers. The German dresses of XVth and XVIth centuries come often under the category, with a low square bodice; full white chemisette; close ruff; hair in plaits; large apron; skirt flowing, but held up by girdle, aumonière bag attached; the tight sleeves puffed at shoulder and elbow with white muslin, the velvet cuff falling over the hand. Occasionally the dresses are made with bodice and skirt in one, or with long bodices coming well down on to the hips, the puffings caught down with beads.

MEDICIS. (*See* CATHERINE and MARIE DE MEDICIS, FRANCIS II., &C.)

MEDORA. Amber satin petticoat, trimmed with gold; Greek bodice and tunic of black satin; hair in plaits, round Oriental satin cap embroidered in gold, with gauze veil.

MEDUSA. Black classic dress of soft cashmere, trimmed with lizards, scorpions, and dragons; snakes in hair, and snakes for ornaments.

MEG MERRILIES (*Heart of Mid-Lothian*). Blue riding jacket with gold lace and bunch of faded flowers in front; hair clubbed like a man's, a plume of broken feathers attached; riding skirt, gloves, whip in hand.

MELNOTTE, WIDOW (*Lady of Lyons*). Plain striped grey gingham dress; black apron; short black cape over shoulders; cap.

MERCHANT OF VENICE. (*See* JESSICA, PORTIA.)

MERCURY (*Girl*). Carries caduceus. Black velvet Phrygian cap, steel ornament in front, white wings at the back, repeated on heels and at back of plaited lace ruff; white short dress with panels of jet and steel, steel sequined cuirass bodice.

MÈRE MICHEL (*French Mother Hubbard*). Gown of flowered chintz; white linen apron; check handkerchief about the neck; white muslin cap; spectacles; blue stockings; feather broom in hand.

MERMAID. Dress with low bodice of eau de Nile silk, covered with drapery of sea green tulle, and a profusion of white corals, shells, marine grass, flowers, and crystallised foam; the left shoulder of the dress ornamented with a cluster of diamonds; the right shoulder and ceinture covered with silvery iridescent gems; flowing hair crowned with coral, pearls, and diamonds, interspersed wirh pendants of seagrass. (*See* WATER-NYMPH.)

MERRY MAID, THE (*Yeoman of the Guard*). Black head-dress made like a small round cap, with the ends standing up high in front; low square black bodice with single spangles, laced with silver cord, a green ribbon edging the opening; full elbow sleeves, under-bodice and over-skirt of yellow material; the skirt arranged in accordion pleats. This over-skirt is turned back with red, black under-skirt, black shoes with silver spangles; black stockings; red, yellow, and blue ribbons from the left shoulder and right elbow, and attached to the tambourine carried in the hand; a loose gauzy scarf falls low round the hips.

MERVEILLEUSE. (*Period of French Revolution.*) Nothing can be too eccentric. Skirt of gold and spotted muslin, with gathered flounces sewn with red, and headed by crossbands; green Directoire bodice, with belt, lined with red; double sleeves, both ending in lace ruffles, the upper one coming to elbow; muslin fichu; large jabot and ruffles; enormous bouquet fastened on left shoulder; crimson satin boots; large hat trimmed with red and green feathers, fastened with tricolor cockade; snuff-box, gloves, and eye-glass; hair plaited in pigtail and tied. The Merveilleuses adopted all the vagaries of their male friends, the Incroyables—the dishevelled locks, the hair *à la victime*, hat *à la* Charlotte Corday, with tri-colored scarf tied under the armpits, stiff stocks, eye-glasses, sticks, and quaint hats stuck on the head anyhow, with trimmings protruding in all directions. The turned-down collar and the revers were also copied, as well as the dangling watches and charms. Underclothing was almost dispensed with, as well as all substantial stuffs; only muslin, organdy, chiffon, gauze, and sometimes, but seldom, taffetas, composed the narrow dresses, which were often embroidered with chain-stitch, and, for evening wear, with gold and spangles, when the robes *à l'Athénienne* were frequently opened at the side and caught up with jewels or bouquets of artificial flowers, just then beginning to re-appear. It was quite a study to slip the train in the belt gracefully or throw it over the arm. The short spencer, or *canezou*, was cut extremely low for all occasions, hence the necessity for always carrying a scarf ready to be thrown over the shoulders when required. Rows of Roman pearls and long gloves covered the bare arms, and the feet were encased in tiny slippers, strapped round the ankles with colored ribbons. Like powder, rouge had been abandoned, and blonde was the color obligatory for the hair. The following are costumes of the period: Narrow skirt of white muslin, or mousseline de laine, ornamented with chain or satin stitch; baby bodice with sash tied at the side supporting a bouquet; embroidered silk mittens; reticule of plush; large hat with soft crown and plume of feathers. Or, kilted skirt of chaudron nun's cloth, scalloped at edge and spotted with gold at every scallop; pointed panel and scarf in bengaline; plastron scarf and left side panel in blue taffetas, the two latter richly embroidered; habit bodice with long tails of pale blue satin, striped with chaudron velvet; stomacher and charm-holder of brown velvet; facings of brown corded silk; silk muslin tie, fastened below the chin in a huge bow; roses and aigrette in the felt hat and on the shoulder. Skirt of fine cream muslin slightly looped up on one side to show the foot in its satin sandalled shoe of a color matching the Directoire coat, of pale pink satin lined with colored silk and with large revers and cuffs of same color. It was cut in a low V at the throat, and filled in with an enormous jabot of soft creamy lace pinned with one or two diamond brooches; bows of different colored ribbons forming shoulder knots; the dress completed by a large white felt hat turned up in front and adorned with pink and olive feathers and diamond clasp; long cream buttonless gloves, and pink and olive reticule on arm. Or, long skirt of nun's veiling, the hem embroidered with pale blue and pink flowers; a short-waisted tail coat, pale pink brocade with revers of blue satin; large buttons, broad frills at neck and wrist; pale blue satin hat, pink and ostrich feathers standing up straight on one side; long cane in one hand and an eyeglass in the other. Or, white three-cornered hat, powdered hair, black silver tipped walking stick fastened with satin ribbon at handle.

MESSAGE, SPECIAL. Powdered hair and cocked hat. Long green satin skirt. Marquise coat with gold brodequins fastening over a flowered waistcoat. Lace tie. Epaulettes formed of loops of ribbon. Gauntlet cuffs and flat pockets. A staff in the hand with a letter attached.

MEXICAN. Short skirt of black and red, with scarf of many colors wrapped round the head and falling on dress. Much gold about the costume; gold sequins, chains, etc. Or, long yellow trousers, opening near the feet on the outside of the leg, and showing a plaiting of muslin beneath; the bodice comes low in the neck, opens on the shoulder, and is embroidered all round in black; a colored scarf is wound about the waist, a round hat on the head; short skirt. (*See* appendix for MEXICAN BOY.) **Mexican Gipsy.** Black satin vandyked skirt, with red satin scarf knotted at the side, and red satin bodice covered with sequins; red satin head-dress and Mexican ornaments.

MICAELA (*Carmen*). Short white cashmere skirt, bordered with a band of blue; blue over-skirt, trimmed up the front; low square bodice, with grenat velvet, revers bordering white stomacher; white linen head-dress, fastened with gold pins, and flowing at the back; muslin cap. **Micaela** (*Le Cœur et la Main*). Short striped red and yellow petticoat; three red tunics above, matching red stay-bodice, cut square at the neck; large straw hat; wreath of flowers.

MI-CAREME. Wears a domino with half black mask, striped pink and white dress with elbow sleeves.

MIDNIGHT. Black tulle, with owl's feather trimming, and silver stars on one shoulder. (*See* NIGHT.)

MIDSUMMER NIGHT. Electric blue satin edged with a ruche of silver gauze, and scarlet poppies at intervals, draperies of blue tulle above, covered with silver stars, drawn up high on one side, with a wreath of poppies: low bodice trimmed with gauze, silver and poppies, epaulettes of blue ribbon edged with silver; bat wings are attached to the back, the veinings outlined with silver cord, the extreme points of the wings attached to silver bracelets; head-dress, bat's head and diamond stars; blue band round the throat, with diamonds; black gloves and stockings; blue satin shoes, diamond buckles; a fan of silver tinsel tied with blue ribbon.

MIDSUMMER NIGHT'S DREAM (*Shakespeare*). (*See* TITANIA.)

MIGNON. The beggar-girl wears a loose grey cashmere dress, with girdle round the waist and hanging sleeves; bare feet and sandals; hair flowing on shoulders. After Scheffer's picture: Peasant's skirt of brown woollen material; cream-colored bodice, blue posy in her belt; 2nd dress; Page's costume of blue velvet; 3rd dress: White silk Watteau trimmed with pink.

MIGNONETTE. Short quilted satin petticoat of palest yellow, with narrow brown braid between the diamonds; pale olive-green brocaded bodice and tunic, the bodice high, turned back at the throat to show the lining of light brown, and laced down the front with brown cord, over a chemisette of pale yellow satin; the tunic has the corners turned back to show the brown lining; plain white kerchief round the throat; hair in a knot at the back; mittens; light brown silk stockings, and high-heeled shoes with buckles; a bunch of mignonette to fasten the kerchief at the side of the hair, and another bunch in an old-fashioned basket on the arm.

MIKADO. The Three Little Maids wear robes so close-fitting that they materially interfere with the free action of the feet and legs; very wide sashes defining the waist, and at the back forming huge bows. Each dress is flowered and embroidered all over. **Yum-Yum** appears in a deep fraise ecrasé shade; **Pitti Sing** in white and gold, and **Peep-Bo** bluish green. Their hairs are dressed in the loops and bows associated with Japan, thrust through with tiny fans. **Katisha,** an elderly lady in love with Nanki-Poo has an elaborate dress in same style, two shades of terra-cotta, almost hidden with gold embroidery.

MILK GIRL. Bodice and skirt of some woollen fabric with tunic; a check woollen kerchief crossed over the neck, and tied at the back; white apron with tucks at the edge, and large pockets on either side; large poke bonnet of straw trimmed with blue ribbons, yokes on the shoulders. Or, a sage green skirt; nasturtium Pompadour polonaise, short sleeves; muslin kerchief and mob cap; and carries the orthodox pail.

MILKMAID. (*See* "MY PRETTY MAID.")

MILLER'S DAUGHTER. Similar dress to Milk Girl, without yokes, in white trimmed with gold. Sometimes for this and **Miller's Maid,** the dress is of white sateen, and worn with powdered hair.

MILLER'S WIFE. Striped woollen skirt with laveuse tunic of plain color; low striped bodice with white sleeves; toy windmill on the top of muslin cap.

MILLINER, WHITE (*Comedy by Douglas Jerrold*). Full skirt of soft white lawn, over-skirt opening in front, caught up in a pouf about the hips; large lace-edged apron with a bunch of white ribbons on one side; pointed bodice laced in front, cut square, with elbow sleeves, fichu and ruffles; high white cap; a white velvet mask edged with lace.

MILLIONNAIRE. (*Same as* MONEY.)

MINNA AND BRENDA TROIL. (*See* BRENDA.)

MINERVA. Tall helmet; hair powdered with gold, and studded with diamonds; red and white classic dress.

MINUETTE. Powdered hair; flowered skirt with large paniers; pointed bodice, elbow sleeves; a cane carried in the hand. This is the costume generally worn for this popular dance.

MIRANDA (*Tempest*). White cashmere dress, bordered with silver, the skirt gathered on to the long cuirass bodice, cut square at the neck, with hanging sleeves, a satchel pocket at the side; silver coronet and veil.

MIRTH, QUEEN OF. Rose-colored skirt, white satin front, and low V-shaped bodice, trimmed with bells, crocuses, shamrocks, and butterflies (emblems of mirth); jewelled coronet and veil; a sceptre surmounted by a butterfly; rose-colored shoes.

MISS MUFFET. Cerise quilted satin petticoat; chintz bodice and tunic trimmed with gold lace; muslin fichu and mittens; spider in large mob cap; a spider embroidered on net apron; bowl and spoon.

MIST. Grey tulle, scattered over with dewdrops; square bodice, and sacque of grey satin, grey shaded tulle veil of the same fastened in powdered hair and to front of bodice, with diamonds; grey shoes, gloves, stockings and fan; diamond ornaments.

MISTLETOE. Crimson satin skirt, sprayed all over with mistletoe; bodice of cream satin veiled with yellow green net; crimson cap with wreath of mistletoe; crimson shoes and stockings; wand of enamelled wood, decorated with mistletoe and ribbon streamers.

MISTRESS OF HOUNDS. Black velvet huntsman's cap; long double-breasted red cloth jacket; short skirt, high riding boots, hunting crop in hand.

MOLDAVIAN PEASANT. High white chemisette fastened with cherry ribbons; corselet of same color, trimmed with lace and embroidered in gold; large muslin apron over short dark skirt; hair plaited with cherry-colored ribbon.

MOLLY MALONE (*Widdy Malone*). Red and blue flannel costume, made like an Irish peasant's, but with a wheelbarrow embroidered on the side of tunic. (*See* COLLEEN BAWN and IRISH POTATO GATHERER.)

MONEY. Dark brown skirt, on it a row of bank-notes printed on white satin; white satin tunic, with purse-shaped pocket and *£ s. d.*

embroidered on it; gold-colored satin low bodice, with long sleeves of gold-spangled tulle; a long netted crimson silk scarf, with a tassel and steel rings at either end, slung round the waist; a satin cap of white, brown and gold satin covered, as is the entire dress, with sequins. (*See* COINS and GOLD.)

MONTE CARLO. Dress, red satin and black velvet and lace, with front of green baize printed with numbers; one shoe red, one black; skirt short, fringed with coins, and trimmed with cards; pointed coronet of red satin, with aigrette of cards on shoulder; croupier's rake carried in hand. (*See* ROUGE ET NOIR.)

MONTESPAN, MADAME DE. Long full plain pink satin skirt, woven with gold; bodice of the same half high, pointed back and front; low fichu folded above and fastened with jewels in front; large puffed sleeves to elbow, slashed horizontally; hair in curls, just touched with powder and sewn with diamonds. Large single brilliant necklace linked with pearls; violet velvet train from shoulders, bordered with gold and pearls.

MONTHS. (*See* JANUARY, FEBRUARY, MARCH, APRIL, MAY, JUNE, JULY, AUGUST, SEPTEMBER, OCTOBER, NOVEMBER, DECEMBER.)

MOONLIGHT, MOONSHINE, MOON, LUCENA QUEEN OF THE MOON, LUNA, CLAIRE DE LUNE. A silver-spangled white (or blue) tulle dress, over white satin; a mantle of the same, bordered with silver lace, attached to the shoulders of the low bodice; an electric star in centre of white and silver scarf twisted round the head, fastened either with diamonds or with silver crescents, which must be introduced on the shoulders, front of the bodice, and skirt; white satin shoes with crescents; silver ornaments. Dark grey and silver is another pretty combination for the character. **Moonshine,** black tulle, with a basque bodice of silver brocade; the tunic edged with delicate fringe of crimped silver, looped at one side with a large star; the head-dress, a close-fitting turban cap of silver brocade, with a narrow fringe of crimped silver; long black gloves, with bands of silver tissue or brocade, about an inch wide, at equal distance; black fan with silver sticks. **Moon,** a dress of soft white silk, trimmed and bordered with brown velvet cut in vandykes, three-quarter moons in gold cloth or yellow silk appliqué on the velvet plastron of the low bodice, and on the short sleeves; blue scarf round waist, edged with gold; gold and silver-spangled tulle round neck;

small silver-spangled cap with a bunch of arrows, surmounted by crescent, on one side. Or, a dress trimmed with moonlight tints on grey and silver; and an electric star in hair. A blue gauze dress, or sometimes green, may be worn. **Moon, Queen of, Lucena.** Pale blue silk skirt; tunic of fire-colored gauze; velvet bodice surrounded by galon and gold crescent; diamond on head; a wand with moon and signs of zodiac carried in the hand.

MOORISH. Maize satin petticoat, embroidered with black; ruby velvet jacket opening wide to show plastron entirely covered with gold embroidery, short sleeves, with long lace ones below worked in gold; velvet shoes to match, embroidered in gold; Moorish embroidered sash; gold coins and red silk scarf in hair, fastened with jewels; Algerian ornaments, bead necklace and bracelets, large earrings; hair in plaits, surmounted by high Moorish head-dress made of white linen bordered with gold.

MORAVIAN PEASANT. Short cotton skirt, dark apron; white full bodice, open in front, sleeves to elbow; low velvet bodice fastening with one button; hair covered with dark silk handkerchief having fringed ends. **Moravian Woman of the XVIIth Century.** Ruff of fine lawn plaited and edged with lace; sleeves puffed to elbow, confined by a velvet band above the elbow; lace ruffles. Head-dress: a gold, embroidered silk scarf, the same at wrist; embroidered velvet bodice high to throat; gay colored petticoat, showing ankles.

MORGAN LE FAY (*King Arthur*). A ruby velvet cloak, with a border of gold applique embroidery inside and out; gown of cloth of gold, heavily jewelled; jewelled bands in hair.

MORGIANA (*Forty Thieves*). White Eastern dress with bands of pale grey, almost covered with sequins; red drapery with gold embroidery; small red head-dress; hair in pendent plaits.

MORNING. Dress of grey dewdrop tulle; a bird on one shoulder; veil of dew spangled tulle; grey shoes and hose; grey fan. Or, skirt bordered with grey, pink and blue tulle flounces and draperies of the same at the back, with paniers of pale grey looped with long bows of ribbon, grey, pink, blue and yellow; grey satin bodice trimmed with draperies of the colored tulle; a large pink rose covered with dew drops on one shoulder; the hair powdered and dressed high with butterflies quivering over it, and a tuft of dew-laden roses; long grey gloves with rosebuds and streamers attached; fan of real flowers veiled with dewdrop lace; pearl ornaments. (*See also* NIGHT and MORNING.)

MORNING STAR. (*See* STAR.)

MOROCCO. Silk trousers, embroidered open jacket ending in jewelled short narrow gold-spangled satin skirt; belt, coins; head-dress and striped veil of gauze in color.

MOSS ROSE. (*See* ROSE.)

MOTHER EARTH. (*See* EARTH.)

MOULIN À VENT. (*See* WINDMILL.)

MOUSSE. Sailor's hat lined with blue. Black velvet jacket trimmed with gold lace and buttons, worn over a white satin waistcoat, large black silk bow in front; the upper-skirt cardinal silk bunched up at the back, displaying the white satin petticoat in front, striped with pale blue satin and edged with narrow lace; pale blue stockings, cloth gaiters, and patent leather shoes.

MOYA. An Irish girl; costume of silver-watered tissue covered with water-lilies and water-plantain; on the head is a large water-lily, with silver grass and weeds hanging down, over the flowing hair. In the hand a long reed, from which hang aquatic weeds.

MUCH ADO ABOUT NOTHING. (*See* BEATRICE.)

MUETTE DE PORTICI, LA. Short blue petticoat bound with light maize; a muslin apron, a Roman scarf about the waist; a low blue stay bodice, with shoulder-straps trimmed with gold braid, and worn over a white muslin chemisette, with long sleeves; square Roman head-dress, fastened with coral pins, coral ornaments.

MUMMERS. These are part of the ancient sports at Christmas-time dating from the time of Edward III. Women wore the horn head-dresses and light green gowns with pendent sleeves lined with silver tissue The long hanging sleeves were cut in quaint vandykes, a girdle marked the junction of bodice and skirt, and the pointed shoes were of velvet covered with a gold lattice work. (*See* EDWARD IV. PERIOD.)

MUSCADIN. White satin waistcoat; maroon satin coat with gold buttons; white satin skirt draped with blue bows, showing petticoat of striped Pompadour satin; open-work stockings, maroon shoes, blue bows, gilt heels; conical cap of silk beaver with roses and blue flowers;

directoire eye-glass, gnarled stick with gold knob; powdered periwig; lace cravat.

MUSE DE LA POÉSIE. (*See* POETRY.)

MUSES, 9. (*See* THALIA.) All wear classic dress (*see* illustration No. 7) with their several emblems. Clio presides over History; Euterpe, Music; Thalia, Comedy; Melpomene, Tragedy; Terpsichore, Dancing; Erato, Poetry; Polyhmnia, Rhetoric; Calliope, Epic Poetry; and Urania, Astronomy.

MUSHROOMS. Pale cream silk dress, trimmed with moss and mushrooms. An aigrette to correspond in the hair, or a cap fashioned like a mushroom.

MUSIC. White satin dress trimmed round the edge with tulle and black velvet, to represent the keyboard of a piano, and above this two rows of notes and lines formed with velvet and buttons; a scarf draped across the skirt has the treble and bass clefs on the fringed ends; the low bodice has winged sleeves, a lyre on the shoulders and in front of the bertha, the same in the centre of the coronet, and on the white satin shoes. Two sisters might appear as Music and Painting. (*See* PAINTING.) Or, soft dress of crêpe de Chine, classic gown, the bodice low and full, fringed with gold; belt embroidered with ivy leaves along the top, the same carried round the pendent sleeves from elbow: head-dress a crown with golden bars lined with blue; a lyre carried in the hand. (*See* CECILIA, ST.)

MY COLOR BOX AND PALETTE. Short cloth skirt with landscapes painted on it, a tunic of coarse linen with paint tubes and brown satin ribbon; the tubes carried as a fringe all round, with alternating shells of gold paint; brown velvet jacket with white muslin shirt; a cord round the waist with palette and knife; old point lace collar, tan gloves; head-dress made like a flat cap.

MY PRETTY MAID. (*See* MAID, MY PRETTY.)

NAIAD. White tulle gown trimmed with silver and water lilies. (*See* WATER NYMPHS.)

NANCE REDFERN. (*See* HUBBARD, MOTHER.)

NANCIEBEL, LADY. Sage green velvet skirt, caught up on left side with gold girdle, showing primrose under-skirt; plain square cut bodice, a jewelled galon round opening; velvet cap with heron's plume; peacock fan.

NANCY LEE. Blue and white striped petticoat; blue or red skirt, looped up with a large silver anchor; full bodice, or blue cloth jacket, with sailor collar; red apron, trimmed with yellow; white cap; red handkerchief over it tied under chin; blue stockings, black high-heeled shoes. Sometimes a black tarpaulin hat is worn with "Nancy Lee" upon it.

NANCY OF THE VALE (*Shenstone*). Olive green silk dress, with a large bunch of daffodils on the short-waisted bodice; narrow skirt. Poke bonnet with yellow ribbons; a reticule hanging from the arm.

NAPOLEON I. (*Time of*) 1800–1815. Narrow pink robe covered with gauze festooned at the hem with garlands of pink roses. Pink silk sash trimmed with silver. Stiff wreath of roses and silver leaves. Veil studded with rose petals. Pink gloves and shoes. Waist short; skirt narrow.

NATIONAL DRESSES. (*See* the Various Countries.)

NAUTCH GIRL. (*See* INDIA.)

NAVARRE. (*See* ISABEL.)

NAVY. Dark blue satin bodice, double-breasted, with gold epaulettes and gold buttons. Black satin skirt trimmed with gold braid and a tricolored sash. Cocked hat.

NEAPOLITAN ORANGE GIRL. Black satin short skirt, hemmed with a yellow band, long green silk apron fringed with red and embroidered with red and yellow silks; low square sleeveless black velvet bodice, worked with yellow, and laced over a chemisette of white batiste; white puff to sleeves from shoulder, the rest velvet, tight to arm; square Italian head-dress striped, colored beads round neck **Peasant Girl.** Pink silk skirt with claret velvet at hem; white silk apron striped horizontally with many colors; claret velvet bodice with pink revers over low-cut waistcoat to match, crossed with gold pins; tambourine in hand. (*See* ITALIAN.)

NEEDLES AND PINS. This dress is after the Mother Hubbard order. (*See* HUBBARD and WORKBOX.) A quilted skirt, with chintz train; low black velvet bodice, fichu; powdered hair; cap and pointed velvet hat. In front of the dress every kind of needle and pin is inserted, forming the motto: "Needles and pins, needles and pins; when a man marries his troubles begins."

NÉGLIGÉ DRESS, 1791. Petticoat and sacque of brocade, with ruffles; pointed shoes; feathers and pearls in powdered hair; mouche on cheek and chin. A négligé is often made of muslin, trimmed with lace, and looped up with ribbons over petticoat.

NEGRESS. (*See* AFRICA.)

NELL GWYNNE. Long pink skirt, with blue tunic; low bodice; full puffed sleeves, slashed at shoulder; hair curled and confined by pink ribbon; low muslin fichu about the shoulders, the ends tucked into the front of the bodice. Or, blue satin skirt draped with brocade; black velvet bodice with the Nell Gwynne hat having loops of satin ribbon; blue stockings and shoes. She is accompanied by a pet lamb.

NEPTUNE, MISS. Cuirass bodice like fish scales; green and silver gauze skirt, all trimmed with shells and seaweed; trident in the hand; a cap fashioned like a fish.

NEWHAVEN FISHWOMAN. (*See* FISHGIRLS, &C.)

NEWSPAPERS. (*See* PRESS.) Bonnet de Paris made in white satin; skirt of the same, with printed headings; a sheaf of papers in the hand.

NEWSPAPER STALL, A PERAMBULATING. A short low bodice of vieux rose silk, and short skirt with newspapers of all kinds attached; an aigrette of paper in the hair; the hanging sleeves formed of newspaper.

NEW WOMAN, THE. (See Illustration, Fig. 29.) She wears a cloth tailor-made gown, and her bicycle is pourtrayed in front of it, together with the *Sporting Times* and her golf club; she carries her betting book and her latch-key at her side, her gun is slung across her shoulder, and her pretty Tam o' Shanter is surmounted by a bicycle lamp. She has gaiters to her patent leather shoes, and is armed at all points for conquest.

NEW YEAR. In the garb of a fairy; wand in hand, bearing the date; a calendar on the front of skirt.

NEW ZEALAND. Dark violet gown with white striped sleeves, bordered with Mongolian goat; feathers in the hair, and a coronet with the constellation of the Southern Cross; wand in the hand.

NICKLEBY. (*See* DICKENS.)

NICOTINE, LADY. Tabac colored velvet and scarlet satin gown, trimmed with cigarettes and cigars; crossed pipes on the shoulder and in the hair.

Fig. 29.—NEW WOMAN.

NIGHT. A long black tulle dress with pendent sleeves; spangled with silver stars and crescents, silver crescent ornaments, silver belt; a crescent on the head, and long crescent spangled veil; a silver wand, with crescent at the top; an owl on the shoulder; black fan, having moonlight scene painted on it. Black gloves, black satin shoes and crescents. With stars only, instead of crescents, this is suitable also for **Evening Star,** or **Starry Night.** A more original dress for Night is a black tulle, with a bouillonné of blue tulle at the edge, trimmed with silver stars; a train of bluish-black satin studded with silver stars and comets; a pale gauze scarf representing the Milky Way; stars seen through it; on one side the constellation Orion; the veil attached to the shoulders by a nightingale and the red berries of the deadly nightshade, surmounted by a bat with outstretched wings. This is sometimes called **The Trailing Garments of the Night.** Or, dark blue tulle over satin, with silver stars dotted all over the bodice, trimmed with shimmering silver fringe; a silver band round the head, and a crescent moon in front; a long blue tulle veil, with stars of various sizes; a dark blue fan with silver sticks, and a moonlight scene painted in white and grey; ornaments, silver stars. **Queen of the Night.** Sapphire blue velvet, studded with silver poppies and bordered with silver fringe in the form of rays; a fringe round the waist of sapphires and diamonds; the head-dress an enormous plume of sapphire blue feathers sprinkled with silver, the hair thickly studded with diamonds; and an enormous black tulle veil enveloping the figure, fastened to the shoulders like wings. **Night and Morning.** Bodice and short dress of velvet and white satin, one-half completely black and the other white; stars and moon on one side, on the other the rising sun in gold embroidery. White and black stockings and shoes; black velvet and white satin cap. **Night and Day.** Powdered hair, the dark purple and pure white feathers fastened in their place by a diamond star; the bodice half dark purple satin, and half white; on one shoulder a bouquet of small stars each one illuminated with the electric light; the skirt, alternate draperies of purple and white satin; on the panel which represents day a clear sky is embroidered, and a sun in gold, with clouds in faint rose-color and lilac, bordered with gold; on the dark purple draperies, for night, a crescent moon and clusters of stars are embroidered in silver. One glove and one stocking purple, the other two white; the shoes also are alternately white and blue, with diamond stars upon each foot.

NINETEENTH CENTURY, EARLY PORTION OF. (*See* VICTORIAN.)

NOAH'S ARK (*as worn at the Empress Eugenie's Fancy Ball*). Toy Noah's Ark on head, with two little silver animals running into it up the parting; long white dress with silver animals in pairs, round; a dove of promise on the shoulder.

NORMA. (*See* DRUIDESS.)

NORMANDY PEASANT, NORMANDY BRIDE, NORMANDY FISH-WIFE. The peasant's dress consists of a bright-colored petticoat, striped or plain, with rows of black velvet; tunic drawn through the placket-hole, or the side-breadths sewn together at the back, so that the inside of the skirt is visible; the tunic should form a contrast to the skirt, such as blue over red, violet over amber. The bodice terminates at the waist, is close-fitting, and has only a shoulder-strap, the linen sleeves having a wide band, coming below the elbow. If this is worn over a white chemisette, it is plain in front; if a muslin lace-edged fichu is worn, it is laced across the front, with colored cord. A gay-colored cotton kerchief may be tucked into bodice, and a large holland pocket worn. In the real Normandy caps there is a great variety, and these are handed down from generation to generation. Two shapes prevail for Fancy Balls, one such as "Evangeline" wears, resembling the Foundling cap, made in thick muslin, with a high crown, low at the back, a shaped piece fitting the head in front, and lappets at the side, like a hound's ears, bordered with lace, a bow at the top, and fastened on with gold pins; the other, a full-dress cap, stands up above the forehead some 12 inches, terminating in a point of 3 inches broad. This upstanding crown is covered with rows of lace and bows of ribbon, and to the top at the back a voluminous lace-edged veil is attached. Large gold earrings and cross, colored striped stockings, and black shoes with colored bows and heels complete the costume. It can be carried out in silks, woollens, and cotton. **A Normandy Fishwife,** in addition, carries a basket of fish at her back, and has a net round her waist. **A Normandy Bride** would wear a white muslin skirt, trimmed with white satin, the apron bordered with swansdown; a blue silk bodice and tunic; a muslin fichu, and high cap, with white flowers. Another variety is the **Cauchoise.** Short petticoat of red satin; square bodice and tunic striped blue and white, the sleeves puffed to wrist. Apron and Cauchoise cap, trimmed with Mechlin lace. The latter high and pointed; the lace fulled on in rows interspersed with red bows. Gold cross and earrings; blue striped stockings; black high-heeled shoes.

NORNAS. The two Scandinavian Sisters who sat round the Ygdrasdil tree; one in a robe of pale green Indian silk, made with a high bodice and full long sleeves; the hem worked in silver, with Runic characters; belt of silver; hair floating, mistletoe wreath. The other sister in the same costume of different coloring, mixed with gold.

NORTH AMERICAN INDIANS. (*See* INDIANS.)

NORTH POLE. Short blue skirt edged with swansdown, the front painted with ships and icebergs and the rising sun. The hanging sleeves and bodice bordered with swansdown and crossed with blue ribbon. A white pointed felt cap bordered with swansdown. Hair powdered, a sceptre in the hand surmounted by a ball and star. Pearls and crystals are introduced on the dress. A small white bear appears on one shoulder, and a large muff in the hand.

NORTH STAR. Black silk gown and tulle veil all spangled with silver stars. (*See* STAR.)

NORWEGIAN PEASANTS, NORWEGIAN FISH-GIRL, NORWEGIAN BRIDE. The peasant woman wears red stockings and black shoes; a short black skirt, striped with red and green; the sleeveless jacket bodice, made of scarlet cloth, terminates in a silver belt, trimmed with green and silver; it has a low red cloth stomacher one mass of silver and beads; a long-sleeved white linen chemisette high to the throat, with an all-round collar, is worn under it, fastened with a silver brooch, and festooned with silver. A large white linen apron reaches almost to the hem of the skirt, and has a band across it of red and green embroidery. The head-dress is of white linen, hiding the hair in front like a fez, and has a pendent point and tassel. The hair hangs down the back in long plaits. Norwegian silver ornaments. **The Norwegian Bride.** (*See* Illustration, Fig. 30.). Stuff gown; white apron and under-bodice; red front magnificently embroidered; nuptial jewelled crown, veil, and ornaments. The **Norwegian Fish-Girl** has a net round waist.

NOURMAHAL (*Lalla Rookh.*) Short amber satin skirt trimmed with blue and gold; amber satin bodice studded with jewels. Or, a pelisse, with bodice and narrow tunic in one, over short skirt; transparent pendent sleeves; blue and gold sash and cap; the hair plaited and entwined with pearls; white full gold-spangled trousers; white and gold slippers; feather fan. Blue and red, or red and green, may be used instead of amber and blue.

NOVA SCOTIA. Skirt of red bunting draped with scarves of red, blue, and yellow, made of Surah silk fastened on with burgees; low bodice edged with gold; a blue ribbon with Nova Scotia embroidered in gold, crossing from shoulder to waist; aigrette of red and yellow ospreys; fan of red, blue, and yellow silk; long Suède gloves tied with red ribbon. This is suitable to a nautical fancy ball.

NOVEMBER. Short kilt pleated grey chiffon skirt over yellow; yellow ribbon coming from beneath the arm tied in a bow in front with a bunch of many-colored chrysanthemums. A deep kilted frill of the material turns downwards from the neck, forming a bertha; two frills below the sleeves; chrysanthemums at the side. A bonnet of the same, crimped, chiffon tied under the chin. Or, a fashionable evening dress of grey tulle to resemble a November fog.

NOVICE. (*See* ABBESS.)

NUBIAN. Dress of rich coloring, red and yellow, with the hair almost hidden by a colored handkerchief twisted about it; an Egyptian harp carried in hand; many coins and beads for jewellery; the sleeves are sometimes long, sometimes short; the bodice is a mere drapery; sometimes a sleeveless jacket is worn over all.

NUMBER, CHRISTMAS. (*See* CHRISTMAS.)

NUN. (*See* ABBESS.)

NURSE. Embroidered muslin cap with ribbons and round crown; striped gingham gown made with high bodice; large muslin lace edged apron; striped stockings; peau de Suède shoes. (*See* AMBULANCE.)

NURSERY RHYMES. Pointed black hat with the names of Jack and Jill or any other nursery heroes or heroines round; black silk stockings, high-heeled shoes, a crutched stick; short skirt of plum-colored silk and plenty of white frilling beneath; round it, effigies of a see-saw, a cat and fiddle, sheep, dogs, or anything associated with nursery lore; bodice of blue velvet cut as a low square with a muslin fichu, a skipping rope round the waist. For the characters from the Nursery Rhymes and for the **Singing Quadrilles** *see* **Jill** (J), **My Pretty Maid** (M), **Bo-Peep** (B), **Mary, Mary, quite Contrary** (M), **Red Riding Hood** (R), **Mother Hubbard** (H), **Cinderella** (C), **White Cat** (W), **Babes in the Wood,** and **Beauty** (B), &c.

NUT-BROWN MAID. Dress of cream-colored nun's veiling, looped and puffed in the old English style; knots of satin ribbon; pointed bodice of pink brocade trimmed with blackberries; Leghorn hat with nuts, blackberries, and loops of ribbon.

NYMPH (*see* WATER NYMPHS.) Dress of silver cloth with coral epaulettes, and silver coronet in the hair; seaweeds and grass introduced on the skirt and low bodice.

OARSWOMAN. Crimson flannel short skirt, trimmed with bands of velvet; brown tunic, caught up high on hips; blue bodice, with revers, and blue and white striped waistcoat, elbow-sleeves, white plaiting round; straw hat, with poppies at side; black shoes, blue stockings; oar in hand.

OCEANEAN GIRL. Head-dress of dark blue and light shaded straw; bodice of red and white striped silk; Swiss belt of red velvet; skirt of dark blue with bead embroidery.

OCTOBER. This is generally rendered after the manner of autumn with trimmings of leaves variegated with all the rich reds and browns of the autumn tints, and with chrysanthemums. A classic cream dress would show such trimmings to advantage. Or, an evening gown of cream and gold satin introducing acorns, with the leaves applied to dress and head-dress.

OCTOPUS. (*See* FISH.)

ODALISQUE. Red slippers; red silk trousers; short embroidered skirt; scarf of many colors, tied round hips; black corselet bodice, embroidered in pearls, half high; white and gold chemisette, with sleeves fastened by silver buttons to elbow, thence falling low on skirt; cap of silk, with crescent and aigrette; plenty of amber beads and ornaments; feather fan in hand.

OLD CLOTHES. (*See* CLOTHES.)

OLD FASHIONED GIRL. Long full skirt of soft silk or muslin; short waist; low bodice made full, short sleeves with just one puff; sash round waist; cap of white muslin, plaited at the edge, cut up at the back; a bow of ribbon in front.

OLD WOMAN WHO LIVED IN A SHOE. (*See* HUBBARD and SHOE.)

OLD WOMAN WHO SWEPT THE SKY. Red cloak; witch's

hat; broom in hand; high pointed bodice with ruff and bunched up chintz skirt.

OLD ENGLISH DRESSES suitable for bazaars and other occasions consist of sateen or quilted satin petticoats; silk brocade or cretonne over-skirts and bodices, laced in front; muslin fichus, aprons, and caps. (*See also* WATTEAU, EARLY ENGLISH, POUDRÉ, &C.)

OLDEN TIME, LADY OF. A favorite character generally carried out by a *poudré* costume, as follows: Quilted satin petticoat; brocaded tunic pinned together at the back; a low velvet bodice laced across a white stomacher; muslin kerchief about the neck; hood and wimple. Or, blue and white flowered tunic or sacque over long cerise skirt; stomacher and low bodice trimmed with blue and cerise, lawn ruffles; powdered hair over cushion, with roses and pearls. (*See* WATTEAU.)

OLD LADY IN THREADNEEDLE STREET. A chintz skirt bordered with bank notes and reels of cotton, an aigrette of bank notes forming an epaulette on the low chintz bodice with a muslin fichu. A tall black hat trimmed with sovereigns, and at the back a couple of needles joined with thread.

OLIVETTE. Tunic of black and gold-spangled satin; over-skirt of blue satin with coral front; black scarf, and pocket embroidered in gold; velvet bodice worked to match with blue, stomacher of gold brocade: blue stockings, black shoes and mittens; gold sequin ornaments; large collar lined with black velvet and edged with gold beads; gold filagree head-dress and necklet. Or, as the Bride, in white satin embroidered with silver beads; Zouave jacket and high collar; small pointed cap with orange blossoms and feathers. (*See* BATILDE, COUNTESS OF.)

OLIVIA (*Twelfth Night*). Long over-dress bordered with gold, having a distinct front breadth; the bodice a low square, pointed at waist, with close-set loops round the point; jewelled buttons fastening the bodice in front; a basque at the back; a ruff comes from shoulder to shoulder, made of a plain piece of muslin edged with pointed lace, not plaited; the slashed sleeves have epaulettes and cuffs, and are puffed to the wrist; a jewelled coif is worn on the head; the hair rolled off the face; a veil floating at the back.

OLIVIA PRIMROSE. (*See* WAKEFIELD FAMILY.)

OLYMPIA. Satin dress, made with close-fitting low bodice bordered with a broad band of embroidery, which goes round the skirt; full sleeves to the wrist, with lace; costly jewels.

ONION SELLER. A peasant dress with white apron and fichu, red handkerchief knotted round the head and a tall basket filled with onions.

OPHELIA *(Hamlet).* Long plain skirt of white cashmere, one end caught up in the girdle, thus forming a lap filled with poppies, corn, cornflowers, catkins, pansies, forget-me-nots, and marguerites; the bodice low and full, with long pendent sleeves, the whole trimmed with rows of silver braid and fringe; the fair hair hangs over the shoulders entwined with flowers; a wreath on the head, and a lisse veil studded with flowers; white satin shoes. It may also be carried out in silver tissue or white silk; long plain brocaded silk bodice opening heart shape, sleeves tight to wrist, puffed to elbow; hair flowing, wreaths of flowers on the head, and on the side of dress caught up with girdle and puffed round waist. As Ophelia, Miss Terry wore a costume of pale pink cashmere, bordered with ermine, cut in V-shape at throat, the skirt draped. Second dress: White satin bodice, studded with pearls; missal suspended from girdle, with string of pearls.

ORACLE DES CHAMPS. (*See* FLOWERS.)

ORANGE GIRL. (*See* NEAPOLITAN.)

ORANGES AND LEMONS. A light blue tulle evening dress, or two shades of yellow, with bunches of oranges upon it, a wreath of orange blossoms having an orange at the side; orange and lemon leaves round the bodice. This offers an opportunity to a recent bride of wearing her bridal wreath once more. Fan with oranges painted on it; basket of oranges and lemons in hand; lemon-colored shoes and gloves. Two sisters might dress the character as follows: White satin dresses over yellow; powdered hair; one trimmed with lemons and foliage, the other with oranges; the leaves arranged as paniers, with clusters of fruit depending, the fruit forming a cap, with the stalk upwards and leaves round; large fan of yellow gauze. Two shades of yellow are sometimes employed for this dress, if the person represents the two fruits.

ORCHARD. An evening dress of light pink and white tulle, trimmed with apples and pears, fruit and blossoms, walnuts and leaves, plums, &c. Or, sacque of brocade with old point, and apples, plums, and pears, &c.

ORIENTAL LADY, EASTERN SULTANA, EASTERN QUEEN, LIGHT OF THE HAREM, &c. All these are rendered with loose silk trousers to ankles; a short satin skirt; and a sort of paletot of satin with pendent sleeves in bright colors, much betrimmed with gold and sequins; the hair in plaits; a round cap on the head. A jewelled aigrette in front. The following costumes are effective: **Eastern Sultana, or Light of the Harem.** Petticoat of white satin embroidered in gold, gold and white trousers to ankles; paletot of crimson striped silk, embroidered with gold and lined with green silk; long sleeves, and white satin ones beneath; Indian gold and white scarf round the waist; yellow-pointed shoes; white satin cap embroidered with pearls; gold jewelled coronet; white muslin veil. **Eastern Dress.** Yellow silk veil confined by gold coins; amber and claret skirt; claret velvet paletot trimmed with amber and much gold; gold sequins and amber beads for jewellery. **Oriental Lady.** Tunic of crimson Dacca muslin; trousers of white muslin spangled with gold; short crimson silk skirt and jacket, the stomacher covered with pearls and jewels; sash of cloth of gold; turban of the same entwined with crimson cashmere; embroidered slippers; gold spangled veil.

ORIENTAL AMAZON. High satin boots, richly embroidered; over this a short kilted skirt of light blue satin; tunic of silver cloth, caught up with a half moon. White metal cuirass, bordered with gold, and draped with aiguillettes; sabre and sheath hang at side; short satin sleeves caught up with crescents; helmet and plume draped in front with blue satin, crescent in centre, surmounted by an aigrette.

ORPHAN GIRL (*Soldiers' Home, Hampstead*). Red stuff skirt and bodice; white muslin tippet, cap and apron, medal suspended at neck. (*See* AMSTERDAM.)

ORTRUDA *(Lohengrin)*. First dress: white flowing skirt trimmed with gold, and velvet over-dress, with cuirass bodice, buttoned on hips; jewels, crown, and veil. Second dress: loose robe of velvet, square cut, long sleeves falling from elbow; silver grey scarf of cashmere about head.

OSTRICH. Ostrich all white and black feathers; an arrangement of plumes at the waist counterfeits the train; head-dress, the bird's head.

OWL. (Rendered as in Illustration). Suitable for a little boy. Brown untanned shoes and flesh colored stockings, the bodice covered with the lighter colored feathers; the wings from the shoulders in one with the cap formed of the head of the bird, eyes and all of the darker tone. An owl is also represented arrayed in brown velvet and satin; white tie; cap like owl's head.

OX-EYED DAISY. (*See* DAISY.)

OYSTERS, QUEEN OF. Dress of white tulle, studded with oyster-shells, coral and seaweed; wreath of same round the low bodice.

OYSTER-WOMAN. Skirt of bright lemon color with fringes of seaweed and coral, which border the tunic and bodice; the latter having revers of lemon satin. The epaulettes are formed of lobster claws and seaweed; the same in the hair. Oyster knife at side. Sometimes this is rendered as a fishwife, with white linen bibbed apron, red handkerchief tied about the head, a basket at the back.

OYSTERS AND CHAMPAGNE. Oyster shells sewn over the skirt. Head-dress formed like a champagne bottle, a cordon of corks on the shoulders.

PACK OF CARDS. (*See* CARDS.)

PAINT BOX. Skirt of dark brown satin with squares of color. Palette fan. Hair fastened with a palette knife.

PAINTING. White skirt with small pictures in water-colors; full bodice, large puffed sleeve with bands over the shoulder. On the top of the sleeves a bundle of brushes. A hat fashioned like a palette with different colors; feathers thrust through the thumb hole, and other feathers peeping over the brim. Or, classical robe of light drab cashmere, low full bodice and belt, short sleeves cut in vandykes, fastened with buttons on outside of arm; long train from shoulders lined with blue, palette and brush on one side; a crown of bay leaves on the head. (*See* ART.)

PALETTE. (*See* PAINTING above, and MY COLOR-BOX AND PALETTE.)

PALMYRA, QUEEN OF. Antique costume of blue satin, trimmed with silver embroidery and ermine; train of sapphire velvet lined with blue satin, bordered with ermine. Jewelled belt, pointed diadem in hair, massive bracelets.

PAMELA. Richardson's heroine wears a black dress, with elbow-sleeves, and white cambric ruffles; a cambric fichu crossed over the front of the bodice, and fastened behind; the hair turned up under a small cambric mob cap, with black ribbons. The dress is sometimes looped over a quilted petticoat. The novel was published in 1741, so the dress is of the last century, and by no means costly, for Pamela was of humble origin. Black high-heeled shoes, silk stockings, and mittens complete the costume.

PANSY. Short light peach crepe de chine dress trimmed with deep rich-colored violet pansies, one large one forming the head-dress, the petals standing well round the head, like a brim; the bodice made of dark petunia velvet, arranged to simulate the flower, the soft peach crepe de chine draped with pansies; a fan in the shape of a pansy. Or, dress of amber-colored soft silk, trimmed with purple bands, outlined with gold; loops of purple and amber-colored ribbons on the top of the sleeves; head-dress in the shape of the flower; white bibbed apron, embroidered in purple; a gold basket of heartsease carried.

PAON. (*See* PEACOCK.)

PAQUERETTE (Easter Daisy). Short upper skirt of white tulle, green satin beneath, with large leaves; gold satin corselet; large collar of the petals of the flower; an aureole of white flowers tipped with gold in hair.

PAQUITA *(Giroflé Girofla)*. Blue and white-striped stockings, blue satin shoes, with high heels; short skirt of blue and white-striped silk, upper skirt of white silk, cut in vandykes, bound with blue, and draped gracefully over the skirt. The low bodice, as well as the upper skirt, is trimmed with gold braid, and over the low bodice is a sleeveless senorita jacket of blue cashmere, bound with gold, having a ball fringe of gold; the silk forms a puff for the short sleeves, with straps of blue over it; head-dress, a white muslin veil attached by a bunch of roses.

PARCEL POST. Conical cap with tinted frills; face the color of brown paper, with red tape tied at the chin. A ruffle of small parcels round the neck. Red skirt covered with small boxes. The word

"Parcel" on a large label fastened to the chest. More parcels round the waist bearing the words "Paid Registered," "Carriage Free," "This Side up," "To be kept dry."

PARR. (*See* CATHERINE.)

PARROT. A yellow gown with cuirass bodice and cap of green feathers like a parrot's head, two long feathers forming the tail on the skirt; the rest of the dress green satin, with wings at the side formed of feathers.

PASQUINETTE. Bodice and sleeves made high; half red, half gold satin, with rosettes down the centre, a wide turn-down frill at the throat, made of lace; skirt of the same, interblending with a pouf all round the waist; one stocking red, one gold, shoes also; high gold-colored hat with red spots, and rosettes of the two colors mixed in colored ribbons.

PATCHWORK. Short skirt and low bodice *à la Vierge*, of patch-work, cut in large diamonds, with alternate black and yellow dividing the other colors; the hair is powdered, and pompons of ribbon of all tints are introduced upon it, as also for the rosettes on the shoes.

PATIENCE. Dairymaid costume, plain skirt flowered chintz tunic, bunched up over contrasting petticoat; low square bodice laced in front, short sleeves; muslin fichu tucked in at waist; holland colored apron; large straw hat, wreath of flowers under brim; carries a water or milk-pail.

PAULINE *(Lady of Lyons).* In first scene: A soft blue cashmere dress, waist beneath the arms, skirt soft and clinging. Silver clasps and buckles. In Act III.: White satin short waisted bodice and skirt, train bordered with cascades of cream lace studded with pearls. The front of skirt and bodice old gold satin with silver clasps and chains of pearls falling in the front of bodice. White mittens. Act V.: Flesh colored satin over-dress, under-gown of pink lisse; the over-dress united by festoons of pearls carried across the front. There are no sleeves, but bracelets are worn below the shoulder. The bodice is filled in with rows of lisse. Three rows of pearls round the neck.

PAVANE. Those who take part in this dance wear Elizabethan costumes, ruffs, puffed sleeves, pointed Marie Stuart coifs, jewelled girdles, hoops, and rich stuffs.

PEACE. A flowing dress of white tulle with loose low bodice, and winged sleeves, trimmed with swansdown, blush roses, lilies of the valley, and bands of silk embroidered with olive leaves; a belt at the waist with pearls, intermixed with the embroidery; the tablier tunic is caught up with olive leaves and holds a couple of turtle-doves. In Paris this dress had the tablier also embroidered with the sentence, "Paix aux hommes de bonne volonté." Flowing veil and olive wreath completes it: It has also been rendered as follows: Dress of pale blue and silver brocade, trimmed with wheat-ears, forget-me-nots, and fruit; a bird's nest with eggs, and silver wheat-ears in the hair; an olive-branch carried in the hand. A white satin banner may be borne, with the word "Peace."

PEACOCK *(Un Paon).* A dark green or lemon-colored tulle dress, bordered with rows of peacock-eye feathers, headed by gold twist; bunches of the feathers are arranged on either side, and bands of the feathers round the train, the skirt draped with crepe; the same bordering the low satin bodice, feather epaulettes; the tail, like a large fan, takes the place of a ruff from behind the shoulders, and the head and neck of the bird form a cap, gloves with gauntlets; bands of peacock's feathers; dark green stockings, green satin shoes with feather rosettes.

PEAR BLOSSOM. (*See* APPLE BLOSSOM.)

PEARL. Pearly white evening dress of gauze over satin; nautilus shell head-dress; pearl ornaments.

PEA, SWEET. (*See* Illustration Fig. 42, SWEET PEA.)

PEASANT, THE COQUETTISH (*La Belle Poule*). Short, striped blue and white skirt, and long jacket bodice, fitting the figure to perfection. It has long sleeves, all trimmed with bias bands, and is cut heart-shape, very open at the neck; a lace-edged fichu over, with a bunch of flowers in front; short draped tunic, and waistcoat of plain blue; coquettish straw hat, with blue ribbons. This is one of many charming French costumes which require to be thoroughly well made; blue stockings and high-heeled shoes with blue rosettes are worn with it.

PEASANTS. (*See* the VARIOUS COUNTRIES.)

PECHEUSE. (*See* FISHER GIRLS.)

PEDESTAL AND LAMP. (*See* LAMP.)

PEDLER (*Woman*). (*See* GIPSY.)

PEG WOFFINGTON (*Masks and Faces*). First dress: Black sacque of figured brocade open at the sides, quite untrimmed, the bodice cut low back and front with a muslin lace-edged fichu over it; the dress skirt beneath of blue figured gauze, and a large black hat trimmed with blue worn with it. Second dress: A red and grey brocaded sacque, quite distinct from the low pointed pink bodice and front breadth, the sacque made very full and low at the back, with elbow sleeves; a round pink wreath accompanies this. Third dress: Brown and maize satin similarly made, the brown sacque caught up on either side of the skirt with large brown and maize rosettes. Or, over-dress of green brocade, pink petticoat, elbow-sleeves, mittens, and kerchief, the ends terminating at the waist and cuff. Peg Woffington is generally represented with a flowered skirt, caught back with colored ribbons, showing a distinct front breadth; a square pointed bodice, and sometimes a lace apron; a large muslin fichu, edged with lace; elbow-sleeves and lace ruffles; and either a lace cap or a straw hat pressed in towards either side of the head and tied under the chin; mittens on the hands. For outdoors, she wears either a hooded scarf or a long mantle and hood. Mrs. Bancroft, as Peg Woffington, wore (first dress) body and train of sea-green, the train lined with paler green showing at the sides; under-skirt of neutral green with three flounces, each headed by puffings; the bodice came well down on the hips, was cut in tabs in front and square at neck, with fichu of lawn and jet; a brocaded sacque fastened to the shoulders; green hat, trimmed beneath the brim with rows of black and white lace. Second dress: Low square gown of silver brocade with high ruff at back and long train; short sleeves with large cuffs of gold-colored satin, and three rows of soft lace below; under-skirt of gold tissue trimmed with Venetian point, and bunches of buttercups and paste ornaments; small stomacher to match; a garland of sunflowers across the skirt relieved by bows and two long tassels of bullion on the bodice; a spangled fichu with gold fringe; head-dress of cream feathers and gold aigrette. Third dress: Sacque of flowered crimson silk looped over a deep red dress with train; broad belt of scarlet fastened by a diamond buckle to match the shoes; hair raised over a cushion and a lace cap tied with black bow under chin, flowers introduced between the hair and lace of the cap; train, full; sleeves, short and tight with fall of lace over elbow. Peg Woffington, in Smallfield's "Old Actors," wears an over-dress of green brocade, pink petticoat, elbow sleeves, and mittens and kerchief, the ends terminating at the waist. Mrs. Bernard Beere dressed it with a curled wig, large hat, long trained princess dress with tabs at the side of bodice; large stick in hand.

PENELOPE (*Wife of Ulysses*). Ancient Greek costume. Long loose dress of white cashmere, trimmed with silver braid in Greek designs, and bullion fringe; over this is the chitonion, a sort of jacket joined on the shoulders, plaited back and front, and falling in points on either side, completely covering the bodice, and hiding the waist; it is bordered with the same braiding, a silver tassel at each point; the diploidon, or flowing cloak, of cashmere, covered with silver stars, is draped from the shoulders; a silver fillet round the head, the hair in a coil at the back; sandals; gold and brown combine well for this dress.

PENWIPER. Short dress and bodice of red and yellow cut in points like a Folly costume; everywhere edged with steel pens. The cap of gold quills. A fan embroidered with gold quills.

PEPYS, Mrs. Green satin dress, with pale pink front of satin, bodice with square tabs at waist, ornamented with pink bows, large pink slashed sleeves; large linen collar edged with point lace; pink shoes; hair in curls with strings of pearls, pearl necklets and bracelets.

PERDITA (*Winter's Tale.*) Shepherdess dress, crook carried in hand, entwined with blue ribbons and roses; short blue skirt with two festooned flounces of silver gauze caught up with roses; tunic of the same; bodice low, and trimmed as a stomacher; wreath on head. Or, as worn by Miss Leclerc for the character: A full white skirt coming just below the knees, trimmed with a blue border of the Greek key pattern; a full low bodice with short sleeves, edged with the same; a blue ribbon girdle; white stockings, and blue shoes, laced across; a wreath of wild flowers on the head, a spray hanging loosely from one shoulder across the bosom, and a crook with wild flowers carried in the hand.

PERI OF OCEAN. (*See* WATER NYMPH.)

PERICHOLE. Skirt of peacock blue; loose jacket of black velvet trimmed with gold sequins; Roman sash; Indian kerchief head-dress; scarlet stockings; gold, silver, and amber necklet and armlets.

PERRINE. Pointed shoes; full lace-edged trousers to ankle; lace bordered short skirt; low bodice, short sleeves; scarf crossing bodice with ball fringe; high hat.

PERSIA. The women wear clinging draperies; the bodice, cut in one with the skirt, fitting the figure closely, made half high, the sleeves tight to the wrist, and armlets over them above the elbow; jewelled girdles round the waist; a sort of coif on the head, with a gold-spangled veil of some soft fabric, the hair loose or in plaits on the shoulders. Oriental-looking satin or cashmere, bespangled with silver crescents and stars, are most appropriate; ornaments of coins and beads. **PERSIAN PRINCESS.** Green satin skirt covered with gold; a black satin bodice and tunic bordered with gold; crêpe lisse fichu beneath, and corselet of cloth of gold; coif, and gold-spangled veil; scarf round waist.

PERTH, FAIR MAID OF. (*See* F.)

PERUVIAN. The hat, senorita jacket and the many colored scarf tunic all edged with ball fringe. Short red satin gown.

PESCHARD, MADAME (*La Branche cassée*). Short striped black and white skirt; blue cashmere tunic, bunched up; long embroidered yellow apron, with bib; a blue low square bodice over linen chemisette and loose sleeves, terminating above elbow. The distinguishing point in this costume is a large white cashmere hood worn on the head, showing the hair, a bunch of roses in front and at the side attaches it to the dress. A spade carried in the hand.

PHARAOH'S DAUGHTER. A soft woollen under-dress drawn in at the waist, cut as a low square and bordered with embroidery. Triple row necklace of beads, the sleeves caught up and showing bracelets above and below the elbow entwined with pearls. A trained over-robe of brilliant coloring falling at the back and brought up in a folded end on the bust with a large Oriental brooch. The head encased in a helmet-shaped metal cap with a falling veil to the shoulders of Oriental brocade bordered with sequins.

PHILIPPA OF HAINAULT. Blue velvet train trimmed with ermine, fastened in front with jewelled clasps; ruby velvet bodice with ermine carried down the front in a double row; a girdle of precious stones about the hips; the front of the dress embroidered with the arms of the family, on gold and silver tissue; a veil hangs at the back; a jewelled coronet on the forehead, terminating in two large circles of gems about the ears. (*See* EDWARD III.)

PHILIPPINA WELSER. Married 1550, when seventeen; famed for beautiful complexion. Bodice of black velvet, very high at throat, with linen ruff; sleeves filled in high to shoulder, bordered with fur; handsome jewels round neck; plain skirt, embroidered in front; hair turned off face, set in jewelled coif and coronet.

PHŒBE (*As You Like It.*) Shepherdess costume of grey cashmere, with bunch of flowers on side of bodice; kerchief, large full leg-of-mutton sleeves; pointed Phrygian cap; leather shoes.

PHŒBE MAYFLOWER. Short skirt of satin, tunic and bodice of chintz laced across the front; muslin sleeves to wrist; apron, and becoming muslin cap with ribbons to match the costume.

PHEDRE. A full skirt touching the ground in yellow satin embroidered in gold of barbaric splendour. The loose bodice is part of it, and it is fastened on the shoulders with jewelled brooches. Over this is a purple velvet mantle richly embroidered with gold falling as a train at the back and passed under the left arm to the right shoulder. Heavy gold band bracelets above the elbow and at the wrist. Etruscan gold necklace and a gold coronet pointed in front and studded with jewels.

PHOTOGRAPHY. A green gauze dress; round the skirt, nestling in the bouillonnés a row of photographs; a scarf of the silk draped across the skirt, with medallion photographs at intervals, all bordered with green galon; the bertha of the low bodice fastened at the front, back, and on the shoulders with them; a cap in the form of a camera; a snapshot carried in the hand.

PHYLLIS. (*See* IOLANTHE.)

PICARDY, PEASANT OF. National head-dress—a broad silk ribbon gaily embroidered, ruched with muslin on top and bottom, and stretched over a shape of cardboard; white chemisette with a broad-belted and embroidered bodice of black velvet over it, black velvet braces, sleeves to elbow. Red or blue petticoat, bordered with gold or silver leaves; lace trimmed white apron and striped stockings.

PICTURE LAND. Skirt and bodice white satin printed with the designs from toy books; A-B-C on the box-plait in front. Powdered hair; an aigrette of colored printed cards; a screen fan of the same.

PIEDMONTESE PEASANT. (*See* BETTINA.)

PIE VOLEUSE. (*See* MAGPIE.)

PIERRETTE. Dress of black and white satin; the back of skirt black, the bodice opens heart-shaped over a lace chemisette, and a wide plaited frill stands out round the throat; another at the waist; the bodice and front of skirt white satin; a black skull cap surmounted by white hat with two red feathers; one black and one white stocking; long white gloves. For a little child the character is often represented with full pink silk knickerbockers, a double skirt of white surah, with blouse to match, fastened diagonally with pompons, same on sleeves; ruff round throat; pointed felt hat with rows of pink velvet round, each secured with a pompon.

PIGEON. (*See* CARRIER.)

PILGRIM. Brown woollen habit reaching to the feet, a cord round the waist, sleeves to wrist; cape, and hood; cockle-shells on cape and on broad-brimmed low-crowned hat; staff surmounted with cross or gourd; sandalled shoon.

PILLAR POST. Long red satin dress; white satin placard bearing V R and hours of collection printed on it; head-dress, square cap, the same form as top of letter-box.

PILOT FLAG. A black tulle skirt and low bodice with a couple of flags draped on the sides, the handles crossing half-way down, made of navy-blue silk, two smaller ones on the bodice, two in the hand and two in the hair.

PINAFORE, H.M.S. Josephine and Hebe wear fashionable morning dresses; the Sisters, Cousins, and Aunts appear in yachting dresses with striped cotton skirts; serge blouses, sailor collars, tarpaulin sailor hats. Little buttercup in an old-fashioned straw bonnet, cotton gown, and black and red shawl pinned across her shoulders.

PINCUSHION, DOLL. Full skirt made of muslin and lace, two deep gathered flounces; plain plastron down the front with steel beads of good size to represent the pins. The bodice has an edging of these pins at the neck and waist; on the right-hand side is a heart-shaped pincushion filled with pins. A coronet of pins.

PIRATES OF PENZANCE. The daughters of Major-General Stanley appear in costumes of bright coloring, made in the fashion of fifty years ago—short flounced skirts, short-waisted bodices with muslin fichus, short sleeves, long mittens coming well above the elbow, reticules hung from the arm, and either poke bonnets or very large hats, with a bunch of roses clustered on one side. This carried out in white satin, pink roses, bright heliotrope or claret, would be effective and picturesque. **THE PIRATE MAID OF ALL WORK. Ruth:** Head-dress of red drapery and coins; red and black short skirt, with much gold trimming; low black gold-bedizened bodice, and gold armlets, with chain of sequins from the shoulder to wrist. **Mabel:** Short pleated skirt; tunic bordered with frilling, bunch of flowers at side; fichu, short sleeves, reticule at side; huge hat and feather. **Kate:** Similar dress without tunic.

PLANETS. White satin short skirt, bordered with a blue silk band and dotted with silver stars; white gauze over-skirt and plaited low bodice bespangled with stars; long wing-like sleeves to match; blue satin Swiss belt cut in points, a star on each; blue coronet with stars; long veil with stars; necklace and bracelets of the same.

PLAYING CARDS. (*See* CARDS, and QUEENS of different suits.)

PLENTY, GODDESS OF. White classic dress, white silk with wreaths of vine-leaves, wild flowers, and fruit; the same in the hair. (*See* GREEK and CLASSICAL.)

POCAHONTAS. Crimson velvet dress; bright colored scarf to match; skirt and bodice covered with beads, coins, and bangles of glass and brass; hair in two long plaits falling on each shoulder; beads strung as thickly as possible round neck; long bead earrings; richly embroidered leggings, Indian work of porcupine quills; feather head-dress.

POETRY. A rich classic dress in light blue and black satin bordered with precious stones; a lyre carried in the hand. Or, under-skirt of blue satin bordered with gold cord, and embroidered with gold in front; black satin train worked with gold lyres; cuirass bodice of amber satin, bordered with a black gold-embroidered band, studded with precious stones; a crown of gold wheat-ears, long gold-spangled tulle veil.

POLAR STAR. (*See* STAR.)

POLICHINELLE. White satin short skirt, striped with crimson, trimmed with gold; tunic half blue and white, forming two ends at the back, bordered with gold fringe and bells, and entirely covered with gold spangles; low bodice of red and white, with basque, trimmed with gold fringe and bells; a blue and white cocked-hat over powdered hair; a fool's bauble carried in the hand. Or, as follows:—Three skirts of alternate black satin and gold tissue, cut in points, a bell at each, surrounded by gold fringe; high bodice of black satin, with a gold diamond-shaped plastron; hair floating on the shoulders, surmounted by a cap; and bells of gold tissue; a bauble carried in the hand, in the form of a small doll dressed in the same way.

Fig. 31.—POLISH COSTUME.

POLISH. The costume in the Illustration, Fig. 31, is white satin with a blue polonaise worked in silver, bordered with swansdown; Polish cap; hair in plaits. **A POLISH PEASANT** at a fancy ball is very unlike the denizens of that country; the correct dress would be a striped woollen skirt; a scarlet bodice laced in front, and trimmed with yellow, over a high white chemisette, with long sleeves; and for a bride, a cap with as many ends of ribbon of all the colors and widths as can be procured, replaced on less gala occasions by a cotton handkerchief folded first cornerwise, then the double-edge turned back twice, about 3 inches broad, and tied behind; a flower stuck at the side. A fancy dress Polish costume is as follows: A plain blue short dress, trimmed with minever; a yellow bodice with tight sleeves like a habit-bodice, with Brandenbourgs in black across the front; the Polish cap edged with minever. This cap is a distinctive feature of the costume; it is square at the top, and hard and stiff, the four sides diminishing in size where they rest on the head; the hair should hang in long plaits beneath it. A beautiful **Cracovienne** dress would be a short blue silk skirt, with a wide band of silver fox fur round the edge; tight-fitting jackét of blue satin, with long hanging sleeves lined with rose color and trimmed with ermine and brandenbourgs; a puffing of white silk passing through the open front of the jacket, fastened tightly round the throat with a band of the same fur; small Polish square cap made of blue satin, bordered with fur; large diamond aigrette and feather wing on one side; hair powdered and dressed high in front with plaits falling to the waist at the back; long bronze boots, with gilt heels and fur tops (*see* POLISH.) **Polish Princess.** Short skirt of white satin trimmed with gold braid, over-skirt of red satin trimmed with gold and swansdown; low jacket bodice and hanging sleeves of black velvet trimmed to match; the bodice, open in front, is filled in with gold braid; black velvet Polish cap, with gold braid and swansdown; white satin boots with black stripes. **Polish Snow.** White silk bodice and short skirt cut in one, bordered with swansdown, and covered with tufts of swansdown; Polish cap. **Polish Skating Dress** of pale blue and crimson velvet; trimmed with gold lace grebe fur. **Polish Hussar.** (*See* HUSSAR.) **Polish National Dress,** as worn near Cracow: Head-dress called Konfederatka, made of red or blue velvet, rim of fur, with gold or silver ornaments at the side, flat crown; sleeveless bodice of same material and color as the cap, trimmed with gold, or silver, or fur, fastened in front under white bodice gathered to the throat; lace-edged sleeves, with bow of ribbon; skirt of colored chintz, with band of velvet; linen apron embroidered with cross-stitch; boots to ankle.

POLLY PUT THE KETTLE ON. Rose-colored skirt to the ankles; flowered tunic, with rose bodice trimmed with white muslin, rose and green ribbon; cap to match; silver kettle earrings; a kettle hung at the side, with a kettle-holder worked with the name of the costume, and surmounted by grey poppies; black mittens; muslin apron, or chintz sacque; muslin kerchief and cap.

POMONA. Either a classic dress or a white evening gown trimmed with fruit; fruit on head; a basket of fruit in hand.

POMPADOUR, MADAME, 1744. The name of this beautiful, graceful, talented mistress of Louis XV. calls up visions of powder, brocade, ribbons and laces, ruffles, plumes, long-pointed waists, and rich embroidery. A pretty costume of hers is as follows: Long embroidered skirt of white satin, with pink rosebuds and silver leaves; tunic of pink brocade; long-waisted, pointed bodice, open in front, laced across, with a stiff and narrow stomacher; sleeves to elbow, terminating in ruffles. Sometimes the upper-skirt is open, and forms a train over an under one, covered with embroidery. Silk, satin, and brocade are suitable. It is with pink and blue combined that she is most associated. The hair should be dressed high over the forehead in numerous small curls, like a *pouf à la neige*, and be ornamented with feathers, pearls, and roses.

POMPEIAN LADY. White woollen skirt, with Grecian border worked in purple; purple chitonian joined on the shoulders, plaited back and front, and falling in points on either side and trimmed with gold lace; hair bound with a fillet, handsome Etruscan ornaments. (*See* ANCIENT GREEK DRESS, and PENELOPE.)

POODLE. Skirt of black tulle covered with small ruches to represent the curly coat; corselet bodice of black velvet. Silver bracelet on the right arm; a collar of red satin ribbon. The hair frizzed; a couple of black velvet ears lined with pink silk at the side.

POPPY. Short skirt of red satin, upright poppies and small buds worked from the hem upwards, a fringe of poppies at the foot; bodice of red crêpe, cut like poppy petals, each sleeve simulating the flower; large poppy on the head; small poppies for ornaments; long gloves, a poppy worked on each. Sometimes it is rendered with red tulle and huge poppies; a poppy for cap.

PORTIA *(Merchant of Venice)* wears either a brocaded over-dress like an academical robe and cap or biretta, wig and bands; a loose black silk under-robe beneath, with scarf about the waist, having tight sleeves; or a loose over-robe of black brocade, collar standing up, slightly pointed, the arms thrust through a wide aperture. The robe opens in front; this is the dress worn by Miss Ellen Terry. Or, a train and square-cut bodice of white or colored satin, over a gold embroidered petticoat, a gold embroidered pouch hanging at the side; velvet tiara trimmed with pearls, or a white satin pointed coif, with gold cord, the hair frizzed and turned off the face, and hanging over the shoulders in curls; a girdle is worn round the waist, a feather fan carried in the hand; the sleeves are large and hanging, over under-sleeves puffed from shoulder to wrist. Miss E. Terry's first dress in this character was a gold-colored brocaded skirt, flowing, and held up one side to show an embroidered petticoat; pointed bodice outlined with jewels, low at neck, with ruff from shoulder; sleeves one puff to elbow and tight to wrist, laced outside. Her last dress was a pink satin petticoat, gown of ruby brocaded velvet on a pink ground, a pink veil secured on either shoulder by a jewel.

PORTUGUESE. Short dark skirts of green or claret; low waist-coat of velvet to match, buttoning down the front with a double row of bright gold buttons; scarf and pocket of velvet going round the hips; a habit-shirt of muslin about the neck, over this a red and yellow handkerchief tucked into the bodice, and bound on the upper edge with red; large slouch felt hat, red or green to match the dress; a half-hand-kerchief pinned to the back to keep off the sun. A more usual fancy dress is a red cashmere skirt trimmed with a deep band of black velvet, grey embroidered over-skirt caught up on either side of the front breadths with a band and bow of black velvet; white silk apron trimmed with embroidered bands and gold; a colored silk handkerchief about the head; gold Portuguese earrings and necklet. **Portuguese Orange-Girl** carries a basket of oranges. **Portuguese Gitana.** Short white satin skirt, with alternate stripes of scarlet and gold; scarlet velvet low bodice, laced and trimmed with gold; a black gauze scarf, the ends fringed with gold, and embroidered in red, tied round the head;

gold chains from short sleeves to wrist; white satin shoes with gold trimmings; gold ornaments.

POSTAGE, POST-OFFICE. Short white satin dress and high bodice; on the skirt the different rates of postage, times of posting, names of the several mails; flowers for the hair made of postage stamps; scarves of different colors on the dress, denoting the mail-bags; enamelled postage-stamps for jewellery.

POSTWOMAN, RURAL. Short red silk skirt with black velvet panels; blue silk blouse bordered with red embroidery on white; small upstanding collar lined with red and white. A red tie loosely knotted. Short full sleeves, wings on the shoulders. Letter satchel on the hip. Blue cap lined with red and trimmed with a small wing.

POSTMISTRESS. Short white satin kilted skirt; red cloth or satin coat, white satin waistcoat; cocked hat; high black boots; satchel of letters carried at side.

POSTILLIONNE. Costume of white satin, ornamented with a military braiding in gold passementerie; epaulettes and cap to correspond; the hair powdered and tied at the back with black ribbons; this would look equally well in pale blue satin, ornamented with silver.

POT-AU-FEU. Steel colored satin dress strung with all kinds of vegetables; black velvet bodice to simulate a saucepan, handles form the epaulettes to the sleeves; head-dress like the lid of a saucepan, all trimmed with vegetables.

POUDRÉ COSTUMES. Powder was adopted pretty well throughout the XVIIIth century by the upper classes in England and France, so that with any costume of that time, not worn by the lower orders, powder is admissible. It was the powder tax imposed by Mr. Pitt in 1795 that sent it out of fashion in England. The following are some pretty poudré costumes: Short blue satin skirt, a Watteau tunic of old brocade, the Watteau plait double, and attached to the bodice only at the neck; the bodice itself pointed, a muslin fichu bordering the square-cut neck; the sleeves to elbow finished off with ruffles; on one side of the powdered hair, a black velvet hat, the brim turned up, and edged with pearls; a bunch of roses under the brim. **Betty, My Lady.** Quilted petticoat; tunic of velvet or brocade; long, pointed, low bodice; powdered hair with pearls and rosebuds; mittens; high-heeled shoes. **My Lady Coquette,** a scarlet satin petticoat; tunic of blue and white striped satin, with flowers between the stripes; scarlet ribbon and white feathers worn in the hair. Pompadour necklace of red roses and blue ribbons. For an elderly lady: Black brocaded sacque, with a large design in gold and feuille-morte; elbow-sleeves and deep ruffles, with robings of pale-colored ruches, opening over a quilted petticoat; old lace and diamonds; the hair powdered. For **Poudré Balls,** ladies sometimes wear powder with evening dress; the gentlemen generally on these occasions have white waistcoats and buttonholes. (*See* Illustrations, DRESDEN CHINA, DUCHESS OF DEVONSHIRE, ENGLISH PEASANT, GEORGE II., GEORGE III., COURT DRESS, Period LOUIS XVITH., MARIE ANTOINETTE.)

POWDER-PUFF. Short waisted bodice; skirt put in with full gathers, made of white, pink, or blue satin, edged with swansdown; the skirt should look as much like the upper part of a puff as possible, and be drawn in just above the feet; shoes, long gloves, sleeves, and bodice are all trimmed to match; earrings and necklace, small powder puffs; circular fan made like a puff; cap of white satin like the top of puff.

PRECIOSA. Double skirt of pale blue silk, the lower embroidered in silver, with pendent silver coins, the upper one covered with a network of silver braid, coins, and tassels; low pointed bodice over waistcoat of silver lace; Roman sash round the waist, with dagger; a tambourine hung at the side; pale blue stockings; black shoes with satin embroidery; necklets and sequins; a blue handkerchief about the head covered with sequins.

PRECIOSILLA (*La Forza del Destino*, Verdi). Short blue skirt with black border, embroidered in silver and gold stars, vandyked at edge; yellow over-skirt, bordered with gold fringe; light blue bodice with gold buttons; short puffed sleeves; senorita jacket of black velvet, trimmed with gold braid and fringe; sash of grenat silk with gold fringe; red velvet cap, bordered with gold.

PRESS, OR NEWSPAPERS. Made entirely in newspaper; the skirt consists of box-plaited illustrations from the papers, reaching to the waist, with names of newspapers pasted across here and there; the bodice made with bertha to match, and bows of scarlet velvet; quill pens, an ink-bottle and sealing-wax stuck in the hair. In Paris the same idea was carried out with a white satin dress, having bands of velvet, bearing the names of Paris papers; a bonnet *de police.*

PRIMROSE FAMILY. (*See* WAKEFIELD, VICAR OF.)

PRIMROSE. Dress of pale green tulle; primrose satin bodice, bordered with moss and primroses; wreath of primroses and grass falling over the hair at the back; small primroses mixed with lace round neck and wrist; green satin shoes, with tufts of moss and primroses on instep; primrose-colored gloves, edged with moss; fan of primrose satin; or, the green bodice cut in a point at the top, and filled in with a kerchief of primrose gauze, fastened with bunches of the flower; skirt of primrose crêpe de Chine with a surah scarf. Wreath of primroses, or cap in form of primrose, stalk at top; primrose gloves and fan.

PRIMROSE LEAGUE, DAME OF. Gown of light primrose tulle, the words, "Peace with Honour" in violets, and monogram of league united, "P.L.," on one side; badges of league on bodice, and as many primroses as possible; primrose gloves; fan, painted primroses.

PRIMULA, EVENING. Mauve dress, trimmed with primulas.

PRINCESS (*Characters from Tennyson's Poem*). (*See also* IDA.) The **Princess Ida,** a classical white robe trimmed with gold. **Lady Psyche,** black velvet hood and tunic over pink skirt. **Lady Blanche** in the same, with grey hair and a crimson brocaded silk skirt. **Melissa,** green tarlatan dress and veil.

PRINCESS IN "FORTY THIEVES." Short white satin skirt, embroidered all over with pearls, and cut in tabs at the edge; between each tab appears a frill of white lace; a scarf of twisted satin, blue and red, is tied over the hips, and from beneath it there are large tabs of brown satin embroidered with brown beads. The white satin cuirass bodice is made long, powdered all over with jewels; a sky-blue and deep-red satin scarf is tied under the arms; the same round the head; ornaments, diamonds and jewelled flies.

PRINCESSE DE CONDÉ. Long white satin robe, the front entirely covered with silver paillette embroidery and numberless small tassels; bodice cut in a low square in front; high ruff, edged with pearls and pearl chains from the points all round the back of the dress; short sleeves, with lace hanging over the arms, and pearl fringes. Hair powdered, and dressed in small curls, with magnificent diamonds intermixed and introduced round the neck and on the front of the dress.

Fig. 32.—PURITAN.

PRINTEMPS. (*See* SPRING.)

PRISCILLA, THE PURITAN MAIDEN (*Miles Standish*). Short black or light grey stuff gown, made in the old style, with tippet, cuffs, apron, and mob-cap of clear white muslin; the over-skirt, which is tucked under, is the same as the skirt; black stockings and shoes, with small buckles. The bodice is quite plain, save the tippet, but it has an all-round untrimmed basque. Or, after the painter Elmore, red striped skirt, green-colored kirtle and bodice; long sleeves; bodice low; sleeves turned back with linen; Puritan cap; linen tippet.

PSYCHE. Loose white dress; low full bodice and belt; silver wings; hair in classic coil.

PULCHINELLE, PUNCHINELLA. (*See* POLICHINELLE.)

PUMPKIN. Head-dress simulating the pumpkin; the bodice potato color trimmed with carrots, parsnips, radishes, cabbages and brocoli. The skirt made like a mushroom. Shoes and stockings green.

PUNTING. Blue skirt with three rows of gold round, and anchors at intervals. Over-skirt draped to the waist with an anchor at the right side. White full bodice, tiny blue senorita jacket and cap; red cap and punting pole.

PURITAN (*as worn in the quadrille at Marlborough House ball*). Long grey satin dress, with three rows of black velvet; round, black velvet, silver-mounted bag hanging at the side. The bodices were made with square basques at the back, and cross-cut gigot sleeves to wrist. Muslin tippets, pointed back and front, were fastened with black velvet bows; white muslin caps trimmed with lace. Another Puritan costume would be a black velvet, or grey or black satin, or stuff dress, with plain skirt to ankle; plain bodice, cut V-shape, with a neatly folded muslin kerchief, plain elbow-sleeves, long muslin apron; square-toed shoes, tied with ribbon, high heels; muslin cap, high-crowned, with plain front. Out of doors the hood with cape attached is sometimes surmounted by a black-pointed hat, like the Welsh. Illustrated in Fig. 32. (*See* ROSE STANDISH, DRESS OF PERIOD 1640, and ALICE BRIDGENORTH.)

PUSSY. (*See* CAT.)

PYRENEAN PEASANT. Scarlet short petticoat, blue skirt, looped up with scarlet and gold; black velvet bodice, trimmed with gold lace; scarlet cap.

QUADRILLES. A marked feature at most Fancy Balls is a specially arranged Quadrille. The choice is a large one. The list includes:—**Watteau, Poudré, Noah's Ark, Cracker, Constellation, Domino, Hobby-Horse, Seasons, Bird, Louis Quinze, Shepherds and Shepherdesses,** when both ladies and gentlemen wear the costumes associated with these characters. For a **Louis Quinze Hunting Quadrille** they appear in the hunting dress of that period; for a **Holbein Quadrille** in the Tudor dress; a **Quadrille of all Nations,** embracing all nationalities, the ladies and gentlemen of the same countries dancing together, the gentlemen occasionally carrying the national flag are all good. In an **Italian and Swiss Quadrille,** each couple preserve the same coloring. In **Black and White** the ladies are entirely robed in white with powdered hair; the gentlemen in black costumes of the time of Edward III., with black masks and pointed shoes, hanging sleeves. **Stuart** and **Georgian** characters make good quadrilles, and **Pierre** and **Pierrettes, Punch and his wife,** and **Spanish Men and Maidens** in various colorings. In a **Toy Quadrille**, toys such as tops, Dutch dolls, battledores and shuttlecocks appear. For an **Octave,** ladies and gentlemen are dressed in black and white, each carry bells which tinkle as they walk. For **Chivalry,** the gentlemen are in armour, and the ladies in the dress of the period. **Scotch, Irish, King and Queen, Army and Navy, Flowers of the Year, Venetian, Vandyke, Pack of Cards, Fairy Tale, Butterflies, Joe Willett and Dolly Varden, Puritan and Cavalier** also find favour. The time when such quadrilles are danced, and the partners, are all pre-arranged. **A Singing Quadrille,** in which the heroes and heroines of the nursery rhymes wear appropriate dresses and sing as they dance, is to be specially recommended for Children's fancy balls.

QUAKERESS. A grey satin dress, touching the ground; short-waisted high bodice, open at the throat, a plain hemmed muslin kerchief, neatly folded inside; leg-of-mutton sleeves to wrist, and turn-back muslin cuffs; a bonnet of the same satin as the dress, with a soft crown and stiff cardboard front; a plaited cap beneath, or a fine cambric cap, without the bonnet.

QUARTERS OF GLOBE. (*See* EUROPE, ASIA, AFRICA, AMERICA.)

QUEEN OF CYPRUS. (*See* VENETIAN.)

QUEEN OF FAIRIES. (*See* F.)

QUEEN OF MAY. (*See* MAY.)

QUEEN OF NIGHT. (*See* NIGHT.)

QUEEN, NORTH AMERICAN. (*See* AMERICAN.)

QUEEN OF THE REGIMENT. Cream satin jacket with gold braid, crimson satin skirt, trimmed with gold cord; red and gold cap; crimson sash, and dress sword.

QUEENS OF DIFFERENT CARDS. (*See* CARDS.)

QUEEN OF THE WOODS. (*See* W.)

QUEEN'S MARIES. (*See* MARIES.)

QUEENSBERRY, DUCHESS OF. (*See* KITTY.)

QUICKSILVER. Fashionable black evening dress made of tulle, and trimmed with silver.

RABBIT. White plush bodice bordered with a lace ruche at neck and sleeves; white satin skirt with rabbits' heads painted or embroidered; cap like a rabbit's head; drum and sticks carried in hand.

RACHEL THE GLEANER. (*See* GLEANER.)

RACING. A short green satin skirt with a steeplechase water jump, and winning post painted upon it. A striped jockey jacket with loops of ribbon on the shoulders; horse-shoe pin. A jockey cap, riding boots, a betting book, and a flag-shaped fan. The character could be also carried out by a dress of any particular racing colors, bedecked with Sandown, Kempton, and other racing badges.

RAG BABY, A. Representing a rag doll, the face being painted to accord with the character. (*See* BABY).

RAGPICKER. Striped cotton gown with loose bodice and basque tied in at the waist. Huge white apron, chiffonier basket at the back, crook stick in the hand.

RAINBOW (*Arc-en-Ciel*), **IRIS.** A pearl-grey dew-spangled tulle evening dress, with low bodice; across it, from left shoulder and under right arm, a tulle scarf of the colors of the rainbow, viz., red, green, blue, pink, grey, violet, and orange, arranged in folds; a half circle of the same on the right side of the dress; a pompon of fringed silks of the color worn in the hair; a veil depending at back; the word "Rainbow" worked in pearls on black velvet round the neck. Sometimes the scarf tunic is composed of tulle of the rainbow shades, bordered with silver, and is drawn in a pouf through a buckle at the side, a veil of the several tints reaching to the feet. Sometimes the dress is of pink, or grey tulle, or gauze, spangled with crystal drops, with a scarf of the colors about it, or a tunic spangled with silver; the bodice pink; silver ornaments.

RANEE. Narrow under-skirt of embroidered white muslin, trimmed with gold lace; tunic of cream-colored silk, having embossed figures in gold; green satin bodice trimmed with gold and jewels; crimson and gold-embroidered native head-dress with gauze veil, spangled with gold and silver; gold shoes, necklace of rubies, emeralds, and diamonds; massive gold bracelets of Delhi and Kutch work. (*See* INDIAN.)

RATCATCHER. A French fancy costume for a child. Short skirt and a double skirt cut in three wide battlements; a low square bodice with jacket basque of white satin, bordered with grey fur; boots to match; a head-dress in the semblance of a cat, with head; a stick over one shoulder, with three rats.

RAVEN. A black evening dress, with clerical muslin band round neck; cap made of bird's head.

READING. The same as ALPHABET.

REAPER. White satin skirt, red satin bodice cut half-high, with puffed sleeves to elbow, profusely trimmed with corn, oats, and poppies; a green satin cap with an aigrette of corn, a sickle at the side, Leghorn hat, and field flowers. Or, a dress of maize tulle, trimmed with tufts and fringes of wheat-ears and cornflowers; wreath of the same. (*See* HARVEST and GLEANER.)

REBECCA *(Ivanhoe)*. As worn by Lady Ernest Bruce at the Queen's Fancy Ball in 1842. White satin skirt just touching the ground; green velvet embroidered pelisse, open in front, showing stomacher; sleeves large and pendent, with close-fitting satin ones beneath; a knotted scarf of many colors encircles the waist, a silk turban on head. Another handsome rendering is as follows: Bodice, skirt, and sleeves of gold or silver tissue; mantle of prune velvet, lined with white satin, trimmed with broad bands of ermine edged with gold galon; velvet and gold turban, with ostrich plumes and diamond aigrette; white satin shoes, brocaded in gold; feather fan, jewelled girdle, and parure of jewels. A veil spangled with gold is generally worn.

RED CROSS NURSE. (*See* AMBULANCE.)

RED MAID OF BRISTOL. (*See* CHARITY.)

RED RIDING-HOOD in the Illustration wears a dark blue stuff gown, white apron, red bodice laced in front, over a white chemisette, red cloak and hood, basket in hand with eggs. Other renderings are a blue silk, quilted skirt; black velvet bodice; red cloak; muslin pinafore; head-dress, corn flowers. (For the **French Red Riding Hood,** *see* CHAPERON ROUGE.)

RED, WHITE, AND BLUE. Short white skirt, striped with red and blue; or a plaited flounce of the alternate colors, five to six inches deep; tunic of the same, caught up with a silver anchor and knots of the two colors; or a silk Union Jack is draped as a tunic over the short skirt. Low satin bodice trimmed with the colors, the bows fastened by silver anchors; sailor hat trimmed to match, or red silk turban intertwisted with blue and white; white shoes, red rosettes, and heels; blue ribbon necklet and bracelets.

RÉPUBLIQUE FRANCAISE. Classical dress of white or pale grey cashmere, trimmed with gold; a long flowing skirt; loose, low bodice, confined by oxidised silver belt; hanging sleeves from shoulders; a tricolor scarf draped from the right shoulder; a Phrygian cap of scarlet cloth, with "Liberté" worked in gold, and a tricolor cockade. Or, white jacket bodice over a tricolored striped skirt; blood-red sash; red cap of liberty; flag in hand with Libertè, Egalité, and Fraternité, or a sword in hand.

RESTORATION, FRENCH. (*See* MERVEILLEUSE.) At first, at this period, the Louis XVIth modes were revived; but in 1830, short dresses, gigot sleeves on whalebone frames, and capote hats, came into fashion. (*See* Illustration of 1830 PERIOD, Fig. 14.)

REVOLUTION *(French)*, 1789. Long dress of striped yellow silk; long skirted coat, *à la* Robespierre, of bottle-green silk, short-waisted double-breasted, made with large lapels, cut steel buttons, and narrow sleeves; it opened at the neck, showing a cravat with lace ends; pointed bottle-green felt hat, with yellow cockade in front, worn over powdered hair. Or, pale pink and green satin redingote, opening over muslin petticoat in bouillonnes to waist. (*See* INCROYABLE.)

REYNOLDS, SIR JOSHUA (*after*). The usual rendering of a costume after Sir Joshua Reynolds at fancy balls is a white muslin dress, with tight sleeves, muslin fichu; powdered hair, a hat of coarse straw lined with blue, or a velvet hat tied under the chin with blue ribbons; black embroidered shoes; a single row of diamonds or pearls round the throat, a diamond brooch in the fichu. Sometimes the dress is made with a deep-gathered flounce round the edge: it just touches the ground, and is always scanty. Sometimes it has a falling collar, and nearly always a blue sash tied in a bow at the back, and the hat is now and then replaced by a mob cap. In a portrait dated 1781, there is a crimson petticoat, canary-colored upper-skirt, brocaded with flowers and trimmed with lace; powdered hair; small crimson hat and feather; pearl ornaments. In his picture of **Lady Cadogan** she wears a white satin petticoat embroidered with gold; lemon-colored satin train; hair powdered; white satin hat, with plume of white and blue feathers; pearl ornaments. And **Mrs. Braddyl,** a satin skirt and train; fulled under-bodice, with turn-down ruff; open stomacher; elbow-sleeves; hair in loose curls. The **Duchess of Gordon** has her hair turned off the face in three rolls, divided by ribbon; low curls on the neck; bodice with stiff ruff; scarf round waist, opening heart-shape; pearls round the neck with miniature; the sleeves made with epaulettes of horizontal bouillonnés, and open sleeves over a puff to the elbow; train of satin. For children, copies from his pictures make admirable fancy dresses. The girl in his **"Rest by the Way"** wears a red short skirt, with a blue band round the low bodice, and elbow-sleeves turned back with white, a muslin kerchief inside the bodice; yellow apron, straw hat. **In the Mask,** high-heeled shoes with blue bows; flowered short skirt; brocaded, bunched-up tunic; square bodice and elbow-sleeves; blue sash; hair cut square over forehead. In the **Angerstein Children** the girl is conspicuous for her large straw hat, trimmed with ribbons, and worn over a fine head of curls, which frame the face. A special feature in her dress is the short shawl thrown over the shoulders and turned under the colored scarf which encircles her waist, forming a bow with long ends on right hip.

RHENISH PEASANT. Short plain cloth skirt and bodice laced in front, over a white muslin chemisette, with full straight sleeves reaching to wrist; a colored silk handkerchief on the shoulders, the ends tucked in to the bodice; hair gathered in a knot at the back, worn with a close-fitting linen cap, the strings tied under the chin; shoes and buckles; white stockings, with colored clocks.

RHEIMS, JACKDAW OF. Short white satin skirt, plain in front with waterfall back, scalloped at the hem, edged with a plaiting of blue satin, in each scallop a round ornament of marabout with ring of turquoise beads in the centre; the upper part of the skirt covered with a festooned lattice-work of narrow gold braid, and turquoise beads at each crossing, forming an apron, having a gold fringe and turquoise tassels; a short panier of black satin bordered with gold lace; bodice pointed at waist and square cut at neck; sleeves of black marabout, trimmed with frill of gold lace. At the back of bodice two tabs of marabout are mounted on stiff wires, like wings; tail of black net and marabout to edge of skirt; streamers of black satin from each shoulder. Turquoise ornaments; powdered hair; head-dress of black feathers, like head of jackdaw, with turquoise ring in beak; black stockings; satin shoes, and gloves; blue fan, jackdaw's head in centre.

RIBBONS. Dress of wide cream-colored chiné ribbon joined perpendicularly. Shoulder knots and flowing ends from the waist. Ribbon aigrette in hair; ribbon necklet and bracelets.

"RICH AND RARE WERE THE GEMS SHE WORE." Dress of soft green tulle, powdered with a variety of jewels; gold circlet over flowing hair; staff, with ring at top; a bunch of shamrocks on the front of bodice.

RIDING-DRESS *(period of Charles II.).* The jacket is made with a basque all round alike, almost as deep as an upper skirt, open at the neck with revers edged by rows of gold or silver braid; the neck is hidden either by a simulated waistcoat of the same material, or by a silk scarf tied once round the neck, the ends laid one over another and pinned down to the waist. This jacket is trimmed with gold or silver braid in a treble row, laid a little from the edge; large square pockets are placed on the outside of the basque in front, with braid to match, as also the mousquetaire cuffs of the sleeves. It can be made in satin and velvet, and is worn with a long trained skirt of the same, caught up on one side over a satin petticoat. Sometimes the cuffs and revers of jacket have the same colored satin under the braid. Large velvet hat and plume, riding-whip and gauntlet gloves complete the costume; large lace collar. Plum and gold is a good admixture of color. **Riding-Dress** (*temp.* George I.). Broad-brimmed satin or violet velvet hat, with large bows of ribbon round the crown; the hair powdered and frizzed at the side, long curls at back; violet velvet habit made with overhanging collar and cape, such as the men of the period wore; it has buttons and frogs on the bodice; the shoes have gold buckles; old point-lace tie at neck.

RISING GENERATION, ONE OF. A favorite fancy costume of the moment worn by children and grown up people. A short, plain frock with a gathered flounce round; low, full bodice with large sash tied at the back, short sleeves in one puff; black shoes buttoned round the ankle; hair in long plaits. It is also rendered by reproductions of some of Kate Greenaway's sketches of children.

RIVALS. (*See* LYDIA LANGUISH, and Mrs. MALAPROP.)

RIVER. Green and silver tissue gown with aquatic flowers. A meandering stream down the side, represented by silver braid and paillettes. A coronet after the same order, deep silver fringe falling from the shoulders and waist.

ROAMING, I'VE BEEN. Plain full skirt of poppy red, bordered with a deep band of pale blue. Square cut bodice with elbow sleeves; tunic of print or cretonne, gathered to bodice; paniers caught back; large muslin apron and kerchief; elbow ruffles; red stockings, black shoes and buckles; hair worn down the back; large straw hat, poppies and wild flowers, wreath round hat; strings of small flowers as necklet and bracelets; palm-leaf fan, painted green, covered with flowers.

ROBIN. (*See* COCK ROBIN.)

ROBSART. (*See* AMY.)

ROCKERY. Dress of fern leaves and morsels of cork, wreathed with rockery plants. Pale green low silk bodice, the skirt covered with trailing ferns; shoes decorated with small fern leaves. Basket of ferns and other rockery plants carried in the hand. Head-dress, a miniature rockery.

ROCOCO. Ecru petticoat, with bands of black velvet and silver;

Fig. 33.—ROSALIND.

tunic and bodice of blue brocade, muslin pelerine looped with black velvet and roses; powdered hair; blue velvet hat; rococo ornaments.

ROMAN *(Ancient).* Long, soft, falling skirt; under-bodice, full and low, the short sleeve buttoned on the outside of arm; loose over-bodice, secured by brooches on shoulder, belt round waist; the lower all-round basque formed by fulness, bordered with gold; over-mantle swathed about figure; hair close to head in waves; veil of woollen cloth; tiara a flat gold band pointed in centre. The dress of course altered in various centuries. Cesare Vitelli's drawings give an excellent idea of the varieties.

ROMAN PEASANT. (*See* ITALIAN.)

ROME. White satin skirt, bordered with a red and gold Grecian border; upper skirt divided into three, edged with gold fringe; the centre embroidered in gold. The side has a Roman standard and eagle in bullion threads, wreaths of bay leaves, etc.; the back, a Grecian gold border; scarf of red and gold looped on right shoulder with cameo, and falling low under left arm; "Roma" on armlets; head-dress, tiara of diamonds, with "Roma" in seed pearls; gold-spangled veil.

ROMOLA. Dress of cream-colored satin, with long hanging sleeves, embroidered in gold and pearls, and caught up with gold girdle; over-petticoat of same material; lace veil fastened with band of pearls; antique Italian ornaments.

ROMNEY (*after*). White muslin dress with short waist, crossing bodice wide sash; tight sleeves. Powdered hair; large black hat, lined with a color, such as vieux rose or blue.

ROSALIND (*As You Like It*) is pourtrayed in the Illustration, Fig. 33, wearing long tan-colored leather boots, a fawn cloth skirt and bodice, with touches of black here and there. A long satin cloak and puffings to the sleeves, the cap of the same with an aigrette. A spear is carried in the hand, a satchel hangs at the side, and a pistol is suspended from the belt. It can also be carried out in a grey doublet, trunk hose, soft velvet hat. **Rosalind** also appears in a dress of brocaded velvet, skirt made full and looped over a satin skirt of the same color with gold braid; heart-shaped bodice, sleeves puffed with gold; gold fillet on head. Her third dress is made loose and full, with belt on hips, pouch attached; puffed sleeves. She carries her boar-spear. Another rendering of the character is a long grey velvet dress with a waistcoat and sleeves slashed with white satin; thick long pearl girdle looped on side. As **Ganymede,** short tunic of grey-green velvet bordered with dark fur; short jacket; long cloak fastened on the shoulders, made of grey silk lined with pale pink; grey stockings and cap; game bag; staff in hand.

ROSAMOND, FAIR. Loose green flowing robe high to the throat, touching the ground; confined at waist by jewelled belt; hanging sleeves; all richly embroidered; jewelled galon bordering the neck, sleeves and hem. Gold coif over flowing hair; pouch pocket at the side. As a nun she wears the full white habit, the large sleeves turning back at wrist; crucifix at side; white drapery about the head; a long black mantle descending to the ground.

ROSE, COULEUR DE. A dress all rose color, with a pair of rose-colored spectacles carried in hand. Can be carried out in satin, silk, or tulle, according to the taste of the wearer.

ROSE. Pink tulle skirt, covered with rose-petals and leaves; bodice of the same trimmed with garlands of roses; long tulle scarf fastened behind; wreath and ornaments of rosebuds, roses, and leaves; balayease of rose leaves.

ROSES, BASKET OF. The head-dress is a gilt wicker basket filled with flowers; the green satin corselet is covered with cross-bars of gold braid also to simulate wicker-work; white gauze skirt over a pink satin, bordered with roses; silk stockings embroidered with roses and the white satin shoes.

A ROSE TREE in the Illustration, Fig. 34, is a light green satin gown covered with green tulle and ribbons over which roses are trailed. A green ribbon outlines the waist, and roses border the shoulders forming a sleeve on one side and a couple of bands on the other. Long ruffled gloves, an erect spray of roses, and green satin shoes with buckles are worn with it.

ROSE, LATTICE. Short silk skirt covered with a black velvet lattice, roses growing in the midst; pointed corselet bodice over white chemisette; a ruche at neck. Short jacket with revers, large velvet puffed sleeves and ruffles; black velvet hat, roses under brim, bow at side. Basket of roses in hand.

ROSE MICHON (*La Jolie Parfumeuse*). High blue boots; pink short skirt, with box-plaited pink flounces round; blue tunic caught up at back, pink apron with two pockets, all bordered with white muslin frilling. Low square blue bodice with plaitings *à la vieille* round it and the short sleeves, a pink rose on one side; a blue ribbon tied in bow round neck; blue rosette at side.

ROSE OF CASTILLE. A Spanish dress. Skirt of black lace over bright-colored satin low bodice; velvet senorita jacket trimmed with gold fringe; high comb; black lace mantilla; black shoes with silk stockings; Spanish fan.

ROSE OF LANCASTER. A dress made with quilted satin petticoat, the front sewn with pearls; gauze train fastened with roses in red, after the same fashion as Rose of York.

ROSE OF SUMMER, LAST. Pink satin ball dress, with low square bodice and elbow-sleeves; pink tulle tunic sprinkled with loose petals caught up with roses and green leaves, a garland of the same on the dress, a few detached petals below them as if they had fallen off; roses in the hair.

ROSE OF YORK. Skirt of white satin covered with white roses and pearls; train of white velvet with roses; a Watteau plait at the back. The pointed bodice square cut at the neck; high ruff, full puffed sleeves; hat of white satin trimmed with ostrich feathers, roses, and pearls.

ROSE STANDISH in the Illustration, Fig. 32, wears a Puritan dress of soft fawn color or lavender-tinted woollen, with a satchel pocket at side. The white linen apron is slightly embroidered above the hem. There is a white linen tippet and a black Puritan cap made of silk or velvet with white linen showing next the face. At fancy balls the dress is enlivened by a red silk sash round the waist, but it would be more in character if this were of a darker tone than the gown.

ROSES, QUEEN OF. Tulle petticoat with bouquets of every colored rose dispersed about it; over-skirt powdered with pink rose-leaves, also the veil, as if a shower of rose-leaves had fallen on them; a wreath of colored roses; earrings, necklet, and bracelets formed of pink rosebuds.

ROSIÈRE. White muslin dress, made high and plain; a wreath of full-blown roses on the hair, and a bouquet of the same at the waist. **A Rosière D'Issy** wears a short red woollen skirt; a linen apron, tied at the back; a red woollen bodice, opening over an écru-colored chemisette; a red woollen fichu fastened over the head, and a large straw hat, ornamented with poppies, and worn quite at the back; blue stockings and plain shoes.

ROSINA (*Barbiere de Seville*). Spanish dress of cerise satin and black lace; black velvet senorita jacket; black lace mantilla, roses at the side; high comb.

ROSINE (Heroine of Whyte Melville's novel, *Rosine*). Striped cambric short skirt of bright colors; square bodice and elbow-sleeves. Muslin apron with bib and shoulder straps, the word "Rosine" worked in red letters on the pockets and corners of the apron; muslin kerchief and mob cap. Silk stockings; black high-heeled shoes; old silver ornaments.

ROUGE-ET-NOIR. Skirt, sleeves, and low bodice of black and red striped satin, with dice embroidered on the front; sleeveless bodice, and diagonally draped tunic of red crape or gauze, forming ends tied at the back, with a bow of black lace and four small toy cards falling from them. These same cards, alternately red and black, in a slanting position, are laid round the edge of the tunic and bodice with a trimming of black lace and gold braid and fringe; a bow on the shoulders with four cards tied together, the same in front of bodice; ornaments, enamel cards and dice; on the head a cornucopia-shaped cap, half-black, half-red, like that worn by FOLLY, with an aigrette formed of a gilt hand holding cards, or a pointed coronet. Croupier's rake in hand.

ROULETTE. Short skirt of red and green cloth, with all the numbers, insignias, and terms of the game, such as "Manque," "Pair Impàir," printed in white; bodice of red and black satin; powdered hair, with small roulette board on one side; a croupier's rake suspended from the waist.

ROUMANIAN COSTUME FROM THE COUNTRY. Full white heart-shaped bodice embroidered in black, the hanging sleeves drawn up at the elbow, narrow black over-skirt opening in the front and covered with gold embroidery, the white under-skirt treated in the same way. A colored scarf round the waist, many rows of beads about the neck. A small fez cap worn at the back of the head and embroidered. Pendent veil.

ROYALIST, LITTLE. A white satin costume with a long skirt. The bodice tabbed at the waist and ornamented with ribbon rosettes;

Fig. 35.—RUBEN'S WIFE.

full elbow sleeves, deep satin collar, and over it one of Irish lace; cuffs of the same; pearl ornament; small, close-fitting satin cap. Hair worn in short curls; white silk stockings and tan cavalier shoes.

ROWENA, THE LADY (*Ivanhoe*). Scanty under-dress touching the ground, the bodice of pale sea-green satin; over this a long-flowing cashmere robe reaching to the ground, either white or crimson, with wide hanging elbow-sleeves, all richly embroidered in gold; a girdle about the waist, a gauze scarf interwoven with gold threads fastened to the left shoulder; the hair entwined with pearls, a gold circlet and gold-spangled veil; gold chain with charms attached; gold bracelets and armlets. Or, sea-green silk skirt, ornamented with pearls; robe of crimson cashmere bordered with ermine; pearl coronet and crystal veil.

ROXANA. Dress of cloth of gold bordered with swansdown, and lined with green satin, over an under-dress of Turkish red.

RUBENS (*After*). The figure in the Illustration, No. 35, can be carried out in straw-colored satin and ruby velvet, the upper skirt bordered with gold ball trimming, the plain bodice edged with white, according with the white satin collar. Large sleeves of the velvet opening over satin. Velvet hat and feathers; ostrich feather fan.

RUBENS' WIVES. Isabella Brant he portrayed in a skirt of white satin embroidered all round with gold cord and pearls; sleeves to wrist with slashings inside the arm and puffings beneath; turn-back cuff of lace; very large ruff round the throat; hair powdered, surmounted by a high-pointed hat, jewelled band round the brim, widening at the side and turned up. **Helena Forman** (*his second wife*) appears in yellow and brown silk and violet velvet, the skirt of the velvet touching the ground; the bodice a low square with square ruff, lace edged; the hair in curls; the bodice, which has a broad rounded point, has jewels in front on a yellow stomacher; the sleeves have an upper puff of violet, the elbow slashed with brown and yellow, puffs of yellow are continued to wrist, with turn-back cuffs; the two colors are blended in the trimmings on the skirt mixed with jewels; a feather fan is carried in the hand; a large-brimmed, low-crowned hat, turned up on one side with ostrich plumes and jewel.

RUSSIAN COSTUME. The dress in the Illustration, Fig. 36, is made of yellow satin bordered with dark fur, the arms of Russia painted on the front. The short jacket of dark crimson velvet ends at the waist, the revers are of satin to match, the skirt bordered with fur; beneath this is a full white satin under-bodice, the band and front richly embroidered in the Russian style. The satin sleeves are covered with diamanté tulle, the lower meeting the ruffled gloves. The Koshnick head-dress is of ruby velvet richly jewelled, a gauze veil depending at the back. **A Russian Baroness.** Rose-colored satin skirt; over it a white satin pelisse, with low bodice and long hanging sleeves, bordered with ermine; cap of rose-color, with jewelled aigrette. This was worn by Baroness Brunnow at the Queen's fancy ball. **Russian Hussar Vivandière.** Short blue velvet skirt; blue velvet polonaise, trimmed with satin; white hussar jacket trimmed with sable; cap to correspond; silver ornaments; high boots with sable tops. **Russian Peasant.** Short skirt of red merino, with bands of green or blue velvet, headed by gold braid; a white chemisette with long sleeves, sometimes a stay bodice of velvet over this, or one coming to the throat crossed with bands of the same, bordered with gold braid passing over the shoulder to the waist in a V-shape back and front, forming a square across the bust, and a band at wrist. The Koshnick is the usual head-dress, with a broad velvet coronet in front dotted with gold coins and swansdown; beads are worn round the neck; a large white silk apron, trimmed with red and gold, almost hides the front of the dress; crimson stockings; high-heeled black shoes. The peasant costume worn in Southern or Little Russia consists of a many-colored woollen petticoat of peculiar shape; linen under-skirt edged with coarse lace; a linen blouse embroidered in gay colors, chiefly blue and red; the head-dress, a broad circlet of brocaded ribbon, with bows of variously colored ribbon falling at the back, and mingling with the thick pendent plaits; an embroidered red and white towel of curious design hangs from the arm; these are worn on certain feast days, and can only be procured at the great fairs; strings of colored beads and a gold cross and chain, or picture of St. Nicholas, complete this costume. **Russian Skater.** Round fur-edged cap; ruby velvet pelisse, edged with fur, opening *en cœur* at the neck, two fur buttons at the back of waist; petticoat of quilted grey satin; high boots edged with fur and bells; silver ornaments; a muff carried in the hand; silver skates attached to girdle.

RUTH, THE GLEANER. (*See* JEWISH.)

RUTH, THE PIRATICAL MAID OF ALL WORK. (*See* PIRATES OF PENZANCE.)

Fig. 36.—Russian Costume.

SABRINA. White spangled tulle dress over light green silver tissue, looped up with silver grass, wreaths of aquatic leaves, water-lilies, and coral; head-dress, large water-lily leaf and silver-spotted tulle veil.

SACK OF FLOUR. A gown made of sacking. Short full skirt with the word "Sample-sack" in front; the bodice loose and cut in one with it, a point drawn up on each shoulder like the ends of a sack. Poppies and cornflowers in the hair.

SACKCLOTH AND ASHES. A tin dust pan filled with ashes for head-dress. The dress made of sackcloth with a hood something like a monk's robe.

SALLY IN OUR ALLEY. Plainly-made cotton dress; with elbow-sleeves; mittens; muslin cap, fichu, and apron.

SALOME. Robe of salmon satin embroidered with fantastic flowers. Loosely-tied sash; bodice square; hair interplaited with pearls, gauze veil and coronet of scarlet flowers. Or, yellow and black draperies, lined with red; head-dress, a kerchief of black silk, embroidered and fringed, gold band with falling sequins round the head and passing beneath chin.

SALT WATER AND FRESH WATER. Suitable dresses for two sisters; both would wear green and white tulle dresses and veils. For salt water these would be trimmed with coral, seaweeds, and shells; the other with water-lilies and grasses. (*See* WATER-NYMPH.)

SALTARELLA. Red satin flounced skirt, edged with gold fringe; pale blue satin drapery, trimmed with gold coins and fringe; tight fitting black satin basqued bodice, trimmed with gold coins and fringe; red satin cap, with gold net and coins.

SANZAGARE, LADY. (*See* SORCERER.)

SANTA-CLAUS. Wears a flowing robe and a pointed hood fringed with toys of all descriptions. A stocking hanging at the side.

SANS GENE, MADAME. Appears first as the **Blanchisseuse** in mauve and white striped cambric to ankle. Bodice cut open at neck, with muslin edging; white linen apron with lace; Charlotte Corday cap with mauve satin bows. Tan shoes and stockings. As **Marèchale le Febvre.** Ivory satin robe embroidered with Byzantine designs in seed pearls, silver spangles and amethysts. Tulle puffed sleeves. Josephine collar of gold and jewelled lace. Jewelled belt beneath the arm-pits. Green velvet royal mantle lined with satin and embroidered with dull gold, studded with jewels. Bouquets on the bodice and handsome jewellery. Period 1793.

SAPPHIRE. Greek robe of pale blue satin, embroidered at the hem with sapphire and blue steel beads; zone and necklet of sapphires. Blue shoes and stockings; blue diadem, with sapphire at top.

SAPPHO. Greek tunic and flowing dress of white satin, trimmed with Greek pattern in gold braid, bordered with gold fringe; mantle of sky-blue velvet, attached to shoulders, trimmed with gold; the hair in close curls, gold head-dress of Grecian design; gold armlets and bracelets, connected by chains; gold necklet of coins; a lyre in the hand.

SAPPHOS, THE TWO. Long trailing black dress with cocked hat.

SARDINIAN PEASANT. Scarlet jacket, with silver buttons and gold lace, over white linen chemisette, with open sleeves; a piece of scarlet silk on head, descending to shoulders; veil over lower part of face. Younger women wear a tight-fitting satin bodice, richly embroidered with gold and silver lace; clasp and belt of the same, and a profusion of rings, chains, and other jewellery; white satin apron, embroidered in scarlet.

SATANELLA. Low black tulle dress, made short, and covered with silver stars; stars in the hair; star ornaments.

SCARLET RUNNER. Short red brilliant poppy silk, veiled with chiffon caught up with green leaves. Shoes and stockings to match. Bodice bordered at the neck with a scarlet runner. An aigrette of the same in the powdered hair.

SCHNEEWITTCHEN (From Grimm's Fairy Tale of *Snowflake and the Dwarfs*). White satin dress made low, and slashed with silver cloth, having long and large puffed sleeves to the elbow, bedizened with pearls. The skirt is looped over a petticoat, on which the seven dwarfs are painted in brown and grey; a silver pointed crown worn at the back of the head, and a long veil floating to the feet.

SCHOOL FOR SCANDAL. (*See* LADY TEAZLE, LADY SNEERWELL, MARIA, MRS. CANDOUR.)

SCOTCH COSTUME, HIGHLAND LASSIE, &c., at fancy balls are generally carried out by a white dress, with Scotch jewellery; a satin plaid scarf draped on the shoulder with cairngorm brooches;

sometimes a Scotch bonnet of black velvet with black plumes, or more generally a ribbon snood or a wreath of ivy or oak-leaves serves for the head-dress. The several clans display their badges in the form of silver acorns and oak-leaves, wheat, &c. This is the fancy dress usually worn at the annual Caledonian Ball. (*See* SCOTCH FISH-WIFE under F.)

SCOTLAND. Black shoes and stockings; white skirt with bands of red; red lion in front. Low V-shaped bodice cut in tabs all round, fastened with silver buttons; plaid under left arm to right shoulder, attached with cairngorm. Scotch cap and heron's plume.

SCRAP BOOK. A white short skirt with an over-skirt of a succession of stole ends all covered with picture scraps. A red satin bodice laced in front. Two sash ends, the word "Scrap" on each. The cap made like a white gallipot edged with a frill of lace, the word "Paste" in front, and the brush for an aigrette.

SEA, THE. Dark blue sailor hat; a kerchief tied in sailor knot, under large square collar; loose bodice of Galatea, and plain skirt with frills of light blue silk or satin; dark blue silk stockings; life buoy supported by blue silk cord. (*See* NEPTUNE, MISS.) **Sea Queen and Nymph.** (*See* WATER-NYMPH.) **Sea Maiden** (*Andersen's Fairy Tales*). Plain loose robe of opalescent moire trimmed at hem with sea-shells; bodice cut as a high square, back and front; short puffed sleeves; coral round neck and wrists; armlets of shells; waist belt of coral and shells, from which seaweed falls on to the skirt. Train of silver cloth, cut like a fish-tail at the edge and trimmed with oyster shells. Pink stockings; pink shoes. Silver band round head; hair floating on shoulders, with red flowers intermingled; miniature of beautiful prince round neck.

SEA GULL. A head dress of diamonds and lace with a bird nestling in the midst. Striped grey silk gown with large white and grey wings on the skirt and sea gulls on the shoulder. Or, short white satin dress draped with white crepe and edged with gull's feathers, large gull's wings on both the front and back of bodice, single sleeves caught up with wings.

SEA SHELLS. White satin under green gauze, caught up in festoons to resemble a shell. A plastron of the same on bodice and an aureole head-dress placed at the back of shells. A wand surmounted by a shell.

SEASONS, THE (for WINTER, *see* W; SPRING and SUMMER, S; AUTUMN, A). Four sisters might personate the Seasons as follows, two should be blondes and two brunes. The dresses made short, the satin shoes matching in color. **Spring** wears pale green tulle, with flowers and a fringe of grasses; necklace of daisies and grass; head-dress, a nest with eggs, and a bird on wire hovering over it. Carries a basket of violets. **Summer** is arrayed in maize and red tulle, with wreath and trimmings of roses; fruit in the hair. **Autumn** in yellow and brown, with autumn leaves, flowers, and ears of corn; holds a sheaf of corn. **Winter** in white satin, with bands of swansdown; a fringe of icicles on the tunic; a miniature fir tree in the hair.

SEMIRAMIS, QUEEN OF ASSYRIA. A loose, long, flowing robe of white satin in classic style, embroidered with lotus leaves; head-dress, a jewelled diadem. Or, skirt of ruby satin lined with gold color, displaying Egyptian emblems and coins; bodice of pale blue satin, fastened round the waist with handsome gold ornaments.

SEPTEMBER. Represented by a white satin dress trimmed with purple grapes, or as AUTUMN. (*See* A.)

SERPENT. (*See* SNAKE CHARMER.)

SERPOLETTE (*Les Cloches de Corneville*). Grey-blue stockings, and shoes with brown heels; short grey cashmere skirt with box-plaiting round, half a yard deep; tunic, forming puff and ends at back, buttoning on to close-fitting cuirass bodice; plain linen fichu, or bib with a point in front; sleeves to elbow with cuffs; white linen cap with blue ribbon band and bow. Second dress, pink brocade long skirt with cuirass; satin hat with three white feathers.

SERVIAN PEASANT. Loose full skirt; Garibaldi bodice, with bishop sleeves to wrist; belt of black leather; gaily striped apron; embroidery at throat; hair plaited with colored ribbons.

SERVING MAID (*Elizabethan Period*). (*See* Illustration No. 17.) Short fawn colored stuff gown, made with pointed bodice; tight sleeves with stuffed epaulettes; ruff at throat; muslin cap; bag hanging at side.

SEVENTEENTH CENTURY. (*See* CHARLES I., CHARLES II., JAMES I., JAMES II., WILLIAM III. PERIODS.) Morning costume of French lady in XVIIth century: Cardinal petticoat; upper-skirt of the same, turned back with dark green; white apron; cape and cap trimmed with lace; red stockings and black shoes.

SEYMOUR, JANE. (1509-1547.) Train of black velvet embroidered with pearls over a brocaded silk petticoat showing in front; long bodice with girdle and châtelaine of pearls, and trimmed with Venetian point; coif of velvet with jewelled coronet.

SHALOT, LADY OF. Long full dress of pale green foulard cut in one from throat to foot and set into a rounded band of primrose satin embroidered with silver thread; silver girdle; at the hem of the skirt narrow silver embroidery. A long mantle of primrose silk fastened on the shoulder, draped below the waist. Circlet of silver in hair.

SHAMROCK. Diaphanous green skirt studded with shamrocks in parllettes; green velvet bodice bordered with gold. A large gold shamrock on the front of the bodice, another forming the head-dress. (*See* ERIN.)

SHELLS. A light green tulle gown with shells attached. A net about the waist. The bodice pink and green. (*See* SEA SHELLS.)

SHEPHERDESS. (*See* ARCADIAN, BO-PEEP, CELIA, DRESDEN, FLORIAN, WATTEAU, and Illustration Fig. 9.) Felt hat, flowers on one side and under the brim; crook; low square bodice filled in with muslin, headed by black velvet braces and stomacher; muslin sleeves to wrist; shott skirt of pink and white striped silk; bodice cut in tabs. **Shepherdess Dress of the Fifteenth Century.** Long blue woollen skirt and sleeves, over which a red tunic to below the knees, and bell sleeves of the same color; the upper dress is confined by a ceinture, in the shape of a loose bag, deep on one side and narrow like a band on the other; head-dress of blue, white, or red linen or merino, folded across the head and left to hang rather deep about the neck and ears; crook. The following are pretty renderings of the character:—White tulle skirt; blue bodice, with pink plastron; blue saucer-shaped hat with roses and long pink ribbons; blue shoes with pink rosettes. Or, short skirt, trimmed with white flounces; lilac silk tunic, looped with garlands of flowers; pink silk tunic draped as paniers; pointed bodice; muslin stomacher crossed with ribbons, rosettes at each side; the bodice bordered with pink passementerie, short sleeves, silk cape, with ruffles; pink hat, lined with lilac, pink roses; crook with flowers. Or, petticoat of blue and white Chambery gauze; bodice and tunic of amber satin trimmed with blue. **Watteau Shepherdess** wears a full, short, yellow skirt, with a deep flounce about two inches from the edge, over which a full all-round panier of yellow and pink ftripes; the bodice with tabs round the waist, showing a white graduated stomacher, over which it is laced with pink cord, a small pink bow covering each of the nine eyelet-holes, four each side of the bodice and one at the point, below the waist. There are two sets of sleeves,—full white elbow-sleeves with pink bows, and short upper-sleeves of yellow to match the bodice; the hat is slightly turned up on each side, and ornamented with pink bows and flowers; the crook, the *sine quâ non* of the costume, has bows and flowers. (*See* WATTEAU and FLORIAN.)

"SHE WENT INTO THE GARDEN TO CUT A CABBAGE-LEAF!" A plain pink dress of the last century with a white muslin cap and apron. Two cabbage-leaves in the hair.

SHILLING. (*See* SOVEREIGN and MONEY.)

SHIP. Grey dress with the badge of any particular ship in gold letters on bodice; wooden ornaments representing torpedoes on one shoulder and in hair. Sometimes a ship in full sail forms the head-dress over powdered hair, and a cannon is painted on one side of the skirt.

SHIPTON, MOTHER. (*See* HUBBARD, MOTHER.)

SHOE, OLD WOMAN WHO LIVED IN A. Short black skirt, over it a chintz sacque *à la* Watteau, cut square at the throat; with elbow-sleeves; powdered hair; high-pointed black hat; a rod in her hand. A large high-heeled scarlet satin shoe, trimmed with gold, slung across the shoulders and filled with small dolls.

JANE SHORE. (1461–1483.) A fair beautiful woman, the wife of a baker, the mistress of Edward IV., who died a pauper in extreme old age. Jewels in the hair. Dress with girdle round waist, flowing skirt, looped over satin petticoat bordered with ermine; stomacher and revers to low bodice. (For style, *see* EDWARD IV.)

SHRIMP. A long pink gown with a cap fashioned like the head of a shrimp. A velvet bodice, the basque at the back simulating a shrimp's tail. Enamelled shrimp ornaments.

SHUTTLECOCK. Short white satin dress with long cock's feathers in perpendicular rows; red skull cap of velvet, bordered with a gold band; red velvet cuirass bodice; white shoes and gloves; small shuttlecocks fastened on red velvet round neck; the same for earrings.

SICILIAN. Close-fitting satin skirt embroidered from the waist with roses. A loose white muslin bodice opening in a V shape to show

Fig. 38.—DRESS OF PERIOD 1640.

an embroidered stomacher. Pendent sleeves and a silk scarf lightly colored round the waist. The hair bound with ribbons, and gold pins inserted.

SILVER QUEEN. Low bodice made of cloth of silver, skirt of silver-spangled tulle; silver sceptre, crown, and ornaments; veil and winged sleeves of silver tulle.

SING A SONG OF SIXPENCE. The maid wears a red petticoat; short, dark blue tunic; pointed bodice, high striped sleeves to elbow; mob cap; satchel at side.

SIREN. Dress of green and white crêpe, over a petticoat of silver cloth bordered with a fringe of grass, shells, and leaves powdered with crystal. Cuirass bodice made of silver cloth, resembling fish-scales, bordered with green satin, to which are attached silver fish and Medusa heads; pearls, mother-of-pearl drops, and dewdrops introduced as fringes; also on the wreath of grasses worn over a crystal-spangled veil.

SISTERS OF CHARITY. (*See* ABBESS.)

SISTERS who desire to appear in costumes which assimilate might choose any of the following: **Apple and Pear Blossoms, Sovereign and Shilling, Cinderella's two sisters, Cordelia's sisters, Brenda and Minna Toil, Brunhilda and Kriemhilda, Salt and Fresh Water, the Roses of York and Lancaster, a Circassian Princess and Slave, Music and Painting, the Two Nornas, Lovebirds, Aurora and the Hours, Oranges and Lemons, Buttercups and Daisies, Rose and Lily, or two flowers of any kind, Nymphs of the Forest, New Year and Old,** and four sisters as the **Seasons.**

SIXTEENTH CENTURY. (*See* CATHARINE OF ARRAGON, CATHARINE HOWARD, CATHARINE PARR, Periods of HENRY VIIIth, MARY, ELIZABETH, and Illustrations of QUEEN ELIZABETH (Fig. 16), ELIZABETHAN WAITING MAID (Fig. 17), TUDOR (Fig. 43).

1640. (*See* Illustration, Fig. 38.) This should be carried out in fawn or silver grey, the lighter skirt trimmed with black velvet, the folded tunic bodice and outer sleeves of a deeper tone. The white kerchief cape turns downwards from the neck, and is made in white linen, a band of the same round the top of the bodice, and the white linen under sleeves are just seen through the opening of the large outer sleeve.

SKATING COSTUME. (*See* RUSSIAN SKATER, POLISH, &c.)

SKIRT DANCER. A kilt-pleated white silk skirt, yards wide, starting from the bust where a sash of ribbons cross below a gold embroidered yoke. A short green velvet gold-wrought sleeveless jacket. Kilt pleated Bishop sleeves; a round cap of green velvet and gold; petticoat all lace and most voluminous.

SLATE AND PENCIL. Slate-colored silk gown edged on the skirt and berthe with fur, slate pencils hanging from the short sleeves; slate-colored gloves to elbow. Slate and sponge suspended at the side. Powdered hair and aigrette of slate pencils.

SLAVE. Flowing dress of white satin embroidered in gold; hair hanging down the back bound with a fillet of gold; gold band round the throat, gold anklets, the hands united by gold handcuffs. Two sisters can be dressed alike, and appear chained together. (*See* CIRCASSIAN SLAVE.)

SNAKE. Black tulle gown with low bodice. A snake formed of glittering paillettes twining round bodice and skirt; another in the same green paillettes embroidered on the stockings. A metal snake for bracelets and necklets. Hair dishevelled, with a serpent coronet.

SNAKE CHARMER. Russet-green gown like the bark of a tree; made in classic fashion—bodice and skirt in one, caught up on hips by cord. The bodice hangs over pouch fashion—snakes in lap, snakes round arm, and clustered on front of bodice. A velvet moveable snake in the hair.

SNAIL. Blue gauze skirt draped with snail shells; bodice of striped yellow and red silk. The paniers of the two colors at the back are cut in the shape of a shell; the neck bordered with feathers. A snail shell for the head dress.

SLEEP. Straw-colored ball-dress wreathed with poppies; cap in the shape of a poppy turned upside down, and worn on one side of the powdered hair, or a wreath of poppies.

SNEERWELL, LADY (*School for Scandal.*) Dress of pink satin, with Watteau sacque; petticoat white satin with lace and pearl embroidery and roses in front. Second dress, walking costume of terra-cotta plush over pale pink; large hat of plush, terra-cotta shaded plumes.

SNIPE. Skirt and bodice of feathers, with cap like head of bird.

SNOW, SNOWBALL, SNOWSTORM. A princesse dress of soft white silk or satin, made high to the throat, or with a square-cut bodice, and very short sleeves; a drapery of Indian muslin put on just below the hips, covered with detached pieces of frosted swansdown, is caught back at both sides with long glass icicles; a wreath of frosted swansdown, with icicles; a veil, fastened either to the wreath or to the shoulders, of frosted tulle; long gloves, trimmed to match, and shoes with swansdown rosettes. Necklace of icicles, drooping snowdrops peeping out beneath; hair down, and frosted with glass powder; or hair powdered, surmounted by black velvet cocked hat, a snowball at each point and over face; the fan swansdown, with an edging of drooping icicles. **Snow Queen.** Same, with crown of icicles. (*See* WINTER and POLISH SNOW.

SNOW WHITE, OR LITTLE SNOWFLAKES. White brocaded satin Turkish trousers; bodice and tunic in one, of white nun's veiling embroidered round the edge with gold; gold girdle about the waist, and a white scarf with embroidered ends; the bodice and sleeves trimmed with rows of gold cord; white cap and veil. (*See* WHITE DRESSES, W.)

SNOWDROP. Skirt and bodice of white tulle, edged with pale green satin; basque and sleeves of white satin, cut in points to represent the petals; trimmed with deep fringe of snowdrops; chaplet of same flowers round the neck; powdered hair, and snowdrop wreath. (*See* FLOWERS and JANUARY.)

SOPHIA WESTERN. Sacque of pale pink, over dark brown satin skirt; long lace apron; kerchief and low bodice, with chocolate stomacher; powdered hair; pointed lace cap; high-heeled pink shoes, paste buckles; tan gloves; copy of "Isabella; or, The Fatal Marriage," in the hand.

SORCERESS. Short costume of black, red, and gold satin, the skirt red, having a black band round with the signs of the Zodiac in gold; a serpent twisted about the waist; a scarf of many colors worn diagonally over the hips; a red kerchief with gold coins on the head; ornaments, beads and coins. Or, a black velvet robe high to the throat, with pendent sleeves covered with cabalistic signs; high-pointed cap entwined with a serpent; a stick carried in the hand; black satin shoes, embroidered with gold. Or, yellow satin over scarlet satin, cut in points, and at each point a copper bell, ornamented with black velvet bats, mice, efts, etc.; a large green snake coiling round the bodice, ditto round the neck and arms; head-dress, gold bat on the forehead, and snake round the head.

SORCERER. The characters include **Lady Sauzagare** in a princess dress of dark violet velvet turned back with pearls. Peach brocaded front. Powdered hair, and black lace; and **Aline** in bridal array.

SORRENTINE PEASANT. (*See* ITALIAN, and Illustration Fig. 25.)

SOUBRETTE, or WAITING MAID (*in Louis XV.'s Reign.*) Wears a pretty *poudré* short dress, generally with a quilted skirt, cap, and muslin apron. For example: Rose-colored quilted petticoat; blue satin tunic; black velvet low bodice laced up the front with blue and bordered with lace; muslin apron trimmed with lace; small lace cap with wild roses; gold ornaments; high-heeled shoes, and pink and white stockings.

SOUR GRAPES. Maize satin dress, covered with bunches of grapes; a wreath of leaves and grapes; more bunches on the low square bodice and elbow-sleeves, and in the muslin apron turned up and forming a lap.

SOVEREIGN AND SHILLING (*for two sisters*). One wearing gold, the other silver. Evening dresses of gold or silver-spangled tulle, liberally trimmed with coins, which fringe the bodice; gold-netted or silver scarf on skirt with coins; rings and tassels at end to resemble a purse; Phrygian cap of satin with the same coins; gold or silver aigrette in front, and coin ornaments.

SPADES, QUEEN OF (*Dame de Pic*). (*See* CARDS.)

SPANISH. The costume illustrated in Fig. 39 has a kilt-pleated skirt and pretty sash knotted at the side, the Bolero jacket trimmed with gold and edged with ball fringe. Large epaulettes overshadowing the shoulder. The felt Spanish hat has a silk handkerchief below and some triple pompons on the edge. Another costume is a satin skirt touching the ground (white, red, yellow, or rose) with black lace flounces headed by bands of velvet or gold; low bodice of the same; senorita jacket of velvet trimmed with ball fringe, made with long sleeves; high comb; lace mantilla fastened over it with red and yellow roses, the hair in a coil at back; gloves, mittens, and high-heeled shoes. The ordinary Spanish dress of to-day is a black silk gown with square-cut bodice and mantilla. The **Women of Carvajales** wear short embroidered flannel skirts, silk mantillas worked with gold spangles, gold necklaces and earrings, and shoes with silver buckles; those of **Dermillo,** short black velvet skirts, aprons embroidered with colored silks, small China crape shawls, and black shoes with silver buckles. The **Women of Toledo,** short silk skirts, trimmed with gold and silver braid; black velvet bodices with gold buttons; red velvet aprons and black velvet shoes; coral necklaces, and the hair tied up with colored ribbons. The **Women of Mercia** have embroidered skirts, black velvet bodices, white shoes worked with gold. **At Malaga** flounced skirts, China crape shawls, and large pearl necklaces are worn. In **Valencia,** short silk skirts, embroidered with silver and gold; satin bodices of different colors, with tight sleeves; silk stockings, and large white satin shoes; a silver comb in the hair with hair-pins and colored beads; necklaces; and baskets of flowers on their arms. At **Saragossa,** with short cotton skirts, the small colored crape shawls are crossed round their waists, and gold necklaces clasp the neck. At **Segovia** the silk skirts accompany black velvet bodices embroidered in gold, with long sleeves; coral and gold necklaces, and black satin shoes; small velvet caps worked with gold. At **Caceres,** silk handkerchiefs are tied round the head, the velvet bodices show silver buttons, the skirts plaited; shoes with silver buttons. At **Ciudad Real,** the black bodices accompany silk handkerchiefs crossed over the chest, and colored skirts. **A Catalonian** has a black velvet skirt with an upper-skirt of yellow; a black velvet jacket; floral head-dress. **A Toledo Woman** a blue satin skirt, trimmed with gold and satin braid; crimson velvet apron to match; a black velvet bodice over white lawn chemisette; velvet shoes, red stockings; coral ornaments. **A Spanish Mandolin Girl** appears in a short red silk skirt, bordered with white silk, with arabesque designs upon it; a low loose cambric bodice, with a black velvet Spanish jacket, trimmed with gold fringe and braid; long scarf sash of black and gold silk, fringed with gold; as much gold jewellery as possible. An **Andalusian,** white silk short skirt, trimmed with pink and black velvet; pink silk tunic, with silver and black velvet; black velvet bodice; silver comb; spangled vest and pelisse; large black fan. The **"Saya y Manta"** is of Andalusian origin, and was formerly worn by the ladies of Lima at processions, bull-fights, and when they went out to shop, but never in church, where the mantilla is *de rigueur.* The "saya," or skirt, is made of rich black satin, lined throughout, and formed into innumerable small plaits from the waist to the edge of the skirt by strong waxed threads. It is then slipped over a board of its own length and from twenty to thirty inches wide, on which it remains for three weeks, so that the satin may retain the creases when the threads are cut to within a quarter of a yard from the waist. A richly-embroidered Chinese scarf, the deeply fringed edges of which fall over the "saya" in front, is fastened at the throat by a jewel. The "manta" consists of a shawl-shaped piece of black Chinese crape, the triangular part of which is tied tightly round the waist by means of a casing, the straight end being drawn up over the head and across the face, so as to show only one eye. It is held thus by the thumb and two first fingers of the right hand, a lace pocket-handkerchief and flower in the left. Silk stockings, and shoes of either black satin or fine bronze kid, embroidered with colored silks and cut very low on the instep, complete this costume. A high Spanish comb is worn (this gives height and elegance to the figure), bracelets and rings, but neither gloves nor fan are admissible. **A Spanish Dancer,** a pale blue satin skirt, trimmed with silver passementerie and grelots; a pale pink satin bodice, with blue satin jacket, reaching only halfway down the back, and ornamented with more silver grelots; a white blonde mantilla; a Spanish comb at the top, and a red rose at the side of the head. **Dancing Girl of Seville.** Blue shoes and stockings embroidered down the centre of foot; short white satin skirt, two gold-colored satin flounces cut in vandykes; white satin low bodice, tight sleeve, a band of red embroidery inside the arm; band at the waist, red epaulettes; red band at waist; gold kerchief tucked inside bodice; gold chain round neck; red ribbons and rose in hair.

SPARROW. Short skirt and bodice of brown feathers; cap like head of bird.

SPELLING-BEE. Orange skirt, striped with black velvet, the letters of the alphabet in black carried round in a double row; the low square black velvet bodice, trimmed with orange, displays the names of dictionaries, such as Webster, Johnson, etc. A bee on the head.

SPEAKER, LADY. Full bottomed judicial wig, black brocaded square-cut bodice. Black silk judicial gown, black shoes and stockings with steel buckles.

SPHYNX. Black satin dress glittering with gold fringe and Egyptian hieroglyphics; short sleeves, and fringed scarf of buttercup colour; Oriental fan at the side. Sphynx head-dress with Ibis; wand in the hand. Black satin mask.

SPIDER. Soft brown silk, the body painted to resemble that of a spider. Brown Japanese spiders fastened about the skirt mingling with the web. Jewellery spiders; gloves, stockings and shoes are trimmed with them.

SPINNING GIRL. (*Fileuse.*) Pink and white striped satin skirt; white satin apron embroidered with roses which taper towards the waist. Paniers and bodice of maize and white brocade. The elbow sleeves have three frills of muslin, and accord with a muslin frilled kerchief; graduated bows of pink satin carried down the bodice to a point, each tied in the centre with the color of the brocade. Distaff and spindle in the hand, decorated with pink ribbon and field flowers. The white silk stockings are embroidered with roses. The black satin shoes have pink heels. The hair is powdered; over it is a hood-shaped cap, the front composed of narrow boullonnés of chiffon over runners of pink satin ribbon, the ends tied in a bow on the top of the head and beneath the chin with a rose.

SPOON, SOUVENIR, as **TWO FRIENDS,** in full white skirts and bodices with waist belts, made in baby fashion, but with a spoon tucked through the belt, and each carrying a large wooden spoon with the words "Souvenir Spoon" on the bowl. An aigrette of spoons.

SPORT. Pink satin waistcoat and lace tie, with brown velvet coat and brass buttons; gold cap trimmed with colors of favorite racehorses; horse's bust on the front of bodice, portraits of racehorses; on the pink satin skirt, insignias of hunting, shooting, and fishing. Ornaments, stirrup, and riding crop.

SPRING. A green or white dress trimmed with spring flowers, daisies, primroses, crocuses, and violets; a gossamer veil falling over the shoulders, a wreath of the same; the flowers may be arranged round the skirt in a lattice-work, the tunic edged with a fringe of green grass. Less hackneyed renderings are as follows; Green silk short skirt trimmed with snowdrops and violets; white polonaise and low bodice, with long hanging sleeves caught up on one side by a swallow; a ruff of lace and flowers round the neck; green and white cap with flowers; green satin shoes. (*See* SEASON, and Illustration No. 26, SPRINGTIME IN JAPAN.)

SPRING CLEANING. Housemaid's costume with a miniature dust-pan, house-flannel, duster, and cake of soap hanging at the side.

SPRITE. (*See* DIABLESSE.)

SQUEERS, MRS. AND MISS (*Nicholas Nickleby*). (*See* DICKENS.)

SQUIRE'S DAUGHTER. Loose satin skirt with three muslin lace-edged flounces; tunic of flowered chintz, open in front, bunched up at side; pointed bodice with blue stomacher; lace elbow-sleeves and kerchief; muslin cap.

STAR, STARLIGHT, EVENING STAR, POLAR STAR, MORNING STAR, NORTHERN STAR, are all rendered after the same order, viz., with either a black, blue, or white evening dress, and veil covered with silver stars; ornaments of the same, and coronet in the hair, frequently supplemented by electric light. Much silver fringe is used on bodices and tunic, a glittering effect being desired. The hair powdered with silver is an improvement, For **Starlight,** a purple dress veiled in star-spangled tulle, with a silver scarf about the skirt, looped with silver stars and fringe; bodice and veil spangled with stars, also front of dress; crown of stars. **A Dark Starlight Night,** a black dress, studded on one side with diamonds, the other with jet stars; one side of the hair only powdered; one glove; and one shoe white, one black.

STARNBERG BRIDE. A short red skirt, full lace-trimmed apron going quite round and reaching nearly to the hem; a black velvet bodice laced across with silver, and filled in with a lace kerchief made with a frill at the throat; long, full sleeves matching the skirt; a bridal wreath. (*See* GERMAN PEASANT.)

STATUARY is represented in white linen robes. The hair powdered, the face, neck and arms whitened.

STELLA. (*See* FILLE DU TAMBOUR-MAJOR.)

STEWARDESS. Short blue satin skirt and loose bodice, with white over-jacket faced with blue; white fisherman's cap with a blue band displaying the word "Stewardess" in silver letters.

STOCKBROKER, LADY. Short pink silk skirt bordered with

Fig. 40.—SUMMER.

white satin, hung with gold coins, and the several kinds of stocks printed upon it. A low bodice, over it a polonaise of star-spangled gauze, caught up with roses, the top trimmed with gold coins and fringe; gold belt at the waist; gold net on the head with coins; a cornucopia carried in the hand, out of which stocks, money, and roses seem to spring; high-heeled pink shoes; black mittens.

STORK. Dress of bird's plumage and satin with head of stork for cap.

STRAWBERRIES AND CREAM. Short skirt of strawberry-colored satin, arranged with deep box-plaits of brocaded cream satin at hem, trimmed with cream lace, looped up with strawberries and leaves and strawberry colored and white ribbon. Paniers of cream brocade edged with a fringe of strawberries; the bodice cream brocade with a long pointed waist laced up the front; epaulettes of strawberries, wreath of same across the bodice; gilded punnet of strawberries for head-dress. Cream fan painted with strawberries.

STYRIAN PEASANT. Short skirt of amber trimmed with black velvet; blue tunic, looped up with rose-color; black velvet square bodice, over high white chemistte; white straw hat with rose-colored ribbons; gold earrings; cross and rosary; white apron.

SUABIAN PEASANT. A plaited skirt of black taffetas, over a starched petticoat, to ankles; red stockings and black shoes; dark-colored cloth jacket trimmed with ruches of black silk, cut *en cœur* in front over white linen bodice; white apron tied round waist; bandana handkerchief about neck; black national head-dress embroidered in gold, black streamers falling at the back.

SUEZ CANAL. (*See* CANAL.)

SULTANA, INDIAN. A robe of cloth of gold and a spangled veil; the seams of the long loose habit embroidered with precious stones; cluster of diamonds on her head; loose under-dress.

SUMMER. (*See* Illustration Fig. 40.) A white or pink gauze, lisse, or tulle dress, festooned with summer flowers, especially roses; a staff entwined with flowers. It is sufficient to wear a wreath of the same, but a veil with butterflies is a more decided fancy dress, or a straw hat, with flowers and butterflies. Scattered rose leaves on the skirt add to the effect, interspersed with butterflies and green beetles; a basket of flowers in hand; necklet and earrings of China roses. A parasol wreathed with roses in the hand.

SUN. A yellow tulle or gauze dress, trimmed with gold; a cap with a gold sun; the same embroidered on the front of the bodice; rising and setting suns appearing on the skirt and one on the wand carried in the hand; ornaments, gold suns, and a wand in the hand surmounted by the same. **Sunbeam.** Yellow tulle, flounced to waist, each flounce edged with rows of gold braid; a large sash round the waist with gold fringe, a gold châtelaine bag at side; head-dress, veil of gold tissue, enveloping the figure, and glittering at every movement; gold ornaments. **Sunrise.** Dress of grey tulle, with rows of ribbon of the rainbow shades round the skirt; veil of grey gold-spangled tulle. Or, grey and pink in alternate skirts; grey tunic, spangled with powdered glass. Wreath of half-opened roses, with dewdrops and birds with open beaks. **Sunset.** Black diaphanous gown trimmed with red and yellow suns; coronet of the same. Or, a red dress, with the setting sun worked in tinsel in front, the rays coming well outside the horizon, slightly blue or grey. Gold gauze veil; gold fringe.

SUNFLOWER *(after Alma Tadema's picture).* A long dress of some dark brown stuff, with loose sleeves, falling back so as to show the arms; embroidered at throat, sleeves, waist, and hem with gold; sunflowers in hand; three gold bands confine the hair. Or, the petals of the flower form a crown and border the waist, making a basque.

SUPERSTITIONS. A black gown with the numbers 13 and 7 in white, together with ladders, skull, and cross-bones, peacock feathers and opals introduced as trimmings, and in the hair, and for ornaments.

SUSAN. Dove-colored stuff gown, rather short, with soft white kerchief and cap, and a pink ribbon in the latter. **Susan, Black-Eyed.** (*See* B.)

SUSANNA (*Figaro*). Wears a Spanish dress of pink satin and black lace, black velvet jacket and mantilla. (*See* SPANISH.)

SUZEL. White silk petticoat trimmed with black velvet; large pink silk apron trimmed to match; white silk bodice slashed with black velvet; black and white stockings.

SWALLOW. Tulle dress, black, grey, and white, with swallows dotted about it; flowers in the hand; a swallow in the hair. **Swallows, Flight of.** White dress with black velvet bodice; the birds sewn on the front of dress, one on each shoulder and several flying across the skirt.

Fig. 41.—SWEDISH COSTUME.

SWEDISH COSTUME, A. (*See* the Illustration, Fig. 41.) Red and white striped skirt, large white linen apron, bodice of green cloth, embroidered in red, gold, and black; straps over the shoulders of black velvet, full thick white muslin sleeves. Hair in plaits, coif head-dress of cloth fitting the head with kilt pleatings at the side. The peasantry wear bright-colored woollen skirts touching the ground; white aprons nearly as long as the dress, with rows of colored embroidery across the lower part; fur-lined jackets over white chemisettes with a red and green corselet rounded at the top, or a half-high square-cut velvet bodice embroidered in silver, with short sleeves, and points at waist, back and front; hair in plaits, a large bow of ribbon at the back. In some parts of Sweden a white linen cap is worn, the shape of a paper bag, the points standing out at either side of the head.

SWEEP, LADY. Dress of dull black satin drawn in at the waist with cord; the word "Sweep" in silver on skirt and bodice; a sweep's circular broom and iron hook attached to girdle; a characteristic smut on cheek. A cap like that of FOLLY, with a point at the top.

SWEETHEART, MY. Dainty dress of pale pink satin; muslin apron trimmed with antique Valenciennes lace; large hat with wreath of wild flowers.

SWEET PEAS, A BUNCH OF. (*See* Illustration No. 42.) The skirt of the rasse terre length, is made of white satin, and so is the full bodice, both entirely covered with sweet-pea stalks, tied in a bunch at the side, to form the girdle. The flowers border the top of the bodice and constitute the sleeves, and a pretty satin hat is fashioned after the form of the flower. Long gloves are ruffled on the arm, sweet peas figure on the fan, and black shoes and white silk stockings complete the costume.

SWEET SEVENTEEN. (*See* WHITE DRESSES.)

SWISS. For the several cantons there are 22 varieties at least of the peasant's costume. In Glarus it is not picturesque; a bonnet very much like a nightcap covers the head; the plain bodice opens V-shape, bordered with a ruche, and the white linen apron contrasts with the dark petticoat. The Ementhal dress is one of those generally copied; a coquettish straw hat covered with flowers; black velvet corselet bodice and yoke-piece worn over a chemisette with sleeves to elbow, the black velvet covered with silver embroidery, and hung with silver chains;

closely-plaited short skirt of green or lilac. The distinguishing feature of the Basle dress is the silver chain round the waist; the head-dress is black silk, like that worn in many parts of Germany. In Schaffhausen the bodice is still more ornamented. In Niedwalden, on the Lake of Lucerne, it is supplemented by a massive silver collar; a silver arrow through the hair. The Geneva girl wears a French muslin cap, tight-fitting jacket, lace-embroidered neckerchief, short apron and petticoat, high-heeled shoes. The Waadtlauderin has a low bodice, with a many-colored chemisette; striped petticoat, silk apron; white stockings; square-toed shoes; straw hat. In Tessin the girls display a multi-colored apron, high square bodice over a white chemisette; head-dress, a tinsel crown with silver arrows; sandals with wooden soles and high heels. In Valois they wear a dark dress and curiously-plaited white cap. In the canton of Uri the gown is dark, the cap large, with a butterfly-wing fastened to the back of head. The girls of St. Gallien have a striped skirt, a silk bodice laced with gold or silver chains, short white sleeves and a black gauze cap with a fan of gauze on either side of the crescent-shaped bandeau which encircles the head. The girls of Solothurn wear the hair in plaits, and the dress high to the throat, in no way remarkable. At Appenzell low, black velvet bodices are fastened with chains carried under the arm to the back of the shoulder, a loosely-tied silk handkerchief round the neck, the red silk handkerchief being a badge of matronhood; a cream-colored plain full skirt; large silk apron reaching to the hem, of a lighter shade. Full white elbow sleeves, neck filled in with white and gathered up to the throat. Hair in two long plaits. Unterwalden. Pale blue skirt, a broad velvet band three inches from the foot. Black silk sleeveless bodice. Full white sleeves, long black mittens, black silk apron, bead necklace. Hair plaited with white ribbon and secured at the back of the head with large silver dagger. Schaffhausen. Plain green skirt, dark prune silk apron. Sleeveless bodice laced in front. Silver chains looped across and carried under arm. Full white sleeves, lace frill round neck, neck-lace. Hair plaited about the head. Large, low-crowned, straight brim, Leghorn hat with roses and prune ribbon; long streamers behind. Argau. Pale grey plain skirt with silk apron to match; square bodice filled in with a stiff chemisette secured at neck by velvet collar which joins the bodice at the back; grey sleeves and round chemisette. Silver chains hanging under arm. Hair in two plaits. At Tiffereggen the head-dress is like an inverted basin. At Puster Thal a large ruff completes the picturesque dress. It is in Schwyz the high wheel-shaped cap is worn, and in Granbundten a striped apron and silk handkerchief about the head. At Zug, a silk bodice trimmed with silver lace, lace-trimmed kerchief over bust, yellow straw hat on one side. At Freiburg the head-dress is a great feature—very large, made of black silk and gauze. The following is a Fancy Swiss costume: Short skirt of silver cloth, with rows of black velvet; muslin tunic bordered with silver, looped up with black and silver; apron of muslin, covered with a lattice-work of velvet and silver; low bodice, with many tabs for basque, trimmed with silver; white muslin head-dress, with silver braid and flowers.

SYBIL. Eastern dress of cloth of gold jewelled and embroidered and richly trimmed with gold lace. The jewelled crown surmounted by three ostrich feathers held by a diamond star.

SWORDFISH. (*See* FISH.)

SYRIAN. Under bodice of muslin or gauze opening in a V-shape at the neck and bordered with gold lace. Corselet bodice of velvet and gold embroidery to which shoulder straps are attached. Open sleeves threaded with gold. A narrow skirt with bright colored bordering. A sash knotted about the waist. Bracelets of coins, two rows of beads about the throat. A bandeau of coins round the head.

TALLIEN, MADAME. Velvet riding-habit turned back with pink silk; a round cape over the shoulders; large muslin tie; hair powdered; broad brimmed black velvet hat, with pointed crown and ostrich plumes drooping over it. Period, 1775–1838.

TAMBOURINE GIRL. Short skirt of black satin, trimmed with crimson, embroidered in gold; bodice of crimson and black satin, fastened with gold buttons; crimson and gold cap; ornaments, gold coin earrings, necklace, and bangles. Or, short black and yellow petticoat; red upper-skirt, trimmed with bands of black velvet, from which depend gold coins; black velvet low square bodice, laced with red and gold; red silk handkerchief about the head, a tambourine hung at the side.

TANGIERS, LADY OF. The turban is of bright orange silk, coming well over the forehead, the ends falling at the back, large pendent jewels hanging on either side, and intermingling with the huge ring earrings; the jacket of velvet has short sleeves, and opens in a circular form to show a stomacher, which like the jacket is a mass of embroidery; transparent hanging sleeves; long embroidered skirt; many-colored silk scarf about the waist; bead necklace, and gold and bead bracelets.

TARGETS. White satin skirt bordered with targets. Bodice draped with lisse, targets on the shoulder, one forming the front of the bodice draped with a sash of the colors. An aigrette of the same in the hair fastened with a silver arrow. A bow in the hand; white shoes with colored bows. (*See* ARCHER.)

TEA. (*See* FIVE O'CLOCK.)

TEAZLE, LADY (*School for Scandal*). A *poudrè* costume of the Georgian period made with sacque; old brocade and satin suitable. For example: Bodice and train of cream-colored brocade; petticoat of lemon satin, trimmed with old point lace, Marshal Niel roses, brown leaves; ornaments, pearls and diamonds. Lady Teazle, in the screen scene, might wear a dress of pale Venetian-red silk, opening over a petticoat entirely covered with plaitings of yellowish lace; stomacher of lace and red ribbons; full neckerchief of cream silk Indian muslin, with double plaitings of the lace, tied in a large knot in front, fastened with a paste brooch, and clusters of pale yellow flowers; either a large cream lace hat, lined with Venetian-red, or a lace turban toque, like that of Miss Gunning in Sir Joshua Reynolds's portrait. Watteau fan; cream mousquetaire gloves; high-heeled shoes of Venetian-red with diamond buckles; black velvet with diamond clasp round throat; a cane might be carried in hand. Or, a white satin sacque with brocaded stripes; the petticoat embroidered in crystal and iridescent beads festooned with yellow roses. A small wreath of roses and aigrette on one side of the powdered hair; satin pointed shoes; long gloves; pearls round the neck, a miniature hanging in front.

TELEGRAPH, SUBMARINE. Bodice and skirt of pale sea-green satin, looped with silver chains, cables, and grappling-irons; seaweed round the throat and top of the dress.

TELEGRAPHINE. Short dress of blue and red satin trimmed with wires, represented by gold and silver braid, and cuffs of blue satin; the upper skirt tulle, looped up with medallions representing the telegraph poles and white satin telegrams; a satin or black velvet cap, with the word "Telegraph" worked in pearls; a dispatch bag at side; pearl ornaments.

TELEPHONE. White satin dress with striped over-skirt. A bunch of strings hanging at the side. Head-dress with the mouth-piece at the side.

TEMPEST. (*See* ARIEL and MIRANDA.)

TENNIS, LAWN. (*See* LAWN TENNIS.)

THALIA *(The Muse of Comedy).* Loose soft drapery caught up at the knee, over flowing skirt; low bodice, with deep gathered basque; sash round the waist; a wreath in one hand, a mask in the other; a tambourine at the side.

THETIS. Dress of foamy white; a beryl-colored peplum with bunches of coral and shells; pale coral and shells about the head.

THIRTEENTH CENTURY, A LADY OF THE, makes a very effective dress. Ruby velvet skirt trimmed with silver lace; cream-colored brocade for front breadth and bodice, with long sleeves; high-pointed head-dress and silver-spangled veil. (*See* PERIOD OF EDWARD HENRY V., BERENGARIA OF NAVARRE.)

THISTLE. Short full skirt of vieux rose satin. Swiss bodice of blue-green satin the tone of the leaf. Chemisette and sleeves of white silver spangled tulle fashioned like a thistle. A bunch of the flowers on one shoulder, and on the other a knot of vieux rose ribbon with long streamers. The motto in white applique, "*Nemo me impune lacessit.*" Tufts of thistles round the hem of the skirt. Green silk stockings with thistle embroidered as clocks, and shoes to match. Gold net on hair.

THISTLEDOWN. Short skirt of pale mauve silk or crèpe; a bunch of thistles on front, back, and on either side, tied with pale green and mauve ribbons; mauve bodice edged with thistles, also the sleeves and waist; there should be a belt of pale green silk and a flounce on either edge, also of pale green, the lower one over 15-in. deep, the upper one reaching the thistles encircling the low bodice about 6-in. deep. Each flounce, cut in deep tapering points, is edged with white pampas grass carefully picked to pieces and sewn on with white sewing silk. These points should be carefully tacked down and lined with stiff muslin so that they may lie flat. Two thistles should be placed like an aigrette in the hair, and a few tied with green and mauve ribbons carried in the hand. Mauve stockings and green shoes, with a thistle on each.

THRALE, MRS. (*Georgian Dress*). White silk sacque, the front covered with lace; powdered hair; white cap.

THREADNEEDLE STREET, OLD, LADY OF. (*See* O.)

TIME. Dress of black and white and orange tulle; with a cuirass bodice, and red Dutch clocks hanging at the side; the several hours in Roman letters round the tunic; an hour-glass and scythe for châtelaine; hour-glass aigrette for head-dress.

TITANIA (*Midsummer Night's Dream*). White or blue robe of tulle, gauze, or some soft floating material, spangled with silver; a tulle scarf fastened on one shoulder with a bouquet of wild flowers, and by another on the opposite side of the dress; for head-dress, either a crown of silver flowers, or a diamond star-coronet, over a veil with butterflies. Necklet and bracelets of small flowers; a wand, with a star at the point; the hair floating.

TITIAN'S BELLA. (*See* VENETIAN.

TOILETTE, MY LADY'S. Pink satin skirt, made short, and striped with pale blue ribbons finished off at the hem with pendent powder puffs, alternately pink and blue. These reappear at the neck of the pointed bodice supplemented by a Medici collar lined with cloth of silver to imitate a looking-glass. Hand-glass on each shoulder. Head-dress a large blue puff surrounded by swansdown.

TOILET TABLE. White muslin dress over pink calico, made with a low bodice, long sleeves, and fichu, trimmed with lace; a looking-glass suspended from waist, with brush, combs, scissors, etc.; powder-puff in hand; cap, like pincushion, stuck with pins; ribbon epaulettes, with scissors, etc., attached.

TOLEDO WOMAN. Blue satin short skirt with gold and silver braid; crimson velvet apron trimmed to match; black velvet and white lawn bodice; black velvet shoes; red stockings; coral ornaments.

LA TOSCA. Satin skirt touching the ground, over-skirt of brocade caught up on one side. A deep sash round the waist and a high bodice with large muslin tie in front, and gauntlet cuffs to the tight sleeve. A stick in hand with ribbons and flowers, and a large velvet hat with feathers.

TOYS. Low bodice and short skirt, with perpendicular gold stripes on a red ground. Loops of cord carried across the waist and on to the shoulders. Cap fashioned like a shuttlecock of red velvet and white feathers. An appliquè of chessmen carried round the skirt.

TRANSYLVANIA. Short flowered skirt, with large embroidered muslin apron almost covering it. Round velvet cape with fur cape above it, and over this a smaller one of white cloth richly braided in black matching the large sleeves to the wrist. Full blouse bodice. Wreath of roses in the hair.

TRIC-TRAC. Short black satin skirt with a row of gold buttons; black satin low bodice, with basque cut in points, bound with gold; bertha of black and white checks; gold-spangled muslin tunic, forming one large puff all round, points falling beneath; black satin bandeau round the head; black shoes with gold heels, check silk stockings; gold ornaments.

TRICOLOUR. Short satin skirt of wide red, white, and blue stripes; blue satin tail-coat, having red and white revers, and old-fashioned buttons; lace collar and cravat; powdered hair, with three-cornered hat.

TRICYCLE. Hair powdered, with a miniature tricycle at the top, the larger wheels towards the face. Grey satin dress, with the wheels on either side in black velvet; black velvet bodice; a bicycle lamp in front.

TRILBY. DuMaurier's heroine wears many dresses on the stage, but the one with which we principally associate her is worn in the earlier part of the story, in the studio. A short yellow and black striped skirt, bare feet, a soldier's dark blue cloth coat, double-breasted, and fastened with brass buttons, epaulets on the shoulders, a belt round the waist, and the corners of the coat turned backwards and tucked under this belt. Then she appears in a simple black dress with white apron and bib, in a fawn stuff gown with muslin cap, long fichu and cuffs, then in an exquisite Empire evening dress of white tulle and gold embroidery with a train of gold tissue from the shoulders, a jewelled bandeau in the hair. In the last dress her hair flows over her shoulders, and she is robed in a loose, diaphanous gown, soft and clinging, hanging sleeves leaving the arm bare.

TROT, DAME. Blue satin quilted petticoat with Pompadour draperies; black velvet hat; muslin fichu and apron; large spectacles; crutch stick.

TRUE BLUE. Carried out entirely in blue; dress, veil, and ribbons.

TUDOR. The Illustration Fig. 43 is a velvet robe touching the ground, pleated; jewelled band round the waist, hanging sleeves; tight white satin ones beneath to wrist; collar and coif of velvet of the period, with bag at the back, taken from old picture. (*See* ELIZABETH, &C.)

TULIP. Skirt of red and yellow tulle caught up with velvet tulips; low bodice of red and yellow satin, the same colored ribbons round the neck, fastened with tulips; tulips in the powdered hair; red satin stockings and shoes; diamond buckles.

TUNIS ORANGE GIRL. Dark blue skirt; red striped apron trimmed with gold; broad orange and white striped silk scarf; black velvet senorita jacket; gold embroidered chemisette; orange silk cap with gold sequins; basket of oranges.

TURKISH WOMAN in Illustration wears full embroidered muslin trowsers gathered above the ankle, short satin skirt just visible over them; an outer robe of green satin; bodice and skirt in one richly embroidered and bordered with gold ball fringe, a belt round the waist jewelled, fastening with two silver circles, gold coin trimming round the open neck. The bodice is cut high at back, the bosom hidden by a gold embroidered kerchief; many rows of gold beads round the neck; long open sleeves, under ones of the gold embroidered muslin, frilled with the same muslin; a yashmuck and a square of muslin folded over the head, often replaced indoors by a round velvet Turkish cap. Velvet embroidered Turkish slippers. In the country they are often worn heelless, but this is not suitable for fancy balls.

Fig. 43.—DRESS OF TUDOR PERIOD.

TWELFTH NIGHT QUEEN. Black satin embroidered skirt. Low bodice and train of red velvet bordered with ermine; short sleeves with a double frill of lace. Gold zone round the waist, jewelled crown with a veil at the back, and a sceptre in the hand.

TWELFTH NIGHT (*Shakespeare*). (*See* VIOLA and OLIVIA.)

TWELFTH OF AUGUST. Gown of cream serge bedecked with heather and cartridges. The cap fashioned like a grouse.

TWENTY-FOUR O'CLOCK. Clock dial on front of high bodice with ruff showing hours from one to twenty-four. At back of head a pendulum swinging; short skirt of striped black, white, and red satin. The cap white satin with a dial in front; the sleeves puffed from shoulders to elbow.

TWILIGHT. May be carried out in four shades of grey tulle, dotted with silver stars, or in dark blue, the tunic caught up with a silver moon on one side; a pink and grey scarf, attached to the shoulders by a crescent, to the skirt by a silver bat. The bodice, *à la Vierge*, is made in two shades of satin or plush, with stars and dewdrops, opening in front to show a pink vest with crescents; a light pink tulle veil, with moths and other insects forming a coronet. Or, black dress of net and silver gauze, bespangled with beetles, grasshoppers, and other insects; silver gauze head-dress, with the same, and silver crescents; beetle's-wing fan, silver ornaments.

TWINS. Two children dressed alike in short-waisted gowns with black velvet shoulder straps, A bow on either side of the waist. A satchel bag attached to one with a doll peeping out of it. Grey satin hoods with points at the back, turning back in front with a piece of black velvet. **The Heavenly Twins** are represented by two sisters in black silk gowns and powdered hair, and **Twins, a Hundred Years Ago,** wear narrow skirts touching the ground, bordered with a flounce. High full bodices and cuffs to the elbow, and huge poke bonnets. Bag hanging at the side. Muffs in the hand.

TYROLESE, A. Short scarlet satin skirt trimmed with black and gold; a black satin tunic trimmed with bands of scarlet and gold; high stay-like black bodice laced in front with gold, bouquet on the left side; a white muslin bodice and sleeves beneath. A high Tyrolese hat with grey ribbons round the crown, flowers beneath; a large muslin apron, embroidered in double lines with gold, almost hiding the front of the skirt, and reaching to the hem. Or, short green stuff skirt, bordered with two bands of black velvet edged with cord; black velvet low square bodice over a white chemisette, with white sleeves to elbow; stomacher embroidered in gold and colored silks; buckled waist-belt made of leather with chain and keys suspended: large apron, embroidered in double lines across; high-pointed Tyrolean hat, with gold cord round, and a bouquet of flowers and feathers at the side; large ruff or wide turn-down collar; multi-colored handkerchief round neck; white stockings, colored clocks; black leather boots cut low on instep, gold buckles in front; gold chain with medal attached.

TWINKLE, TWINKLE, LITTLE STAR. Short dress of blue and white gauze, with low bodice *à la Vierge* trimmed with silver stars; a tulle spangled veil attached to a silver band for head-dress.

UNA. Long, full robe of white cashmere with gold girdle; hooded cape, hair flowing. She is accompanied by lion.

UNDINE. Plain skirt of glittering silver tissue, edged with a narrow ruche, into which are placed at distances water-lily buds and leaves in small clusters; two broad scarves of pale and dark green are draped across the front, and arranged to fall low at the back; a large cluster of grass, lilies, and dark brown leaves at the left side; the bodice of silver tissue, trimmed with grass and water-lilies; a large open water-lily on the head, and a great deal of grass falling over the long, flowing hair; ornaments, pearls, shells, and bits of pink coral all threaded together; shoes pale green, with silver tissue rosettes, and a lily bud and leaf in the centre; strings of shells, &c.; and a mother-of-pearl fan, with water-lily leaves and flowers arranged on pale green satin. (*See* WATER NYMPHS.)

UNION JACK. Dress made of Union Jack flags; anchors on the shoulders; sailor hat; a flag carried in the hand. Or, red short cashmere skirt cut in long points, with plaitings of red, white, and blue between; the front draped with silk flags; corselet bodice of dark blue velvet over white chemisette; an aigrette in the form of a small flag; fan of the same.

UNITED KINGDOM. England, Ireland, and Scotland. England wearing a white dress and large hat with roses; a plaid on one shoulder clasped with a cairngorm, and heather on the other; a shamrock attaching an Irish harp.

UNITED STATES. Short white satin skirt with red, blue and white stripes. Blue satin tunic edged with silver fringe covered with silver stars. White satin waistcoat, blue satin jacket with revers at the neck, coat tails at the back trimmed with red and silver. Mousquetaire cuffs, all round collar, muslin tie, blue satin shoes; diamond ornaments; wand with eagle at the top. (*See* AMERICA.)

UNIVERSE. Short blue and white dress made of cashmere or soft silk cut in classic fashion, with stars and spheres and ornaments; star-spangled veil; a sceptre with globe in hand.

UP-TO-DATE. (*See* NEW WOMAN.)

UTOPIA. Gossamer skirt trimmed with long pendent leaves from the waist. A tinsel bodice. The hair falling on the shoulder, encircled by classic crown.

VALENTINE. A soft classically draped white satin, the skirt garlanded with roses, a quiver and a couple of red velvet hearts tied at the side. A low classic bodice caught up with hearts; a sash belt of roses across; hearts forming the belt; wings at the back, smaller wings in the hair with a couple of arrows thrust through a red velvet heart; bows and arrows in the hand.

VALENTIA PEASANT. (*See* SPANISH.)

VALENTINA (*The Huguenots*). Dress of velvet or brocade with front breadth of quilted satin, long slashed puffed sleeves to wrist, with epaulettes; pointed stomacher, small ruff at throat; velvet hat and feather, or pearl and gold coil.

VALLIÈRE, MADAME DE LA. Blue satin gown, worked with gold leaves, the petticoat having a gathered flounce and double heading; the train, with two bows at either side; low pointed bodice, with white folds of tissue above; large loose puffed sleeves from elbow to shoulder; hair in curls, not powdered. Or, gold-colored satin petticoat, embroidered in gold thread; crimson and gold bodice; dark ruby velvet train, worked in gold; powdered hair.

VALOIS. (*See* BERTADE and MARGUERITE.)

VANDYKE. (*See* CHARLES I., PERIOD OF.) Full plain skirt; muslin apron, edged with pointed lace; bodice with revers; sleeves to wrist, turnback cuff of Vandyke lace; hair in curls.

VARSOVIENNE. Skirt of violet satin trimmed with a flounce headed by amber satin, tunic edged with gold braid; sleeveless bodice; Hungarian hat; sash round waist; hair braided in long plaits; gold ornaments; Hussar jacket; Russian boots.

VAUDOIS. (*See* FLOWER GIRL.)

VELASQUEZ (*born at Seville,* 1599). For a portrait of a child by this artist, *see* accompanying Illustration. It was lent by the Duke of Devonshire to the Exhibition of Fair Children at the Grafton Galleries, 1895. She wears a tunic in two tones of red, the satin underskirt profusely embroidered, and the red velvet bodice with gold threads. The stiff linen collar has a lace edge, also the cuffs. The hair turns back from the face and has a wreath of tiny sparse white primroses at the back.

VENDANGEUSE (*or Grape-picker in the south of France*). Short white cashmere skirt, trimmed with blue satin and gold fringe; bodice of a blue and white striped woollen stuff, turned back with blue; blue satin apron, trimmed with lace; white cap, with blue ribbons; black leather shoes; basket of grapes on the arm.

VENETIAN COSTUMES. The Illustration, Fig. 44, shows magnificent materials applied to a most ornate style of dress. The brocades worn by Venetian dames when Venice was in the height of her glory were highly floriated, some pure silk brocade, some velvet on satin grounds. The skirt is a rasse terre length, full all round. The bodice has a round point outlined by a jewelled girdle. The bodice is cut with a small open square apparently straight across the front, where it is met by handsome embroidery carried over the shoulders, a jewelled chain and ornament borders this square, and more jewels encircle the neck. There is a red ruff of muslin edged with lace at the back. The tight sleeves have lace ruffles, and vandyked lace cuffs, and the puff at the top of the arm is slashed with the dominant color in the brocade or with white. A small jewelled crown is worn in the hair. It would be scarcely possible to have a richer style of dress as painters have handed it down to us. At the Marlborough House Ball, in 1874, the Princess of Wales headed a Venetian quadrille. Her Royal Highness's dress was of

Fig. 44.—VENETIAN COSTUME.

pale blue satin, nearly covered with gold embroidery and precious stones, forming the front breadth to a train of ruby velvet, embroidered in gold and silver, and lined with blue satin, fastened back with precious stones; the close sleeves to the wrist were of ruby velvet, with blue satin puffings, also gold embroidered; the small ruff was edged with gold, and the bodice of the dress covered with strings of pearls; the small round Venetian cap, of ruby velvet, was one mass of jewels. The Duchess of Manchester wore white and gold, with olive-green and gold-embroidered sleeves. The Countess of Craven, in the costume of Ignota, detta la Bella di Tiziano, green embossed velvet, embroidered with gold, slashed with red and white brocade over a white satin petticoat, also embroidered in gold; a gold chain round the neck; the bodice cut low; the sleeves to wrist, with a puff at the top, and perpendicular slashings along the front of skirt, which was much embroidered. A notable Venetian dress is as follows: Train and bodice of white and gold brocade, with long open sleeves hanging from the shoulders, finished off with gold fringe, and worn over tight sleeves of crimson satin, embroidered with pearls and gold; crimson satin petticoat, worked in gold; gold girdle and pouch; ruff and white and gold gauze veil. White and black gauze veils were in fashion among Venetian dames, and fine lawn and reticella for ruffs. The hair was arranged in small curls and puffs above the forehead, and formed a knot at the back of the head as a support to the veil. The fan was made of ostrich-feathers, suspended from the girdle by a chain of gold or silver. The most usual make of Venetian dresses was a full all-round or trained skirt, long stiff pointed bodice, cut as a high square, with a ruff coming from the back of the shoulders; sleeves to wrist, with cuffs; a jewelled girdle; pointed cap and veil. In winter, robings of fur were introduced. Venetian mantles, made of black silk lined and embroidered with the same colors, are occasionally worn over ordinary evening dress in lieu of a fancy costume.

VENETIAN FISHGIRL. Old gold-colored satin petticoat; crimson silk tunic, with gold lace and crimson fringe; black velvet bodice, with gold trimmings; white silk under-bodice, open at neck, with sailor collar; red silk handkerchief about the head, with gold fringe; a creel and fish.

VENEZUELA. Short yellow and black skirt edged with ball fringe. Full white under-bodice with a linen collar turning back from the throat. Gold embroidered bolero jacket. Multi-colored scarf round the waist with dagger, gun in hand, bracelets above and below the elbow. High crown large round hat bordered and trimmed with pompons. A striped silk handkerchief round the head.

VERNON, DOROTHY. (*See* DI VERNON, D. for riding dress.) In ball costume she wears a satin skirt trimmed with lace; pointed bodice and bunched-up tunic of brocade, with abundant trimming of lace; hair powdered.

VESTAL VIRGIN. Swathed in white from head to foot. Dress made after classic fashion. Tunic and peplum of white cashmere, draped *à la Greque;* gold bands in the hair.

VICAR OF WAKEFIELD AND FAMILY. (*See* WAKEFIELD, W.)

VIERLANDER *(Hamburg Flower-girl).* Scarlet petticoat bordered with green, having many gatherings at the waist; black apron; black bodice, one mass of embroidery worked in gold, silver, and colors in front; white chemisette; curious straw hat, with a circular trough round the crown; and at the back of the head a black leather bow, the ends reaching to the waist; basket of flowers in hand. (*See* FLEMISH FLOWER-GIRL.)

VICTORIAN, EARLY. The early portion of this century has found favor at Fancy Balls of late. Gowns with narrow skirts, short waists, long gloves, and large bonnets. But it is the 1830 costume which is most popular, as illustrated in Fig. 14. The skirt is full, made of moire, the bodice pointed and close fitting, with a turned down collar of satin edged with lace, the sleeves low on the shoulders, with triple bouillonnés below, and one full puff to the wristband. A silk scarf embroidered and fringed at the edges thrown loosely about the shoulders, and the large satin bonnet is trimmed with frillings of lace and flowers introduced inside and out. The Illustration, Fig. 13, depicts a Nineteenth century dress with many tucks; bodice long; sleeves falling over the hand. Large bonnet.

VIGO, WOMEN OF. Green stuff short skirt, bordered with red, which is carried up the side; the low bodice is blue, showing a red under-bodice peeping over the other; full linen chemisette to the throat; coral necklace and earrings; hair turned back from the face, and in a coil at the back.

VILLAGE GIRL. (*See* COLETTE, in *La Cruche Cassée*).

VIOLA (*Twelfth Night*). As a page in trunk hose; Elizabethan habit and ruff; epaulettes formed of satin loops; a sword with bows and rosettes. Tudor, low-crowned velvet hat and feathers.

VIOLET (*Violette, La*). Short light peach tulle dress covered with violets, a fringe of the same round waist and at hem; powdered hair; a wreath of same flowers on one side, or a cap like a violet. (*See* FLOWERS.)

VIOLETS, BASKET OF. Plain short skirt of violet satin covered with a trellis pattern of straw, laid on to simulate a basket, with green leaves peeping out between trellis ends; the skirt from below the hips to the waist is covered with perfumed artificial violets sewn on close together; violet satin bodice trimmed with green leaves; wreath of violets; powdered hair.

VIOLETTA VALERIE (*Favorita*). First scene: Ball gown of peach brocade and violets. Second dress: Pale blue silk made *en Princesse*, covered with point de gaze. Third dress: Silver brocade. Last scene: clinging robe of crêpe de Chine made as a tea-gown.

VIRGIN OF THE SUN. Long classic dress of tulle or soft silk covered with tufts of swansdown; skirt touching the ground, falling softly; low bodice; loose belt round the waist fastened on the shoulders with a brooch; the hair floating; long veil, gold band round the head.

VIRGINIA (*Roman Maiden*). Classic robe of white cashmere embroidered with gold. (For style, *see* ROMAN.)

VIRGINIA (*Paul and Virginia, by Bernardin de St. Pierre*). White Princesse dress, pendent elbow-sleeves with band round waist; palm-leaves. Or, the dress made as a white Indian muslin, sacque, over pink silk, opening in front to show the pink under-skirt, trimmed at the hem with a deep box-plait; the bodice square cut, with a soft fichu of muslin and fine lace, and ruffles of the same at the elbows; a bouquet of oleander blossoms fastened in the fichu. A wide shepherdess hat, lined with pink taffetas, should be carried on the arm, and a palm-leaf screen in the hand. Long gloves of white Suéde without buttons. The hair dressed high from the forehead, and falling in curls on the neck, but not powdered. A ruching of pink ribbon or double falling frill of white lace round the throat.

VITTORIA COLONNA, DONNA. As worn by Lady C. Villiers at the Queen's Ball, on the 12th May, 1842. Skirt just touching the ground, of sky-blue brocade; low square red velvet bodice and tunic, the latter cut in battlements and bordered with gold; gold girdle; low chemisette under the velvet bodice; leg-of-mutton sleeves puffed, the puffs divided by gold cord; diamond circlet, tulle veil edged with gold.

VIVANDIÈRE. The Illustration, Fig. 45, shows an excellent vivandière costume carried out in green cloth, trimmed with scarlet, a white waistcoat, white cuffs, and gold buttons. Black forage cap, lace ruffles, barrel slung with leather strap. An admirable dress for the **Daughter of the Regiment,** viz., the opera of *La Figlia del Reggimento* has given this character particular prominence. But there are many varieties in this class of dress, such as **Vivandière Polonaise.** She wears a jacket of blue satin, braided across the breast like a Hussar's, which is slung from the shoulders; a pelisse of scarlet satin, braided to match, and trimmed with fur; white satin skirt embroidered with gold; sabretache of scarlet and gold; Polish boots, and Lancer cap. **Vivandière des Mousquetaire de la Garde du Roi Louis XIII.** wears a short crimson satin skirt, trimmed with gold braid, and black velvet bows; pale blue satin doublet faced with crimson and gold lace; white satin pelisse lined with satin, trimmed with gold braid and Astrachan fur; blue satin cap; small barrel, and sabretache; black satin high boots. **Vivandière des Grenadiers de la Garde Imperiale Napoleon III.,** dark blue cloth skirt, with broad scarlet band, and gold lace; jacket of blue cloth, with gold epaulettes, braid, lace, etc.; facings white, collar and cuffs scarlet, revers of white and scarlet, with gold lace and braid; Hessian boots with gold tassels; kepi of gold, scarlet, and blue; small white muslin apron, with tri-colored ribbons; canteen, with arms of Napoleon. **Hungarian Vivandière.** White silk skirt; blue satin vest, braided in gold; crimson satin jacket, with white facings; blue satin boots, trimmed to correspond; aigrette on tri-cornered cap with gold. **Vivandière Francaise.** Scarlet cashmere skirt, bands of white satin and gold braid, white satin scarf trimmed with gold fringe and braid; jacket of same material cut in military style; facings of satin, trimmed profusely with gold; epaulettes and cords on the shoulders; three cornered black satin hat; black strapped boots with diamond buckles, scarlet silk stockings; scarlet and white barrel and white gauntlet gloves. Or, blue and red epaulettes, lace skirt; coat in mousquetaire style, the skirt buttoned back; cocked hat. (*See* also RUSSIAN HUSSAR, MEDIÆVAL VIVANDIÈRE.)

Fig. 45.—VIVANDIÈRE.

VIVIEN (*Idylls of the King*). A long grey robe of brocade; a gold belt at the waist; a gold band over the flowing hair; the bodice a low square; the sleeves puffed.

VOLUNTEER, LADY. In the grey color of the Inns of Court; satin skirt and velvet bodice, the drapery of the Union Jack forming a sash. Silver braid trimmings. A volunteer helmet.

WAITING-MAID (*French*). Striped black and red petticoat; over-skirt of deep gold color, lined with red, forming a puff at the back; black velvet bodice, and white plastron, barred across with black velvet; small muslin cap with plaiting *à la vielle*, black velvet round it, and a bow; a gold cross tied about the neck; red and white striped stockings; black shoes. (*See* ELIZABETHAN WAITING-MAID, and Illustration, Fig. 17.

WAKEFIELD, FAMILY OF THE VICAR OF. Olivia and **Sophia Primrose** wear quilted skirts, bodices with elbow-sleeves and ruffles; muslin aprons and kerchiefs. In Maclise's picture, "Preparing Moses for the Fair," the two sisters appear: one in a long quilted satin petticoat touching the ground, a white muslin apron surrounded by frilling reaching to the edge of the skirt; a bodice and skirt all in one of chintz or brocade; the skirt drawn away from the front and caught up at the back, so that the inside is seen at the sides; there is a large bow at the back of the waist. The bodice is low, and a muslin fichu crosses the shoulders, and is pinned down to the waist in front; a knot of ribbons on the dress; a band of black velvet with bow at the throat; the sleeves come to the elbow, finishing off with a puff of muslin and a frill; the hair is drawn over a cushion above the face, and a cap with a bow of ribbons at the side is pinned to the back, so that the lace just shows above the roll in front. The other sister has her hair dressed in similar fashion, wears a large ruff round the throat, a white dress with a low bodice cut in one piece with the skirt, a black lace shawl over her shoulders. Miss Terry, when acting Olivia, wore several notably pretty costumes; one was a short skirt bordered with a gathered puffing, a large white muslin apron with lace-edged frilling; a bunched-up tunic and low bodice, a muslin fichu knotted in front showing a white chemisette with frill; the hair dressed very high, with curls and the Olivia cap over it; long white mittens. Another dress was a brocaded sacque opening to show a distinct front breadth, and a long apron of embroidered net matching the figured net fichu; the hair in curls and no cap; elbow-sleeves and mittens. And then again she wears a hood, cape, and white tippet. After the elopement, the sacque and front breadth are of red brocade made with a pointed bodice, elbow-sleeves, and muslin apron. The cap is most becoming. It has a large full crown and a close double plaiting of lace round forming two scallops in front like a window curtain. High-heeled shoes are necessary parts of this costume. **Mrs. Primrose**, the Vicar's wife, has also a quilted skirt touching the ground; a train looped over this so that it reaches the edge of the skirt; a muslin kerchief tucked inside the low pointed bodice, having merely straps across the front, the white muslin showing through; the sleeves coming to the elbow, and the head is covered bv a black silk hood.

WALLACHIAN PEASANT WOMAN. Blue cashmere short skirt embroidered with gold; stay bodice with blue straps over a muslin chemisette, the sleeves having bands of scarlet; a crimson satin sash with gold fringe round the waist; apron of many colors; hair in long plaits, tied with a ribbon; small red cap embroidered in gold; bracelet and necklet of beads and coins.

WALLFLOWERS. (*See* FLOWERS.)

WAR. A classic dress (for style, *see* Illustration, Fig. 7, CLEOPATRA, DRUIDESS, ANCIENT GREEK, &c.) made in flame color, blue and gold, a flag and sword in hand, erect wings attached to back. Scarlet mantle fastened to shoulder; helmet on head with plume.

WASHERWOMAN, LAUNDRESS, BLANCHISSEUSE. Short skirt of yellow sateen, with a band of blue sateen round it; blue tunic, turned up *à la laveuse,* with a piece of yellow; blue bodice cut square, with fichu; cap and apron of clear muslin; blue stockings; black shoes; an iron at the side and a piece of soap. Sometimes for the French laundress the dress is red and white striped print, with a cambric cap. A Normandy cap would be correct; also shoes to resemble sabots. Another rendering: Dress of grey and white print, muslin apron and cap; skirt reaching to the ankle; high-heeled black shoes, buckles, and black stockings. A cord slung across the back with miniature clothes as if drying. A white label on the front of the bodice with "Laundress and Clear Starcher, Clear Starching done here." A small flat iron and a packet of Sunlight soap hanging at the side together with gauffering irons and packets of starch.

WASP. (*See* BEE.)

Fig. 46.—WASTEPAPER BASKET.

WASTEPAPER BASKET. The gown in the Illustration, Fig. 46, must be carried out in any fabric which most closely resembles the wicker basket work, the trimmings being entirely confined to waste paper, which should be sewn with some skill round the hem forming the sleeves and cap.

WATER. WATER NYMPHS. (*See* WATERFALL, RIVER, UNDINE, NAIAD, AQUARIUM, LORELEI, LURLINE, MERMAID, SABRINA, SIREN, PERI OF OCEAN, AMPHITRITE, WATER-LILY, WATER-WITCH, SEA QUEEN.) All these are arranged in much the same style, viz., as a dress of frosted gauze or silvered tulle over green, looped up with seaweed, coral, shells, crystal, and aquatic flowers, for the salt-water nymphs; water-lilies and grasses for those who rule over lakes and rivers, such as **Undine** and **Lurline.** A veil of tulle to match the dress falls over the hair, which should be covered with frosting powder and be allowed to float on the shoulders. A cuirass bodice of silver gauze, the tunic silver gauze, is a good rendering of the character. The bodice, whether a cuirass or made *à la Vierge*, should be trimmed with a fringe of the shells, etc., a dragon fly on one side of the hair. The silver tulle that is used should as nearly as possible resemble water, an effect best produced by waved stripes. Diamonds, coral, and aquamarine with silver are the most appropriate ornaments, and silver fringe should be introduced wherever it can be placed. **Undine,** the Nymph of the Rhine, has invariably water-lilies intermixed with the rest, and often lotus-flowers, and these should be dew-spangled. **A Mermaid** may be carried out as follows: Over the green and white and silver skirt the cuirass bodice should be made entirely of scales or sequins of mother-of-pearl, or of cloth imitating fish-scales, coming down well on to the hips. A girdle of seaweed, etc., is appropriate to most of the characters, and many of them have pendent sleeves bordered with the same; but no seaweed must be used on **Lurline's** or **Undine's** costumes. For **Aquarium,** the dress should not only be trimmed with marine plants, but with fish. **Water-Lily** is the same sort of dress, trimmed with water-lilies. **Water-Witch:** Short white satin skirt, completely covered with silver tissue and fringe; low body to match; scarf of sea-green satin tied tightly over the hips, and fastening on one side, powdered with silver cockle-shells and silver fish; silver cockle-shells in the hair. A head-dress made of a single spiral shell as a cap is appropriate.

WATER-CARRIER. Short, light pink skirt; light blue tunic turned up in front; low square muslin bodice; over this, a long jacket with revers and fastened with gold clasps down the front; high pointed hat; pink and blue striped stockings; black shoes; water pail attached to yoke.

WATERCRESS GATHERER. White tulle dress with garlands made of glistening green leaves in all the cress shades, which are very numerous, from dead yellow to brightest emerald; basket of lattice-work, with *santé du corps* in green letters, carried in hand. Or, black shoes, red stockings, short red skirt, bodice, and tunic of chintz, Bandana handkerchief buckled at throat; straw hat, cherry colored ribbons: basket of watercresses.

WATTEAU COSTUMES are so called because they attempt to reproduce the charming picturesque beings delineated by Watteau, who died in 1721. A sacque in most cases forms a part of these costumes. It is fastened to the bodice (which is either high to the throat, or a low square at the back) in a double box-plait. Sometimes it is merely caught to the top, and then falls loose, so that the bodice may be seen distinct from the plait; but more generally the plait forms the back of the dress. The sacque may be tacked to the front breadth, or it may be quite loose and distinct from the skirt and bodice. Sometimes it is looped up as a tunic; or it reaches to the hem of the dress. Watteau dresses are as follows: High-heeled shoes, coming well up on the instep, diamond buckles, silk stockings; a skirt of silk or satin, often quilted, short or just touching the ground, or of muslin with small plaited flounces to the waist; a sacque of silk with square-cut bodice, pointed in front, trimmed with lace; elbow-sleeves and ruffles; narrow black velvet round neck and wrists; powdered hair; a muslin apron. (*See* Illustration of DRESDEN SHEPHERDESS.) **Beadle Parisienne.** Watteau overskirt of pink satin, cut square at neck, and showing a silver cloth stomacher; petticoat of grey satin, slashed with silver cloth, having two gathered flounces; pink satin shoes with high grey heels; grey satin hat, worn on the side of the head over powdered hair, with pink ribbons. **Bouquetier in Watteau's Time.** Striped skirt and full bodice with long basques and sleeves, fichu of muslin over the bust, white muslin cap with frill.

WEALTH AND PROSPERITY. Dress and train of gold and silver cloth, covered with jewels, and strings of gold coins, with a gold crown

Fig. 47.—WELSH COSTUME.

WEATHER. Classic dress of silver gauze trimmed with silver fringe and simulated rain drops, gold tinted to resemble sun shining through the rain. A weathercock in the hair.

WEATHERCOCK. Dress of black lace over white satin; low bodice; black gloves; black velvet pointed cap surmounted by a vane.

WELSH COSTUMES. The Illustration, Fig. 47, portrays the Welsh peasant in a red striped flannel skirt, long check apron, red and black shawl; high hat; thick white muslin sleeves. The skirts are mostly flannel; the tunics turned under at the back; the bodices either open heart-shape or are low. Many of the sleeves have a white over-sleeve to elbow. A white apron and a small colored shawl across the shoulders, and a high beaver hat over a cap. The shapes differ in North and South Wales; at Swansea the cockle-shell hat is made of straw, and has a flat crown. Fancy Welsh dresses are as follows: Striped red and black satin short skirt: upper skirt and bodice of black velvet, with revers of red satin; white muslin neckerchief tucked inside, high hat; mittens; knitting in hand. Or, a dark blue stuff skirt, striped red and black upper skirt, bunched up; black and white check apron; tall beaver hat over cap. Carmarthenshire Peasant: Plain red cloth skirt; low purple bodice; white muslin handkercief tucked inside. White cap; white sleeves below elbow; short white apron; mittens.

WHAT-A-TAIL. Skirt of drab plush; bodice of feathers; cap like head of the bird.

WHEAT-EAR. Green satin bodice and tunic over gold-colored tulle skirt, the tunic embroidered with wheat-ears, and looped up with the same; coronet of the same in the hair.

WHERE ARE YOU GOING TO, MY PRETTY MAID? A pink cotton dress, and blue apron caught up on one side nearly to the waist; puffed full sleeves above the elbow; a white kerchief open at the breast; a large shady sun-bonnet, with a long point, and a milk-pail in the left hand. (*See* M.)

WHIG, THE LITTLE (*younger daughter of the great Duke of Marlborough.*) Petticoat of yellow satin with point lace flounces, and headings of pearls; green velvet pointed bodice and train bordered with ermine; high head-dress with yellow gauze twisted in hair; patches.

WHITE CAT. (*See* CAT.)

WHITE CHICKEN. (*See* C.)

WHITE CHINA. (*See* C.)

WHITE DRESSES. Pure white dresses at balls are most becoming to youth. (*See* WHITE LADY OF AVENEL, POWDER-PUFF, WHITE MILLINER, MILLER'S DAUGHTER, &C.) **The Ghost of Queen Elizabeth,** the costume of her time, all white; a **French Peasant** in white cambric jacket and skirt; white cap, apron, and stockings. **Snowflakes,** white velvet bodice, and spangled tulle veil, with swansdown on tulle skirt. (*See* HOAR-FROST.) **Sweet Seventeen:** Soft white muslin dress made with short waist, broad white sash, small puffed sleeves, long white mittens; white sandalled shoes; hair powdered; white satin bag suspended from arm.

WHITE WITCH. In the Illustration, Fig. 48, wears white satin shoes, the petticoat quilted with pearls, which are also introduced on the front of the stomacher, and as ornaments on the bodice. There are lace ruffles to the sleeves; a close ruff surrounds the neck. The white felt pointed cap has pompons at the side, and the staff is tied with white ribbons. It can also be carried out in white satin and gauze, with a white velvet bodice; white ruff, satin stomacher of silver cloth; and sugar-loaf hat, worn over *poudré* hair, with an electric star on forehead; silver broomstick and cauldron.

WHITE LADY OF AVENEL wears a long dress of some soft white material, crêpe, gauze, or tulle, one skirt over another; the low full bodice drawn in with a string at the neck, without tucker; shoulder-straps with wing-like sleeves at the back, falling on skirt; flowing veil; the hair loose, an old-fashioned bodkin or hairpin thrust through it; a gold girdle confines the waist.

WHIST. Red satin skirt and bodice bordered with playing cards; scarf of white gauze crossing the front and falling on the skirt with clubs, spades, diamonds, and hearts scattered over it in red and black; bracelets, necklet, and earrings, in enamel, with the same devices.

WHIST, LIVING. The cards enter in procession and go through shuffling, cutting, and dealing, indicated by certain manoeuvres. The players over ordinary evening dresses wear large cards of the pack hung both at the back and front, like sandwich men. The King, Queen, Knave, and Ace of Clubs are in robes of dull grey trimmed with white fur, the emblems of the suit in black velvet; the crowns showing rows of small

Fig. 48.—WHITE WITCH.

clubs, the knave and ace in picturesque head coverings of grey, outlined by jet. The Heart suit is robed in green with the emblems in vivid red; the diadems and sceptres being carried out in the same style for all the suits. Spades wear rose color with black velvet. The Court cards in gold color with red diamonds. The game is played on an olive-green cloth to represent a whist table. The pages in white satin suits herald the procession of fifty-two cards; music playing as they go through the different performances.

WIDOW WADMAN. Large white muslin cap, surrounded by a black velvet band and broad lace frill, fastened under the chin, a velvet bow at side. Black dress, large open sleeves, with broad lace; bodice, a low square, filled in with folds of white Swiss muslin, terminating in front under the dress.

WIFE OF BATH (*Chaucer.*) Striped stuff skirt; close fitting blue bodice; beaver hat, with muslin kerchief knotted above the brim, and one end tied beneath the chin, the other falling under the hat; distaff carried in the hand.

WILD FLOWERS. (*See* FLOWERS.)

WILL-O'-THE-WISP. Flowing hair falling over a black tulle dress worked with irridiscent sequins. Dark lantern carried in the hand; star of electric light in the centre of the forehead.

WIND. Short costume of pink satin, with low yellow satin bodice and white stomacher, laced across with the two shades; powdered hair, the four arms of windmill placed at the back of the head; windmills also on left shoulder in enamel; a pink satin ribbon, with bow at neck, windmill depending. The satin skirt has a landscape on one side, on the other Boreas.

WINDMILL. Short black satin skirt, a ladder of white satin two inches wide with crossbars of satin one inch wide begin at either side of the waist, two in front and two at the back, proceeding downwards. The ladder should widen from three inches at the top to twelve inches or fifteen inches at the hem, and the bars be placed two inches apart. On the low, black satin bodice, front and back, are two smaller ladders V-shaped from the waist to the shoulder. These should be well made on stiff cardboard, and reach two inches or three inches above the shoulder, in white satin. Sleeves of black satin, a toy windmill on each sleeve and in the hair. A long white wand with a toy windmill at the end might be carried. Black stockings and white shoes; hair powdered. Or, small sacks of white satin tied at the neck with black ribbon might replace the windmills.

WINTER, CHRISTMAS, DECEMBER, SNOW, FROST, ICE, ICICLE, HOLLY, &c. For these a white tulle or lisse dress and veil, either crystal spangled or gauze is used, covered with tufts of swansdown or white wadding. For **Winter, December,** and **Christmas,** holly leaves, ivy and mistletoe, and berries are *en regle;* Christmas roses and a robin appear on the head, shoulders, and dress. Sometimes the dress is black, tufted with swansdown. December is also rendered as a pale blue gown fringed with icicles; a blue-grey cloak attached to shoulders; or sometimes with black tulle and tufts of swansdown and holly. **Snow** and **Frost** have icicles and glittering crystal drops, with crystal fringe introduced. Satin is more suitable with the tulle than silk, and bands of swansdown make admirable trimmings. Silver is often employed, but crystal is more appropriate, though a tunic and bodice of silver cloth veiled in tulle has a good effect for **Frost** and **Snow.** The hair should float on the shoulders, and be covered with frosting powder. Satin shoes, and long gloves bordered with swansdown. **For a Snowstorm on a Dark Night,** black is used instead of white, trimmed with jet and swansdown. Fans painted with snow-scenes and robins are adapted to any of these dresses. Sometimes blue satin is worn with the white, but it does not make the dress so distinctive. The adoption of a blue-grey mantle, covered with tufts of swansdown, is meant to show that winter is not always bright. Crystal or diamond ornaments are the most appropriate. Or, dress of green satin, bordered with twigs and evergreens; marabout feathers scattered over skirt and bodice; a veil treated in the same way enveloping the figure. **An Arctic Maiden** or **Arctic Queen** wears the same style of white dress, trimmed with tufts of swansdown, and forked with tongues of talc cloth to imitate icicles; white veil; silver and crystal or diamond crown; a white wand in the hand. **Arctic Queen,** the same, with crystal crown. (*See* JANUARY.)

WINTER'S TALE (*Shakespeare*). (*See* HERMIONE.)

WITCH. (*See* HUBBARD, MOTHER; MACBETH, and WHITE WITCH, Illustration Fig. 48.) Short quilted skirt of red satin, with cats and lizards in black velvet; gold satin panier tunic caught up with a bat; black velvet bodice with muslin ruff at shoulders, a bat's head, tabby color, appliqued in front; small cat on right arm, a broom in the hand, with owl; tall pointed velvet cap; shoes with buckles.

WIVES OF WINDSOR. (*See* ANN PAGE.)

WOMAN, OLD, WHO LIVED IN A SHOE. Short, black quilted satin skirt; Watteau sacque of flowered chintz or brocade, cut square in front, with elbow sleeves; a mob cap, and a large high-heeled scarlet satin shoe, trimmed with gold cord on the shoulders, filled with small dolls; a rod in hand.

WOMAN, NEW. (*See* N.)

WOOD. Short skirt with paniers and low crossing bodice striped to resemble pieces of wood. The head-dress made like a bundle of wood. A log on one shoulder.

WOODS, QUEEN OF THE. Leaf green satin, fringed with gold for the skirt and low bodice. A quiver full of arrows slung across the shoulders, birds nestling in the hair, and about the dress, brown and green leaves form the fringe to the hem of the skirt and at the waist.

WOOD NYMPH. Green tulle gown, trimmed with leaves, wild flowers, blackberries, hips, acorns, &c., forming a fringe round the train or tunic, a bird nestling here and there. The skirt should be bordered with a puffing, out of which peep violets, primroses, and other spring flowers, and so placed that they seem to be growing; the bodice must be trimmed to match. Flowers to be placed in the hair, which should float on the shoulders, beneath a veil of green tulle. Natural ivy may be used on this dress; each leaf should be painted over with oil, and thoroughly dried; this makes them bright and shiny.

WOODLAND WHISPERS. Short brown stuff gown, and straw hat all trimmed with flowers; a squirrel on the shoulders.

WORK-BOX. A short red quilted skirt; blue tunic at the back, with the rhyme, "Needles and pins, needles and pins, when a man marries his troubles begin," formed with pins. A white linen apron, the end turned up to form a square pocket, in which are needles, pins, tapes, cotton cord, scissors, &c.; blue bodice with reels round the top; muslin cap and fichu, a chatelaine of scissors, bodkin, thimble, housewife, &c.

WURTEMBURG, PEASANT OF. Full plaited skirt, over another rather larger; belt of silver braid; red stockings, and shoes with buckles; gilt comb; close-fitting black cap; hair plaited in two long tresses and tied with ribbon; white chemisette, with stomacher of crimson velvet or cloth over black bodice; black open jacket with long sleeves.

WURTEMBURG, LADY OF in Illustration No. 49, wears a short round skirt with a triple band of embroidery, long narrow muslin apron made of linen, close-fitting, bodice with velvet, introduced down the front and at the cuffs, single pleated ruffle at the throat, appearing above the collar band, hair in two pendent plaits surmounted by a small flat biretta cap with a jewelled band; jewelled satchel at the side.

YACHTING. Blue and white striped stockings, white pointed shoes, white tunic caught up on left side over a dark blue petticoat, vandyked and edged with gold at the hem, the fullness bordered with gold; a gold anchor painted on left side. The tunic forms one pleated end, and a life preserver hangs beside it. The close-fitting blue and white striped bodice descends to the hips. There is a cape half blue, half white, which covers the shoulders. Full sleeves to elbow, where there is a rounded turn back cuff of blue; white cap with peak.

YACHT. At balls at our seaports, the dresses of the ladies are associated with certain yachts by means of scarves carried across the bodice bearing the name, such as the *Swallow*, the *Raven*, and so on. A white tulle skirt is draped with flags and the burgee; the national flag falls from one shoulder. (*See* FLAGS, SHIPS, and NOVA SCOTIA.)

YEAR, OLD AND NEW. Full short skirt of white satin; low bodice with sash about waist; hours printed round the hem; calendar with the old year on one side, the new year on the other.

YEAR, OLD. Quilted satin petticoat, hours printed or tacked round it; scythe fastened to the side or carried in the hand; hair powdered; large pointed hat with the date of year in front, partially hidden by gauze. The wearer should assume to be old and infirm; a clock on left side of dress. The tunic black, with silver letters telling of any remarkable occurrences of the old year.

YEAR, NEW. A radiant young girl in the heyday of youth wearing a plain long full satin skirt, with the hours in silver round it: silver cord about the waist; the bodice made full; pendent sleeves from elbow, caught up with roses; wreath of roses and veil in hair.

YSEULTE OF IRELAND. Under-skirt of olive-green velvet, embroidered with silver; under-sleeves of primrose-colored nun's cloth;

Fig. 49.—A LADY OF WURTEMBURG.

bodice tight-fitting, fastened at the back; veil of pale yellow Indian muslin bound to the hair by a diadem of silver; antique silver baldric with large pouch bag of olive velvet worked with silver, and lined with silver and primrose; olive velvet shoes; no gloves; antique bracelet and necklet of silver.

ZEALAND, NEW. (*See* N.)

ZELICA (*Lalla Rookh*). White satin petticoat, richly embroidered with gold, over-skirt and bodice of red satin, cut low at neck in a point; gold-embroidered white zouave jacket bordered with gold lace and fringe. A jewelled girdle and silk scarf round waist; gold-spangled muslin trousers to knee; bracelets on wrist and round upper portion of arm; anklets; a Persian cap of crimson and gold, hair in plaits, entwined with pearls.

ZENOBIA. Full Greek robe of dull indigo red; veil of fine gauze of a soft grey interthreaded with gold and fastened to the diadem. Ribbon sandals. Jewelled feather fan to match. Or, full Greek robe of deep red India muslin; veil of fine gauze; diadem; sandals; jewelled fan, and handsome gold antique jewellery.

ZERLINA (*Don Giovanni*). A Spanish dress. (*See* SPANISH LADY.) Short white satin skirt, trimmed with black lace, ornamented with gold and cerise; Spanish bodice of black satin, braided with gold; gold dagger; black lace mantilla; crimson roses.

ZINGARI in Illustration, Fig. 50, wears a red satin skirt richly embroidered in gold, coins, paillettes, cord, and thread, a scarf of many colored silk encircles the waist, which is bordered with a coin fringe. The black velvet Spanish jacket is edged with gold balls, a coronet of balls forms the head-dress, with two ball-headed pins thrust through the rich coils of hair. Gold bracelets at wrist, and on the upper part of the arm are united by chains, the tambourine displays many colored ribbons. Indeed in this dress, yellow, black, and red, with as many gold ornaments as possible, are essential.

ZITELLA. Red cap with coins; black velvet bodice and red waistcoat, embroidered and laced with gold; red gold-embroidered tunic, studded with coins and bound with black velvet, and bordered with gold fringe; petticoat of black velvet, with a broad band of hieroglyphics in gold, and gold fringe; silk sash in red, gold, and black.

ZURICH. (*See* SWISS.)

APPENDIX.

A FEW DRESSES SUITABLE FOR BOYS.

ARCITE (Chaucer). *Juste-au-corps* of brown moire antique; gold belt; dark blue trunk hose.

ASTROLOGER. Long velvet toga, with wide hanging sleeves, bordered with satin, bearing the signs of the zodiac in gold; high pointed velvet cap, entwined with a gold snake; wizard's wand, large spectacles, book, and telescope; long pointed shoes.

BABY'S OPERA (*By Walter Crane*). The costumes in this are very suitable for children. **Musicians** in tabards, the stockings of two colours; shoes, square toed. **King Cole:** Fat burly figure; loose brown flowing robe, with ermine; large beard, and regal cap. **Boy:** Trousers to knee; loose shirt; hat with band round; trumpet in hand. **Jack Horner:** Blue cap; slashed jacket, with three rows of buttons; breeches.

BEAU, OLD FASHIONED. Long skirted coat; silk stockings, high boots, breeches, and waistcoat; hat, and stick; watch and seals.

BEAST. (*Fairy Prince, as worn by Duke of Connaught at Marlborough House Fancy Ball.*) Ruby velvet doublet; grey satin tights; ruby shoes; a leopard's skin, with claws attached to shoulders by jewels; small round ruby cap and feather.

BECKFORD, MASTER HORACE (*From Cosway's Picture*). High hat and feathers; hair hanging down in curls; tight jacket and breeches; with lace collar and turn back cuffs; silk stockings and shoes; scarves tied round leg, with bows on outside of leg; stick in hand.

BEEF-EATER (*or Yeoman of the Guard*). Long-skirted scarlet Tudor coat, trimmed with black velvet and gold, crown and Tudor rose embroidered on breast; close plaited muslin ruff at throat; full sleeves to wrist; low-crowned black velvet hat, blue, red, and white ribbons round; rosettes of the same on black shoes and at the knees of breeches; red stockings; sword in belt, halberd carried in hand.

BLUEBEARD. Flowing Eastern robe; red silk turban; scarf of many colors round waist; loose silk trousers to ankle, one yellow the other red; red pointed shoes; beard, blue; carries key.

BOY BLUE. Dressed as Gainsborough's Blue Boy, Black shoes, with large blue rosettes; the same at knee; blue stockings, velvet breeches, and close-fitting jacket, buttoning in front; blue satin cloak, fastened to shoulders, bordered with gold braid: the sleeves to wrist, slashed twice inside the arm, showing white under-sleeve; Vandyke lace cuffs; large lace collar; plumed hat: hair curled.

BUNTHORN (*Patience*). Velvet jacket and breeches; large flat velvet cap, with wig of light hair beneath; velvet shoes, and silk stockings.

CAVALIER DRESS (*For boy, after Von Hughenburg*). Dutch type. Broad-brimmed Flemish hat, with ostrich feathers; doublet and waistcoat; breeches to knee; swordbelt crossing bodice; tie at throat; hat and plumes; shoes with bows; gauntlet gloves.

CHARLES, PRINCE OF WALES (*Son of Charles I.*). (*See* Illustration.) As Vandyke painted him, is clad in satin breeches and habit with vandyked lace collar, ribbon bows at knee and waist, sleeves slashed inside the arm. The shoes have large rosettes coming well up on to the instep; the hair is cut square across the forehead and curled at the back. This is a favourite dress for Pages at weddings.

CHRISTMAS, FATHER. Long loose robe of white, red, or brown, the shoulders covered with tufts of frosted wadding; a belt round waist; wallet, staff, white hair and beard; holly wreath.

CLOWN (*Ordinary*). Black or white shoes, white stockings with blue or red clocks; short white calico trousers with frills at knee, and a close-fitting dress fantastically ornamented with blue and red; face painted white, triangular patches of red on either cheek, very red lips; close curling stiff red point from back of head, which shakes at every movement. (In Louis XV's reign). Loose trousers to knee; full jacket with large collar, confined at waist by belt; sleeves to wrist, with pendent ones over the hand, all made in white cotton or merino piped with red, and large red buttons in front; white felt pointed hat, with colored ribbons.

COCK ROBIN. Short brown pleated skirt, with rows of Marabout feathers; round bodice with pointed basque at the back, like the tail of a bird, made of feathers or plush; red waistcoat, high collar; red necktie; cap with a peak as much like a bird's head as possible.

CONSCRIPT. Long kid gaiters fastened with buttons to the knee; yellow breeches with gold embroidery at the pockets; red cloth coat with yellow epaulettes, cuffs, and facings; Lancer cap.

COLE, KING. (*See* BABY OPERA.)

COOK, BOY. All in white; shoes, stockings, knee breeches; loose blouse, with frilled collar; round cap; apron, the corner tucked in at waist. Or, jacket and breeches of white satin slashed with blue, white linen apron; muslin ruffles; shoulder sash of blue moire, to which is suspended a huge carving knife; white cap with blue puffings; white stockings and shoes, and blue rosette.

CUPID. Dress of blue and silver gauze, smothered in roses; bow and arrow, and silver gauze wings.

DICK TURPIN. Scarlet coat and waistcoat, with gold braid and buttons; lace cravat and ruffles; high jack-boots; leather breeches; three-cornered hat and flowing wig; belt and pistols.

DUTCH FISHER BOY. Wooden shoes; full breeches, coarse knitted stockings; striped blouse; red tie and cap.

FRANCIS I. A flat-brimmed cap, sometimes jewelled, and always bordered with an ostrich feather; doublet of plain or figured silk, with slashed puff sleeves to the elbow, and tight to the wrist; over the doublet a breastplate as part of armour; Norman chaussés or hose, striped and fitting exactly to the limbs; broad toed shoes with slashed tips.

FERAMOZ (*Poet of Cashmere*). White gauze and silver turban, with jewels; satin jacket embroidered, having hanging over sleeves; under-vest and sleeves of brocade; full white lawn shirt, showing Indian scarf round waist; velvet breeches, with silver buttons to the knee; silk stockings, small low shoes; a guitar in hand.

FIGARO (*Barber of Seville*). Dark green velvet Spanish jacket embroidered in silver; white satin waistcoat; green velvet breeches with pink buttons; pink sash with silver fringe, and necktie; Spanish hat; pink bows on shoes, white silk stockings; mandoline in hand.

FLY COSTUME FOR BOY OF FOUR. Golden yellow satin skirt, ornamented with black braid and studded with small gauze flies. The short upper skirt forms a sort of long basque, and is sewn to the waistband; rows of gold braid across the high bodice, and round the short sleeves; loose jacket ornamented with gauze; fly in the centre of back, and smaller ones in front; black velvet toque, with gold band round; a gold fly securing the aigrette.

FIANCÉ, (VILLAGE). Striped blue and white silk trousers, silk stockings of a darker shade of blue; black shoes with buckles; red silk waistcoat; white shirt; dark blue cloth jacket, with revers and large buttons; large bouquet of flowers, fastened to the jacket with a bunch of ribbons; high hat.

GARIBALDI. Red shirt and grey trousers, with silver stripe; large felt hat and ostrich feather.

GOBLIN. Tight-fitting red justaucorps with red vandyke tunic; winged hood with cape; fork in hand.

GREEK. White plaited fustanetta, or petticoat, wide silk belt, ornamented with gold; short embroidered vest, buttoned at throat; jacket; full trousers to knee, and gaiters; fez; dagger stuck in belt. Made in satin, cashmere, or cloth.

GRENADIER (1760). High white gaiters buttoned to knee; blue coat turned back with red; red cuffs; white waistcoat and breeches; red and white pointed cap; sword; hair in pigtail.

HAMLET. Long black cloth cloak; scalloped black velvet jerkin trimmed with jet, black velvet sword-belt, and bonnet with black plume; black silk tights, black velvet shoes slashed with satin.

HEARTS, KING OF. Red and white striped stockings; blue justaucorps, cut in points, and covered with hearts; a large satin collar, in the shape of two hearts; red cap, with hearts; tight and hanging sleeves; sceptre with hearts.

HENRY VI. wears a felt hood or bonnet, with short tippet and single feather; a doublet of braided silk, cut round even with the shoulders, a separate scarf covering the latter; loose sleeves trimmed with fur; tight hose; high boots of brown leather, long-toed and spurred.

HERALD. White felt hat with feather; the tabard coat yellow, green, or blue, with the arms embroidered in gold or silver, and a shoulder jacket of contrasting color; tights, silk hose; trousers striped or parti-colored. A trumpet in hand.

HIGHLAND PIPER. Boots, white gaiters, plaid stockings; kilted skirt; sporran; uniform coat; plaid, fastened with brooch on left shoulder; bagpipes.

INCROYABLE. Short-waisted long brown coat, with wide lapels; yellow satin waistcoat; cloth breeches having blue ties at knee; striped stockings and shoes; a watch and watch-chain hanging at both sides; lace frills at wrist and neck; large necktie; cocked hat.

IRISH CAR DRIVER. Green coat patched with cloth, brass buttons; brocaded waistcoat; drab breeches with patches; high collar and red tie; blue darned stockings; leather shoes; hat trimmed with green and sprigs of shamrock.

ITALIAN. Stockings crossed with colored ribbon; blue cloth breeches, buckled at the side; a leather waistcoat fastened with silver, steel or leather buttons, cut low and straight, showing the shirt; a short jacket bordered with gold, and a pointed hat with ribbons; coins and amulets. The **Pifferari,** in addition, have a long brown caped cloak, and carry their musical pipes. **The Italian Fishermen of Naples and Barri, Masaniello, &c.,** are represented with silk tights, striped trousers rolled up well above the knee; a shirt of the same, open at the neck to show gold charms; earrings in the ears; a red or brown cap; and a brown jacket slung from the shoulders; a scarf round waist.

JACK HORNER. Blue breeches; a long waistcoat; long-skirted red coat, with gold buttons down the front, and on the wide turn-back cuffs and pockets; a black tricorn hat bordered with gold braid; a plum dangling from the watch-chain.

JACK (JACK AND JILL). Smock frock and round felt hat. Or, breeches and long waistcoat, long-skirted coat of velvet, cambric shirt, velvet cape, ruff at throat red rosette on each cuff and corner of coat.

JAMES EDWARD, PRINCE, SON OF JAMES II. (*after N. de Largillière*). He died in Paris, 1746. The costume of the Prince of Wales resembles the one worn by courtiers towards the end of Charles II's reign. Wig formally curled, and no longer flowing; three-cornered hat, low in the crown and wide in the brim, with feather edging; a neckcloth or cravat of Brussels or Flanders lace, tied in a knot under the chin, the ends hanging down square; short doublet or coat of dark green, blue, or drab cloth, with buttons and buttonholes all down the front, the cuffs and pockets similarly adorned; the skirts of the coat terminating above the knees, and its sleeves reaching to the elbows, with shirt sleeves bulging out, ruffed and adorned profusely with ribbons and lace; short trousers of dark velvet, loose to the knees, with a fringe of lace or a cambric edging; blue or scarlet stockings, with silver clocks; high-heeled, lace-edged shoes, with diminutive buckles in front, fastening a lace bow to the instep.

JESTER, FOOL, AND FOLLY. Pointed shoes; tights, the legs of different colors; parti-colored short full trunks; close-ftting habit with basque cut in points, bordered with gold, a bell at each point; sleeves with the same points and bells; hood, with cape of two colors, also cut in points; a fool's bauble in the hand. Red and blue is the usual mixture, also green and gold, amber and blue, amber and violet.

JOCRISSE. Jacket and knee breeches of puce-colored satin; waistcoat of strawberry plush; buckled shoes; silk Madras handkerchief round the throat, high linen collar; gold buttons; puce felt hat.

JOCKEY. Top-boots; satin breeches; jacket and cap of two colors; whip in hand.

JOHN BULL. Top-boots and breeches; long coat; low-crowned hat.

JOHN, LITTLE. Green cloth doublet trimmed with squirrel fur; green breeches slashed with satin; white and green satin sleeves, under the pendent ones, belonging to a doublet of green silk; green stockings and buckskin shoes; green velvet cap with eagle feather; hunting-horn and knife.

KING (*Sing a Song of Sixpence*). Long flowing mantle trimmed with gold braid or fur; puffed satin habit; breeches and silk stockings; diadem on head.

MALTA, KNIGHT OF. Silk shoes and stockings; black puffed trousers and jacket with ruff; red round cloak to waist, bordered with gold braid, a cross on either side; flowing hair, hat, and feather. A ruff and cloak over boy's ordinary dress would suffice, if a saving of time and trouble be an object.

MALTESE WATER-CARRIER. Sabots, blue stockings, white trousers; red silk sash; blue jersey, striped jacket, red cap barrel; and cup.

MARLBOROUGH, DUKE OF. Full wig; large lace neckcloth; hanging cuffs and ruffles; square-cut coat and long-flapped waiscoat; a sash over the right shoulder; blue or scarlet silk stockings, with gold or silver clocks, drawn high up over the knee; square-toed shoes, with high heels and small buckles.

MARQUIS, LOUIS XVI. Blue velvet coat and breeches embroidered in gold; lace sleeves and cravat; white satin vest worked to match; three-cornered hat edged with gold lace, having white plume; shoes with diamond buckles; sword.

MARQUIS OF CARABAS. Tights; velvet shoes; velvet habit bordered with gold; belt round waist; hanging sleeves; large hat and feather.

MASHER. Suitable for a boy of very tender years, who appears in the exact counterpart of a man's dress suit.

MEPHISTOPHELES (*Faust*). Silk tights, full short trunks round hips; tight-fitting habit; short cloak attached to shoulders; a cap with two upstanding feathers like horns. This is generally carried out entirely in red velvet, or in scarlet satin and black velvet.

MERCURY. Mantle attached to shoulders, and drawn through the girdle at the waist; peplum and skirt all made in white veiling; caduces carried in the hand; sandals laced up the leg; wings on the cap and heels.

MEXICAN BOY. (*See* Illustration). Long jean breeches or some thick woollen stuff of white or nankeen color, a pancho over the shoulders of bright red, green, and black woollen stuff, easily reproduced, coarse pointed straw hat, black shoes.

MIGNON OF THE COURT OF HENRY III. Black shoes,

white stockings; full knickerbockers to the knee; a blouse, confined at the waist by a belt, long full sleeves to wrist; a shoulder-cloak, and round cap made of striped satin or calico; a close muslin ruff at the throat.

MONK. Long brown ample robe, with wide sleeves, and a cord round the waist. The Franciscans have a small cape and hood; the Capuchins' cape is as large as that of an Inverness wrapper. Rosary at side.

MUSICIANS. (*See* BABY OPERA.)

NIGHT AND MORNING. Half black, half white satin tights, *juste-au-corps*, and round hat; the face half black, the hair powdered on one side; one glove black, one white; the same with shoes.

OLDEN TIME, GENTLEMAN OF. Silk stockings; shoes with buckles; knee breeches; very long flowered waistcoat, with flap pockets; long coat, steel buttons, and ruffles; a frill to shirt; bald head or white hair; a stick in the hand.

PAGE (*The Betrothed*). Tights; long skirted habit; sleeves with double puffs, slashed from elbow; wide lace collar. (*Temp.* Charles I.) Velvet coat and breeches, with ribbon rosettes; silk stockings, shoes with bows; vandyke collar and cuffs; satin-lined coat; large hat and feather; all to be of the one tone. (*Temp.* Elizabeth.) Silk stockings; trunks; satin habit and shoulder-cloak, elaborately braided; ruff and low-crowned hat. (*See* also CHARLES, PRINCE OF WALES).

PANGLOSS, DR. A black velvet suit in the Georgian style, with long skirted coat and waistcoat, breeches, and silk stockings, buckled shoes, white wig and spectacles.

PAUL PRY. High boots, trousers of red and white striped calico, tucked into them; waistcoat to match, with large watch and chain, powdered bag-wig, blue tail-coat and brass buttons, umbrella under arm.

PIEMAN, in white suit and apron; cook's white cap,

PIRATES OF PENZANCE. Frederick. In undress uniform. **Pirate King,** cocked hat; coat with epaulettes; plaited petticoat and loose under-bodice; belt with pistols; stockings and shoes; banner with death's head and cross-bones. **Samuel,** similar dress to PIRATE KING, only a sailor's cap instead of cocked hat; sailor collar, and no epaulettes. **Sergeant of Police** in policeman's uniform.

PROSPERO. Black velvet robe trimmed with sable and gold, made with long hanging sleeves, scarlet under sleeves, barred with gold; large collar facings of scarlet and black with hieroglyphic signs; skull cap similarly bordered; flowing grey wig, beard and moustache; red stockings, pointed shoes.

PUNCHINELLE. Bodice and tunic in yellow satin, striped with black bands, bound with gold; skirt of red velveteen; red pompons and belt; black lace ruffles, cuffs and basque glittering with gold; red and black hat with gold spangles and tufted plume; wooden shoes.

PURITAN BOY. Brown velvet breeches; brown cloth coat and cloak; white tippet; felt hat.

PUSS IN BOOTS. Cat's head and bodice; groom's coat made of white fur with leather belt; top boots, and breeches.

REYNOLDS, after SIR JOSHUA. There is a good dress in "Feeding the Chickens;" black shoes with black bows; red stockings; blue petticoat with blue band; high white pinafore with red sash, made with a wide falling collar, bordered with a frill; sleeves to elbow; a red bow at throat. Another, in "Doubtful Security," the child wears shoes with straps; a yellow and blue skirt; low white pinafore with pink sash. **The Angerstein Children.** The boy has a frill and a turned-down collar, edged with lace. The manner in which the boy's hair is arranged is characteristic of the period—short over the eyebrows, and falling in curls on the shoulders, most becoming to youthful faces. **The Affectionate Brothers:** The attire of the three boys is quaint and picturesque, and the group as a whole would make an admirable *tableau vivant* enacted by children—the eldest boy with coat, waistcoat, and breeches of maroon-colored or black velvet; the little boy with jacket and trousers combined, and made of light colored cloth; and the baby all in white, with a gaily-trimmed Gainsborough hat in miniature, and a cherry-colored sash round its tiny waist.

RICHARD I. (*Coeur-de-Lion*). A maroon velvet tunic trimmed with gold lace, three lions couchant embroidered in gold on the breast; white silk tights; velvet trunks; gold and satin shoes; jewelled belt, sword, and dagger.

RISING SUN. As a schoolboy, with a large linen collar bordered with a frill; shell jacket with many buttons; trousers buttoned over that.

ROBINSON CRUSOE. Knickerbockers and long coat of fur, with robins sewn about it; belt round the waist; silk tights, sandals, green parrot on shoulders; fowling piece, pistols, hatchet, and umbrella.

SAILOR, ENGLISH. A favorite costume at fancy balls. It is best to obtain the real sailor dress from a nautical outfitter, either in white drill or serge; viz., loose trousers, loose jacket tucked into them; a belt round the waist; the sleeves of the jacket fastening at the wrist, having a sailor's collar, very open at the neck, with a silk handkerchief tied in a sailor's knot beneath it; a man-of-war straw hat, or a sou'-wester and peajacket. The drill suits have the jacket trimmed with blue down the front and on the cuffs and collar.

SCHOOLBOY. For a tall boy; green jacket, with triple row of buttons down the front; large frilled collar; grey trousers, short, and buttoned over the jacket; shoes with straps; a satchel with books slung over shoulder.

SCHOOLMASTER. Cloth coat made long, with gold buttons; striped blue waiscoat; nankeen breeches, fastened at the knee with the same buttons; white and blue woollen stockings; high collar, and blue silk necktie; spelling book under the arm; Madras handkerchief escaping from the pocket; periwig, brown jersey; quill pen in the ear; birch in the hand; muslin frilling round the waist.

SHEPHERD. Blue stockings, black shoes; figured blue cotton bodice showing only at neck; and breeches, bunches of ribbon at knee; Holland smock, long sleeves bordered with pink and blue ribbon, embroidered in silk with flowers; white wig.

SHEPHERD (FRENCH, OF 14th CENTURY). Loose blouse reaching to knee, sleeves tight to wrist; high stockings, long pointed shoes; girdle with carved horn attached; a crook with spear-like point.

SHEPHERD OF ABRUZZI. Brown trousers and garters tied with strap of leather; brown coat, and sleeves slung to waist, colored scarf round waist; sheepskin at back; high hat.

SHEPHERD, WATTEAU. Pink knee breeches, with blue puffings down the outer side of the legs; a white waistcoat with small frill; a coat coming slightly below the hips, showing the waistcoat, and having tight sleeves to the elbow, with big white puffings and ruffles to the wrist, a band of pink with blue rosettes inserted over the upper part of the puffing; a circular cape of violet and yellow; a Gainsborough-shaped hat; silk stockings, low shoes with large blue rosettes on the instep; and a crook with a bunch of blue and yellow ribbons on the top.

SIMPLE SIMON. Old-fashioned smock; corduroy trousers; hob-nailed shoes.

SLOPER. Tight brown trousers; blue coat, brass buttons, handkerchief coming out of pocket; old black gloves; white hat and black band; large green umbrella, and distinctive false nose.

SURFACE, CHARLES (*School for Scandal*). Silk stockings, shoes with buckles; breeches; long-tailed coat and waistcoat; powdered hair and bag wig; lace ruffles and lace necktie, fastened with a diamond star. This is always a most elaborate costume, the coat, waistcoat, and trousers made of light satin, and richly embroidered in gold and silver. For example, blue satin coat, with white satin vest and breeches; or lilac or light pink satin suit.

TOUCHSTONE. Red and white Folly dress, with bells and fool's cap.

TRADESMAN IN THE REIGN OF LOUIS XI. Brown velvet doublet bordered with blue; yellow sleeves, large blue collar lined with red; yellow leather purse fastened to the belt; brown hat turned up with red and yellow feather.

TURKISH (*see* Illustration). The pointed cap in the illustration is encircled with black, which could be rendered by black beads. The full breeches are blue, the habit white with an oriental shawl crossing the breast, the right arm is tatooed, and a black ribbon and bow surrounds the other.

TYROLEAN. Brown or grey coat, and breeches ending above the knee; white stockings; black shoes. The coat bound with green, having green collars and cuffs, is wide and open, showing the shirt and vest, across which there are bands of black velvet; and round the waist an elaborate silver embroidered belt. High pointed hat entwined with silver cord; flowers at the side.

WALTER OF SALUCES (*Chaucer*). Dalmatic of green and gold brocade; purple velvet belt; silver ornaments and clasp; crimson cloak lined with fur; wreath of ivy.

WHITTINGTON. Light brown pointed shoes covering front of foot; loose brown habit with belt round waist, open at neck to show chemisette; tight sleeves with puffed epaulette; stick on shoulder with bundle; short brown breeches; blue worsted stockings.

YANKEE. Skirt and trousers of striped cotton, with high collar black necktie, and large-brimmed hat.